# Baba Josie's Kitchen

## B. Matsalla, T. Mudry

### Edited by: M. Waddell

To: Kaylee
FR: Baba Ella
    2021

ISBN: 978-1-7774576-0-0

# Table of Contents

# Introduction

Welcome to *Baba Josie's Kitchen*: The loving home to a lifetime of cooking, baking, gathering of family & friends, and collecting brilliant love-filled recipes.

This collection stems from Josie's overstuffed binder of handwritten and photocopied recipes that she had assembled throughout her life. Our mom treasured time with her family and friends and she loved sharing food and the traditions that came with preparing these dishes. With her passing in February of 2020, her family has decided to commemorate her through sharing her collection along with some memories of her farm life in Tiny, Saskatchewan. We hope you enjoy our story and take the time to experience the recipes with your loved ones.

## Farm Location: Tiny, Saskatchewan

Tiny Saskatchewan is no longer on the map, however the Canadian Northern Railway originally registered it on October 3, 1965. In the early days, the CNR decided to make Tiny a central point. There was not enough water to supply the railway's requirements, so Tiny was abandoned and the railway moved its interest eastward to the nearby town of Canora (name was derived from the acronym of the CNR, aka the Canadian Northern Railway).

*Matsalla Farm north of Tiny, SK.*

In its prime, the hamlet of Tiny had a population of 36 people, 3 elevators, a blacksmith shop, a large livery barn, a hotel, a store (complete with a dance hall on the second floor), a church, and a general store. Although it was officially removed from maps, a revival occurred and it can now be found on some online maps. The nearest village was Buchanan, population 392 (1981), 14 km west of the farm. Canora was the closest town, 18 km to the east with a population of 2667 (1981). The nearest city was Yorkton, population 15,339 (1981), located 68 km south.

## Our Mom Josie

Josephine (Josie) was born on November 18, 1924, in Hamilton, Ontario, to Joseph and Pauline (Belitsky) Zarazun. She was the second child in their large family of eleven children.

Our mom was always the heart of any gathering, tasting and sharing the recipes contained in this book. She often would refer to the recipes she cooked by using the name of the family or friend that shared the recipe with her.

Her dad, Joseph Zarazun, was born in Holbiczek, Poland, and immigrated to Canada at the young age of seven. His parents settled on a farm in the R.M. of Buchanan area of Saskatchewan. Josie's mom, Pauline, lived nearby in the Dobrowody area near Rama, Saskatchewan.

*Joe and Pauline Zarazun and family. Josie circled.*

Josie received her childhood education at Norway and Forest Hills schools.

As one of the oldest children of the family, Josie had a lot of responsibilities looking after her younger siblings while her parents were out working on their farm. Josie primarily enjoyed her time in the kitchen and garden, but one of her hobbies was sewing clothes for herself and the entire family. There was nothing she couldn't sew with or without a pattern. When she traded-in her manual foot pedal style sewing machine for an electric sewing machine, both her skills and production increased. Sewing was something she would do when there was bad weather or when it was late in the evening to pass the time. Josie also made crochet doilies and knit scarves, she even made the famous siwash sweaters or jackets.

In the early 1980's, Josie found part-time employment as a Home Care technician. Her clients would request her personally for her incredible cleaning and cooking/baking skills. Often, she would care for people much younger than her own age.

In her later years, Josie was a regular bingo player and she was proud to attend the bingo when the donations were going to the church. She had her favourite lucky spot and snacks to share with her friends. Josie always said, "it isn't about winning at bingo, it's about visiting and having fun", but she still loved to win and would always manage to use her previous winnings at her next bingo outing.

## Our Dad Joe

Joseph Matsalla was born on November 1st, 1915, to Michael and Frances (Sliwa) Matsalla. He was the ninth child in a family of eleven children. As a boy, Joe attended Badgerdale farm school that was located a few miles north of the family farm, often walking or riding horses to and from school.

*Michael and Frances Matsalla and their children. Joe circled in picture.*

Joe loved to go fishing, with Josie and the kids joining him to fish whenever they could. When the catch was good, some fish would be frozen or canned. When Josie canned Jackfish (Northern Pike) it tasted just like canned salmon.

*Joe with his Northern Pike (jackfish) catch, with Brent.*

On stormy days music would waft over the Matsalla homestead as Joe accompanied himself playing fiddle and harmonica simultaneously, with the assistance of a harmonica holder he had fashioned from galvanized fencing wire.

Joe not only farmed full-time, but also occasionally worked driving a gravel truck for Wilson Construction or as a wrangler at the Buchanan Community Pasture. He was in addition a talented woodworker, certified welder, and blacksmith. Blacksmithing was a skill passed down through his father as the original Michael Matsalla homestead included a blacksmith shop.

In later years, Joe was elected and served the community as a councillor for the R.M. of Buchanan and sat as a director on numerous boards and organizations, which included the Canora Hospital.

Aside from his passion for playing music, Joe had many hobbies that kept him busy during the long winter days. He made flower planters from tires and wall hangings from spray-painted tin cans twisted into beautiful artwork. He made his own twine ropes by twisting and braiding the rope to the length he desired. He enjoyed paint by number detailed kits to pass his time. Joe also loved to sing, and since lyrics were not readily available, Josie would write down the words to the song as one of the children with steady hands lifted the needle off the record. Joe would focus on remembering the words to help Josie write them down. He also loved to entertain, especially when sharing a taste of his latest batch of root beer, moonshine or chokecherry wine.

*Joe during his cattle wrangling days.*

## Love Happens

On October 23, 1943, Josephine Zarazun married Joseph Matsalla at the Ukrainian Catholic Church north of Tiny, Saskatchewan. The Matsalla homestead has been in the family since 1902, it was located on a section of farmland SW 12-32-5, three and a half miles north of Tiny. Joe and Josie would raise five children on the farm: Eleanor, Bernice, James, Theresa, and Brent.

At various times the grain farm produced oats, barley, wheat, and canola. They also farmed cows, pigs, chickens, and sometimes ducks, geese and turkeys. The livestock also included horses that were trained to pull work sleds when

*Joe and Josie Matsalla*

cleaning out the barn. The horses were trained and managed by Joe by way of making clicking noises when he needed them to pull or stay put. In addition to the livestock, Josie and her family would maintain huge gardens that provided the essential ingredients for the amazing recipes in this book.

*Left to right. Back: Eleanor, Bernice, Joe. Seated: Francis (Joe's mom) Josie holding Brent. Front: Jim, Theresa.*

The Matsalla homestead was located approximately a mile from the country church Kowalowka - St. Mary's Roman Catholic Church (built 1905 by the region's homesteading pioneers). The family's involvement and attendance at Sunday mass is central to many of our memories. The names of the contributing pioneers are still etched into the church's history, captured in stained glass that adorns the windows of the quaint church.

St. Mary's still celebrates its history with one special mass each summer. This tradition shares a big meal with worshippers after the service, cooked by the once-parishioners. Josie stayed active with St. Mary's until she'd move to Canora in the mid 1980's where she joined the Catholic Women's League at St. Joseph's Roman Catholic Church. Josie was also a very active member in the Canora Gateway Lodge Women's Auxiliary.

## Heartbreak

After 29 years of marriage, sadly Joe passed away suddenly of heart complications on February 6, 1972. After her husband's passing, Josie continued to operate the family farm, however with a much smaller garden and they minimized the livestock solely to chickens.

*Josie's house in Canora, 1984.*

Josie retired in 1985 and moved into the town of Canora. In town, she would still plant a garden and loved to pick berries, rhubarb, and mushrooms any chance she would get. Josie gladly embraced more time to entertain, her circle of friends broadened and even more recipes were collected and shared.

## Josie's Recipe Collection

Some people collect stamps, others fancy salt and pepper shakers, recipe collection on the other hand, costs only pennies for the paper and the black binder they were bound into with love. Many of the precious recipes contained in this book, Josie made over and over again for family and friends. Some of the recipes lack some instructions as she would only list the recipe's ingredients, but they were too interesting to exclude from the book. We debated trying all the recipes prior to publishing however it was not a task without many tears, especially when you'd reach for the phone to call mom for clarification.

*Josie and granddaughter Mandelle making cabbage rolls.*

*Josie barbequing at a family event.*

If you ever spoke with Josie (phone or in-person), one thing was for sure; the conversation would always include food, from ingredients to what was on each other's menus in the following days. Josie never stopped collecting recipes her entire life of 95 years, so this collection is a multi-decade collection that as mentioned includes recipes contributed by family and friends.
We've also included a few more recent individual family favorites for newer generations to enjoy forever.

*Josie cutting the cake at a Zarazun reunion.*

Nobody ever went hungry when you visited Josie's house. A huge pot of soup was almost always on the stove and her fridge and freezer were full of the best ingredients she could get her hands on. "Baba" noodle soup (chicken broth with homemade egg noodles) or borscht were favorites requested by grandchildren when they'd visit. At holiday gatherings family from out of town would always be sure to stay until fresh soup was served the following day, and they would surely leave with an ice cream pail full of cookies for the road (if not sandwiches, etc.) and she'd also be sure to pack a treat for the dog!

Josie was never afraid to try a new recipe and she bravely made her own modifications. Even after curtailing her baking after the age of 90, she would still remember a recipe's ingredients, how to execute the dish, and above all, the name of the person that gave her the recipe. If you were stuck, all it took was a phone call with her to help you through the "how-to" and to pass on her expert tips.

*Mom's recipe collection.*

Through recipes Josie was able to share her love for cooking, but her cooking and recipes also became the link to her heart full of love. The Matsalla family hopes you will enjoy this cookbook as much as we have enjoyed Josie's cooking and baking our entire lives.

## Saskatchewan Family Farm Life

Farm life in Saskatchewan was filled with hard work that changed with the season; always prepping to ensure the family had plenty of food for the entire year. Nothing went to waste, as the surplus was always offered to other families.

*Matsalla Farmyard.*

Everyday chores included tending to the livestock in feeding and milking cows or picking the eggs. Livestock was free-range but also fed with "chop" (chopped grains from crops grown and processed right on the farm).

Separating the milk from the cream using the cream separator after milking twice a day was the largest chore by far. Cream would be placed in a cream can and taken to market at the local creamery in Canora, Saskatchewan. Before heading to market cream would have to be stored in a large fridge, and before power and the luxury of affording a fridge the farmyard had an icehouse. This was basically a roof covering a hole dug into the ground, with straw bales and ice housed inside.

Joseph and Josephine Matsalla Homestead

Pond

Home Pasture

Chicken Coop and Chick house

Oil House - Fuel Tanks

Shop

Barn

Ice House

Pigpens

Garage

House

Grain Bins

Garden 1

Garden 2

Blacksmith Shop

Original Michael Matsalla Residence

Pond

Beginning of 80 Acre Pasture

*Map of Matsalla Farm*

In summer the cows free-grazed in the 80-acre pasture. It was the children's job to bring the cows home for milking, but the dogs always helped to herd the cattle. The kids knew a storm was brewing when the cows would come home early all on their own. When milking cows by hand, the cats would gather in the center of the barn mouths open in anticipation that you would send a stream of milk their way. Hand picking roots and stones became other important family tasks. With newly broken land, tree roots would continuously break the ground, potentially causing damage to farm machinery. Roots would be piled and burnt on the land next to the stone piles.

Telephone service at that time was through a shared party line. The phone call was for our farmhouse if it had 1 long ring and 1 short ring; other rings belonged to the neighbors. If you wanted to make a phone call, you had to pick up the phone and listen to ensure the line wasn't being used.

## Spring

When the cold Saskatchewan winter finally subsided, it meant the family would soon be gathering together to go out on a quest for the most amazing morel mushrooms. Morels were picked and sliced, then added to a cream sauce that included green onions and fresh dill. If you've never had morels cooked this way, it's a must to experience at least once in your life, and you will remember the taste forever. On good years, many morels could be frozen for future use.

Despite the promise of delicious morels, spring was not Josie's favourite season, she would always say it was dirty and lots of hard work to clean up and set up for the rest of the year. This season was also a bigger expense with the need to buy grain and garden seed.

Gardens and crops needed to be seeded and planted. In order to prolong the short Saskatchewan growing season, some seeds were started in the house from seeds collected from past years. The gardens were large enough to supply produce for the entire year.

Winter onions would be the first to sprout in the garden. These were a perennial onion that could be enjoyed in a creamy sauce with a little salt and pepper for seasoning. Green onions were not available in the stores so early in spring and it was considered a treat to our family to have them.

Rhubarb would begin to grow and eventually provide many tasty treats. There are a variety of rhubarb recipes shared in this book, as Josie loved using rhubarb in dessert recipes.

Springtime also meant Josie would order her chicks for the season and this also meant preparing the chick house for their arrival. This was a different building than the chicken coop that housed older hens and a rooster. The chick house was equipped with heaters and a secure fenced yard for when the weather would get warmer and as the chicks got older, allowing them to venture outside.

The farmhouse contained a potato bin (8'x8' cold room) in the basement to store our yearly supply of potatoes. By springtime, these potatoes usually began to sprout and were used as seed potatoes for the current gardening season. The remaining old potatoes were cooked and mashed and used for pierogi filling. Pierogies were made and frozen to last throughout the busy summer season as a fast and easy meal. The pierogi supply never got too low, as we enjoyed them throughout the year.

Easter meant the tradition of making paska and babka breads that were enjoyed alongside boiled eggs topped with horseradish shavings. The horseradish always provoked a challenge with who could tolerate eating the most at one time. Ukrainian and Farmer sausages were always brought out on Easter Sunday, in addition to the other holiday snacks.

## Summer

As vegetables grew in the fertile Saskatchewan soil, simple salads were made with lettuce, radish, and green onions.

Fresh young potatoes from the garden were cooked in cream with dill and green onions. This was one of Josie's favorites. Young potatoes also meant potato salads that were often taken to a picnic at the lake on a Sunday afternoon after church.

Summer meant that the raspberries, chokecherries, Saskatoon berries, and strawberries were ripening and needed to be picked. Some were stored as jams and jellies, but fresh fruit was always a treat to add to Josie's cake or pie recipes.

Gooseberries were planted on the edge of one garden, as kids, we would pick them before they were ripe and challenge each other, as well as friends and cousins that visited, to try to eat one without making a sour face. Selecting the big brown ripe gooseberries for you was the trick, as these tended to be sweeter.

Soon the cucumbers would start to produce which meant it was pickling time. Fresh baked bread and homemade butter with slices of cucumber was a lunchtime treat. Often fresh cucumbers would be made into a salad with green onion and dill in a creamy vinegar dressing.

In late summer, the rhubarb stalks got bigger. We would simply dip the large red stalks in sugar to counter the sour flavor, and as kids we would entertain ourselves playing with the large leaves.

In July, an annual church picnic was held, where everyone contributed to a smorgasbord lunch. There were games for young and old including a softball game after we'd clear the parking lot of cars and toss down the makeshift bases. The men would gather aside to chat and likely get a sample or two of their neighbor's latest batch of homebrew. Very often the homebrew was a brandy made from overripe local foraged berries.

Josie also made her own cottage cheese, the milk curds would be wrapped in cheesecloth and hung in the basement with a drain bowl underneath until dry.

Summer also meant preparing young chickens for the freezer before they got too old. Josie would preserve chicken in jars. Canned chicken was quick, easy, tender and tasty, so it was very convenient and often used when company would arrive unannounced before mealtime. The canned chicken would form a jelly in the jar when slow cooked in a canner for hours. This jelly ensured the chicken remained moist.

The canned goods were placed in storage on an entire wall, floor to ceiling, in the basement of the farmhouse. By springtime the shelves were full of empty jars that would be filled by the time autumn rolled around.

*Hay stacks to store more hay to last the winter.*

As soon as the sloughs (ponds) dried out from winter runoff, hay would be cut and baled. It was a family effort to bring in the bales that were stored in the hayloft on the second story of the barn. Bales would be hauled off the fields in pickups or tractor pulled trailers and placed one by one onto a bale loader that would lift the bales up to the hayloft. Once the hayloft was filled the remaining bales were stored in long haystacks beside the barn. Often these haystacks also served as a playground for us children, jumping off them into piles of broken hay bales or we would make forts out of them for upcoming snowball fights.

*Joe making chop for livestock feed from grains.*

The Saskatchewan summer often included unpredictable weather. The weather could often turn extreme and hail would thrash the garden and fields of crops. When this would happen, the community of friends, neighbors, and family always came together and offered any produce they had to make up for your loss. Sharing will always be the Saskatchewan-way of doing things.

## Autumn

In early autumn, Josie would pick wild cranberries to bake her cranberry tarts, creating the filling from scratch tasting and adjusting depending on how many berries she had. In later years when unable to go picking, she would ask others if they would pick some for her, so she was still able to enjoy her favourite tarts. The family would also travel to relatives and friends yards to pick crab-apples to freeze for pies or can the apples with syrup to enjoy all year.

Besides fishing, Joe also enjoyed wild game hunting, often seeking whitetail deer and moose. This helped to stock the freezer with meat during the winter. Hunting was followed by butchering and a lot of sausage making. Along with the wild game, the freezers would be packed with farm meat for the upcoming winter.

The fall grain harvest was the most important task of the entire year; it was both labor heavy and held the most financial weight as well. Focus shifted to ensuring the crops would be harvested timely and stored in the wooden grain bins on the farmyard. When the grain was dry enough for harvest it became all hands on deck. Josie would jump from preparing meals to hauling grain to the bins.

*Joe unloading grain from the combine hopper.*

Harvesting often meant very long workdays while the weather was good and the grain was dry. These long days would always include lunch and dinner in the field. The menu was often fresh cucumber and/or tomato sandwiches, and hot coffee with sugar and fresh farm cream, always served in a mason jar. This meal tasted so good we would joke that the secret ingredient must be the Saskatchewan dirt you'd find inside. Pepper or dirt, you couldn't be sure, but it always tasted amazing.

While the men were in the field harvesting, all the vegetables needed to be cleared from the gardens and prepared for the freezer. Beets were of course cooked into borscht. Peas, beans, corn, and carrots were frozen. Onions and garlic were hung and dried in cold storage. Women did double-time as lunches still needed to be delivered to the men harvesting the crops. The men would help with the garden as well when waiting for the grain harvest to dry, when combining wasn't possible after rain.

Once the first frosts of autumn killed the tops of the potato plants it was time to harvest the potatoes. The whole family participated in the potato digging, gathering and sorting in order to restock the potato bin for the year ahead. A tractor with trailer would be used to transport the massive potato crop to the house, although sometimes dad would use the horses and sled. A wooden ramp for potatoes was built to unload the potatoes through the basement window into the potato bin, allowing us to stock the bin directly from the trailer or sled by emptying the large burlap bags of potatoes we filled in the garden.

The end of the potato harvest included gathering up all the garden waste and burning the pile in a bonfire right on the garden. We would toss potatoes into the fire to cook while enjoying the warmth on the cool autumn Saskatchewan night. The potatoes would be totally burnt on the outside but the insides were so flavorful and fluffy when you added fresh farm butter. The ashes from the bonfire would be spread over the garden providing nourishment for next year's crop.

With cabbage coming off the garden it meant time to make sauerkraut. A huge ceramic or wood barrel would need to be cleaned and the heads of cabbage shredded (shredded cabbage was also frozen for future use in soups and other dishes). The shredded cabbage would be salted and weighed down by a heavy boulder. Whole heads of cabbage would also be placed on top of the shredded cabbage for weight and to be later used as sour cabbage leaves for cabbage roll making. This barrel would be the source of many sour smells as it fermented. When done the sauerkraut would be stored in mason jars.

## Winter

The Saskatchewan winters were very long and often harsh to endure. Regular winter tasks were taking care of the livestock and pushing the snow to clear the long driveway with a tractor and plow.

It was the time of year to dive into those treasures previously canned and frozen. Josie's intuitive organization of the canning shelves was pivotal to her easily rotating through the storage to use everything up in order of stocking, making sure nothing ever went to waste. Part of this was ensuring all Christmas goodies were made timely to the ingredients expiry. Christmas was all about the good food and baking to share with family and friends throughout the holiday season.

During winter Joe would do some of the cooking. He made potato chips by slicing the potatoes really thin using a knife he'd made himself, and frying each chip in the electric frying pan turning each chip only once. Often they were eaten faster than he could fry them. Joe would also impress with cutting baloney sausage circles to resemble flower petals, this would ensure they didn't curl when frying but the kids thought they were pretty fancy.

Winter meant there was more time to spend visiting and playing cards. Josie loved playing cards her entire life. Often the game of choice was a Ukrainian card game called Troika. This game was played in teams of two and spawned many competitive card games that would last into the wee hours of the morning. When done the oldest child in the family was sent outside to start the car, so it would be nice and warm for the trip home during the many -40 degree prairie winter nights.

Christmas was centered on the traditional dishes of Poland and the Ukraine. After the Christmas feast, it was often the men that washed the dishes to pay homage to the fabulous cooks and bakers of the family, which kept us all well fed throughout the entire year. Sometimes dishes were just cleared and we would move on to the snacks for the evening, food was always the heart of the celebration.

## More Farm Memories

*Joe's winter homemade horse-drawn caboose so the family could travel in warmth to church in winter.*

Walking into the house after church to smell a cream chicken roasting is an unforgettable memory. Before leaving to Sunday mass at St. Mary's, Josie often put a chicken in a roaster along with cream, dill, celery and onions. Of course visiting after church alongside vehicles in the parking lot was a common occurrence and part of the Sunday traditions as well.

On summer Sunday's, we'd rush home from church and quickly pack a picnic basket to share with family and friends at Goodspirit Lake (previously named, Devil's Lake). The huge sand dunes at the south end of the lake were a favorite spot for us kids. Occasionally, we'd go down to the Assiniboine River, but the leeches there made us prefer the lake.

*Burgess Beach on Goodspirit Lake, 1966.*

The food at the Sunday picnics always filled the table with everyone contributing to the meal. Meats were prepared in advance for barbequing over coal briquettes. It was hard to bring such fun to an end, so we pushed it until the evening fell then rushed home to do the chores in the dark, milking the cows, feeding the pigs and closing up the free range chickens in their coop before we turned in for bed.

Keeping livestock meant you couldn't go away for extended times to visit relatives without ensuring help would tend to the animals. For this reason it was very difficult to visit Grandpa and Grandma Zarazun in Winnipeg, Manitoba, a six-hour trip from the farm. When we did see them it was usually a wedding or other organized family celebration. However, family from Winnipeg often visited the farm and helped with the seasonal farm work while we all visited and had a good time. Josie always made sure they went home with produce care packages.

Josie's kitchen was where everyone got together and visited. The dining room table was used for big holiday celebrations or if the kitchen table couldn't hold everyone. Kids played in the living room or upstairs unless it was summer, then it was outside until dark. Kid's outdoor activities were games such as Anti-I-Over. This game consisted of two teams on opposite sides of the farmhouse, taking turns throwing a ball over the roof. When the ball was caught, the catcher and his team would rush to the other team's side, if you were tagged by the ball carrier you joined that team. Teams changed sides after a catch. This got extremely challenging around dark when the dogs ran with you.

There was also Kick the Can; a version of hide-and-seek where you defeat the seeker and hence end the game by successfully hiding from them while simultaneously kicking an actual old oil can and yelling "KICK THE CAN". This allowed everyone hiding to hear the current game was over and to come out from the hiding spots. If the seeker spotted someone, they would touch the can and call a person out from their hiding place. Other fun activities included baseball if there were enough players, if not, we went bike riding on the gravel driveway and grid road that passed by the farm.

Being a farm kid meant lots of chores to help with the upkeep of the farmhouse and land including kitchen duties, washing the cream separator parts daily, dishes, feeding livestock, cutting grass, and shelling multiple 5-gallon pails of peas and beans.

Indoor plumbing was not installed into the farmhouse until the late 1970's. Our toilet was an outhouse or in winter was a pail that had to be emptied often outside. The daily wash-up sink was in the kitchen where the family washed up and brushed our teeth. The farmyard wasn't fortunate to locate a water well on the homeland. Our drinking water came from a cistern in the basement and was hand-pumped into the kitchen. This water was

*Early 1980's farm house in winter.*

hauled from Amsterdam, Saskatchewan, a few miles east of the farm. Manual heating of water was required when cooking or bathing.

The basement also included a coal bin, a dedicated room that stored the coal used in the furnace to heat the house in winter. This furnace took up most of the basement space. The large floor vents or registers were often used to dry winter clothing or quickly warm you on a cold winter day. In the 1970's an oil furnace was installed to replace the manually operated coal furnace.

The bathtub was made of galvanized metal and was stored in the basement along the shelves of preserves. Every Saturday, water from the cistern was heated for the tub. You washed quickly and dressed even faster as the basement was always very cold. The bathing order was usually youngest to oldest as the depth of water would always increase over time, adding more warm water as it cooled.

*1952 Minneapolis Moline Model U with homemade cab and snowplough.*

Before rural mail delivery, the mail would need to be picked up in Tiny. Often that meant treats for the kids in the form of chocolate bars (Cuban Lunch or Bounty Bars), maybe even a bag of potato chips with a Cream Soda, Root Beer, Mountain Dew, or if really lucky we'd get an Orange or Grape Crush.

As a farm kid you learned to drive a stick shift and a tractor at a young age in order to help with duties such as delivery of lunch or parts for a machine breakdown. Every family member knew how to drive the tractor; we had a 1952 Minneapolis Moline, a valuable workhorse on our farm. Occasionally, the family would visit the city of Yorkton. These trips included getting farm grown wheat ground into flour at the mill for use in Josie's recipes. The trip home almost always included fresh slices of bread and a hand-broken chunk of newly purchased Ukrainian garlic sausage. Sometimes this included mustard, but only if it was on the shopping list!

Josie lived on the farm until her retirement in 1985. Her son James would continue to farm the land for many years to follow. The farm is now owned and run by a cousin of the family and it still produces some of the world's best canola.

*Josie's house in Canora in the mid 1980's.*

Josie's first house in Canora had a garden that included a rhubarb patch. In her later years, Josie would move into a senior's condo still maintaining a small garden there, until her age prevented her from managing her own garden any longer. Despite not having her own plants planted she still took joy in looking out her window and watching her friend's gardens grow, and sometimes still managed to score a sample of the harvest.

Even in her later years you'd often find Josie sitting outside her home with friends enjoying a coffee or treat that they took turns bringing to the gathering. Food was a huge part of Josie's life, right up until her passing in February 2020, at the age of 95. We hope that through sharing this lifelong family archive of Josie's recipes, it will bring to you and your family, as much love as Josie's loving hands put into countless dishes she prepared and served to her family and friends.

This book was created for a family archive and is not for profit. Any profits generated by sales of this book will go directly to supporting local Canora, Saskatchewan, charities that Josie loved and believed in.

*Jim, Bernice, Eleanor, Theresa, Brent and Josie seated.*

On behalf of the Matsalla family, we thank you for purchasing the book, *Baba Josie's Kitchen*, and sincerely hope you enjoy these recipes as much as we have, and will continue to enjoy for the rest of our lives and for generations to come.

## Bacon Brittle

| | |
|---|---|
| 1 1/2 cups sugar | 1 tsp. vanilla extract |
| 1/2 cup light corn syrup | 1 tsp. baking soda |
| 3/4 cup cold water | Room temp butter, just to coat the baking |
| Pinch of salt | sheet |
| 1 lb. crispy and crumbled bacon | A hammer! |

Brush a 9" × 13" baking sheet with butter and set aside. Combine the sugar, corn syrup, water and salt in a medium saucepan. Bring to a boil over medium-high heat, stirring until the sugar has dissolved. Cook, swirling occasionally, until mixture reaches the softball stage on a candy thermometer (238 degrees). Stir in the crispy and crumbled bacon, continue to cook, stirring often so the bacon doesn't burn, until the mixture is amber in color! Carefully stir in the vanilla and baking soda. The mixture will foam up in the pan. Pour the mixture onto the prepared baking sheet and quickly spread it evenly. Set aside until it's completely cool. Gather everyone around and take turns breaking the brittle into pieces with a hammer. *Contributed by Brent Matsalla.*

## Bacon Wrapped Jalapeno Poppers

| | |
|---|---|
| 1/2 cup cream cheese | 12 jalapeno peppers, halved lengthwise, |
| 1/2 cup shredded sharp Cheddar cheese | seeds and membranes removed |
| 1/4 cup finely chopped onion | 12 slices bacon |
| 1 can crab meat (optional) | |

Preheat the oven to 400. Line a baking sheet with parchment paper. Mix ingredients in a bowl until evenly blended. Fill each jalapeno half with the cheese mixture. Put halves back together and wrap with a slice of bacon. Arrange bacon-wrapped peppers on the prepared baking sheet. Cook until crispy, about 15 min. Also, can be put on the bbq. *Contributed by Brent Matsalla.*

## Baked Popcorn Coating

| | |
|---|---|
| 1 cup margarine | 6 quarts of popped corn |
| 2 cups packed brown sugar | Peanuts (optional) |
| 1/2 cup corn syrup | 1/2 tsp. baking soda |
| 1 tsp. salt | 1 tsp. vanilla |

Melt margarine stir in sugar, syrup and salt bring to a boil stirring constantly. Then boil 5 min. Without stirring. Remove from heat. Do not boil after adding the next 2 ingredients.

Stir in: Baking soda and vanilla. Pour over popped corn stirring quick to coat all corn. Turn into shallow pan, bake at 250 for 1 hour. Stirring every 15 minutes to break apart. *Contributed by Antonia Hladun.*

## Candied Peanuts

1 cup sugar
1/3 cup water
2 cups peanuts
1 tsp. cinnamon (optional)
1/8 tsp. nutmeg (optional)
1/4 tsp. cayenne (optional)

Heat ingredients on medium stirring constantly until texture is gritty and all syrup mix is gone. Place on a parchment lined cookie sheet and bake at 300 for 30 minutes, stirring every ten minutes. Store in sealed container. *Contributed by Brent Matsalla.*

## Cauliflower Hot Wings

1 head of cauliflower, washed and broken up into small florets
3 tsp. extra virgin olive oil
1 tsp. garlic powder
1 tsp. paprika

1 tsp. chili powder
1/2 tsp. salt
2 Tbsp. butter
1/2 cup of your favorite hot wing sauce

Preheat the oven to 425. Place cauliflower in a bowl with a lid, add olive oil and shake to distribute evenly. Combine garlic powder, paprika, chili powder, and salt in a small bowl. Toss spice mixture over cauliflower and shake well, making sure all the cauliflower is coated in the spices.
Spread cauliflower out on a rimmed baking sheet a roast for 20 minutes.
Melt butter and add wing sauce. Pour wing sauce over baked cauliflower and let stand 5 min before serving. Serve with your favorite dressing for dipping. Enjoy!

## Dill Pickle Egg Rolls

8 oz. pkg. of cream cheese
Dill pickles, sliced lengthwise
1/4 cup of old cheddar
Bacon, chopped and fried
3 garlic cloves, crushed

Egg roll wrappers
Dash of dry mustard
Onion salt
Pepper
5 chopped green onions

Blend cream cheese with cheddar, bacon, garlic, spices and green onion. Spread cream mixture onto egg roll, place a sliced pickle on and roll up and seal. I use a cornstarch and water wash to seal the egg wrapper. Fry in a pan with hot oil until brown. Serve immediately as an appetizer, delicious!
*Contributed by Darla Wolkowski.*

## Nuts & Bolts

26 cups cereal, pretzels, Shreddies, Cheerios, Cheese sticks, etc.
1 cup oil

6 tsp. dill weed
1 1/2 tsp garlic powder
2 pkg. Ranch dressing powder

Mix cereals in a large bowl. Mix remaining ingredients together and pour over cereal mixture. Mix every 1/2 hour until dry. Put in bags. *Contributed by Twila Hadubiak.*

## Popcorn Coating

1 cup margarine
1 cup un-popped corn, cooked and popped
1 1/3 cups white sugar

1/2 cup corn syrup
1/2 tsp. cream of tartar
1 tsp. vanilla

Combine margarine, sugar, syrup and cream of tartar. Boil gentle 3 minutes. Remove from heat and add baking soda and vanilla. Pour over cooked popcorn and mix. Cool in large pan.

## Shreddies Snack Appetizer

4 cups Shreddies Cereal (could alternate with Life cereal etc.)
1 cup salted peanuts (optional)
1 small pkg. pretzels (of choice)
1 small pkg. cheddar cracker (goldfish crackers work)

1/2 cup margarine
1 Tbsp. Worcestershire sauce
1 tsp. garlic powder
1 tsp. onion powder
2 Tbsp. dry ranch seasoning

Mix the cereal, peanuts and pretzels in a shallow baking pan; spread evenly. Melt margarine, add Worcestershire sauce, and seasoning, and blend well. Pour over cereal mixture and toss to coat. Spread mixture evenly in a pan. Bake at 300 for 25 minutes or until cereal is toasted and crisp. During baking turn mixture several times. Cool on paper towel. Makes 6 cups. Alternate: add 1/4 cup grated parmesan cheese after 5 minutes of the cereal being in the oven. Store in airtight container. *Contributed by Theresa Mudry.*

## Spinach Dip Loaf

1 small pkg. frozen spinach, chopped, thawed, squeezed dry.
1 cup mayonnaise
1 cup sour cream
1 pkg. dry Knorr vegetable soup mix

4 green onions, chopped
1 can water chestnuts, chopped
Salt and pepper to taste

Mix all ingredients together and let chill overnight to blend flavors.
Slice the top off 1 round French loaf or pumpernickel loaf. Scoop out the inside of the loaf and cut bread into cubes for dipping. Fill bread with chilled mixture. Bake at 325 for 30 minutes. Serve hot with bread cubes. Can be served cold as well.

## Stuffed Mushrooms

About 20 - 30 mushrooms washed, set aside to dry well and stems removed.
2 pkg. of cream cheese, room temperature
1 small onion, finely diced
3-4 cloves of garlic, finely diced
2 small cans of crab meat (optional)
1/2 lb. of bacon, fried and finely crumbled or finely chopped
1 1/2 cups finely shredded mozzarella cheese
1/4 cup grated parmesan cheese
2-3 Tbsp. of dried basil and parsley

Wash, dry and stem mushrooms and place them on a lightly greased cookie sheet. Fry up the bacon, set aside to cool and crumble or chop it fine. Using the leftover bacon fat, fry the finely chopped onion and garlic until the onion is clear and see-through. Warm up the cream cheese in the microwave so that it is soft and pliable. Add to the cream cheese, the bacon, onion, garlic, crab meat, ½ of the Mozzarella and Parmesan Cheese and combine with the dried basil and parsley. Using a teaspoon, spoon the mixture into the mushroom caps generously until they are heaped up nicely. Top each mushroom cap with the rest of the Mozzarella and Parmesan Cheese. Bake in a 350 degree oven until they are all nicely browned. Serve warm. *Contributed by Brent Matsalla.*

## Summer Sausage

1 tsp. mustard seed
3 Tbsp. tender quick
1 cup cold water
1/2 tsp garlic salt

1/2 tsp onion salt
1/8 tsp. pepper
1 1/2 Tbsp. liquid smoke
2 lbs. hamburger

Mix all seasoning in cold water. Pour over hamburger, mix and shape into roll. Wrap in foil, press together tightly. Let stand in fridge 24 hours. Then bake 1 hour in 350 oven on a cookie sheet, cool in foil. Keeps in fridge for weeks.

## Surprise Spread

1 package cream cheese
1/2 cup sour cream
1/4 cup mayonnaise
1 can small shrimp, drained (optional)
1 small jar seafood sauce

2 cups shredded mozzarella cheese
1 green pepper, chopped
1-2 tomatoes, diced
Chopped green onions

Mix first 3 ingredients together; beat well until smooth. Spread into a 12" pan or dish (or 2 smaller dishes). Add seafood sauce, then layer on remaining ingredients. Cover and chill. Serve with crackers. *Contributed by Jenelle and Mark Breker.*

# Beverages

## Crab Apple Juice

5 quarts boiling water
4 quarts crabapples
6 tsps. cream of tartar

Sprinkle cream of tartar on washed and quartered crabapples. Pour boiling water over and let stand 24 hours. Strain through a cloth. Bring juice to a boil and add sugar to taste. The juice maybe processed for later use by boiling juice for 10 minutes and sealing in hot sterile jars or place jars in canner in boiling water to boil and seal or it could be frozen but don't fill to full.

## Ginger Rhubarb Punch

1 cup sliced ginger root
4 cups frozen chopped pink rhubarb
4 cups water
3/4 cup sugar

2 cups ginger ale
1/4 cup lemon juice
3 cups ice cubes

In a large saucepan cover and bring ginger and 4 cups water to a boil. Add rhubarb and sugar, reduce heat and simmer until sugar is dissolved about 10 minutes. Strain into large bowl or pitcher. Cool. Cover and refrigerate 1 hour. Serve with ginger ale, lemon juice and ice cubes. *Contributed by Theresa Mudry.*

## Iced Coffee Mix

1/2 cup instant coffee granules
1 1/8 cups sugar
1 cup boiling water
1 tsp. vanilla

Serve on ice mixed with milk or cream of choice. Store in fridge for about a month. This recipe makes about 8 - 10 servings. This recipe doubles well. *Contributed by Theresa Mudry.*

## Mojitos

10 fresh mint leaves
1/2 a lime, cut into 4 wedges
6 tsp. white sugar or to taste
235 ml ice cubes
45 ml white rum
120 ml club soda

Directions: Place mint leaves and 1 lime wedge into a sturdy glass. Use a muddler to crush the mint and lime to release the mint oils and lime juice. Add 2 more lime wedges and the sugar and muddle again to release the lime juice. Do not strain the mixture. Fill the glass almost to the top with ice. Pour the rum over the ice, and fill the glass with carbonated water. Stir, taste and add more sugar if desired. Garnish with the remaining lime wedge. *Contributed by Linda Matsalla.*

## Slush

2 cups boiling water into 4 tea bags to set to cool.
Heat 7 cups water and 2 cups sugar (don't boil)
Mix in 1 - 12 oz. can frozen lemonade
1 - 12 oz. can frozen orange juice
1 - 26 oz. vodka

Freeze for 24 hours. Serve with 7-up or sprite.

## V8 Juice

10 large ripe tomatoes
1/2 cup celery chopped
1/4 cup chopped onion
3 Tbsp. chopped fresh parsley
3/4 cup water
1/4 tsp. basil

Then add: this to each quart sealer.

1 Tbsp. lemon juice
1 tsp. salt
1/4 tsp. sugar
1/2 tsp. Worcestershire sauce

Cook covered over low heat for 30 min. *Contributed by Linda Matsalla.*

# Breakfast Dishes

## Apple Pancakes – Baked

2 - 3 Tbsp. butter
2 medium apples
2 Tbsp. sugar
1 tsp. cinnamon or pumpkin spice
2 eggs
1/2 cup milk
1/2 cup flour

Preheat oven to 400. Peel, core and slice apples. Place on bottom of greased 8" x 8" pan. Sprinkle sugar and cinnamon over. Combine eggs, milk, then add flour and stir until no lumps are visible. Pour batter over the apples. Cut butter and dot on top of pancake. Bake for 25 minutes. Serve with maple syrup or any other pancake toppings. This recipe easily doubles.

## Austrian Pancakes

1/4 cup butter
2 eggs
1/2 cup milk
1/2 cup flour

Melt butter in a pie plate/skillet. Beat eggs slightly. Add milk & flour to eggs. Stir slightly but leave a bit lumpy. Pour into pie plate/skillet. Sprinkle with cinnamon. Bake at 400 for 15 mins. *Contributed by Adam and Mandelle Waddell.*

## Baba's Special French Toast

2 eggs
1/4 cup milk
4 slices of bread
1/2 tsp. ground cinnamon (Baba would add this in sometimes for something special when I stayed at her place)

Beat egg, cinnamon, and milk in a shallow dish. Dip bread in egg mixture, turning to coat both sides evenly. Cook bread slices on lightly greased non-stick griddle or frying pan on medium high heat until browned on both sides.
Top with your favourite toppings; syrup, whipped cream, and/or fruit compote. *Contributed by Caley Eikelenboom.*

## Bacon, Egg & Cheese Biscuit Bake

7 eggs
2 Tbsp. milk
1 can Pillsbury Grands Flaky Layers refrigerated Original Biscuits

1 pkg. thick pre-cooked bacon cut into ½ in pieces
1 cup shredded cheese (of your choice)
Salt & pepper

Heat the oven to 350. Grease a 8" x 12" in glass baking dish with butter. In a big bowl, beat the eggs & milk with a whisk until smooth. Add salt & pepper to taste. Separate the biscuit dough & cut each into 4 quarters. Gently stir biscuit pieces into egg mixture to coat evenly. Add the cooked bacon & cheese. Gently pour mixture into buttered baking dish; making sure to arrange biscuit pieces into single layer to make sure it cooks evenly. Bake at 350 F for 20-30 mins until golden brown. *Contributed by Caley Eikelenboom.*

## Blueberry and Mascarpone Stuffed French Toast

3- 8 ounces French baguettes

8 ounces mascarpone or cream cheese, room temperature

2 tsp. vanilla

2 cups powdered sugar

2 cups fresh blueberries

6 eggs

2 cups milk

3/4 cup granulated sugar

1 1/2 tsp. ground cinnamon

Step 1 Grease a 3-quart baking dish. Cut each baguette into 1" slices, cutting to but not through bottom of loaf. For filling: In a medium bowl beat mascarpone and 1 tsp. vanilla until smooth. Beat in powdered sugar until combined. Fold in blueberries. Spoon filling between baguette slices; arrange baguettes side by side in prepared dish.

Step 2 In a large bowl whisk together eggs, milk, 1/2 cup granulated sugar, remaining vanilla, and 1/2 tsp. cinnamon. Pour over bread. Cover; chill overnight.

Step 3 Preheat the oven to 350°F. Uncover dish. In a small bowl stir together remaining 1/4 cup granulated sugar and 1 tsp. cinnamon. Sprinkle over bread. Bake, uncovered, 40 to 45 minutes or until egg mixture is set, covering with foil the last 15 minutes if necessary to prevent over browning. Remove; let cool slightly. Makes 12 servings. *Contributed by Caley Eikelenboom.*

## Crispy Maple Bacon

1 lb. bacon
Drizzle of maple syrup

Fry bacon until lightly crispy. Place cooked strips on paper towel to drain. Put bacon on a plate and drizzle maple syrup over crisp bacon strips. *Contributed by Ivy Miller.*

## Delicious Pancakes

2 cups flour

2 tbsps. melted margarine

2 tbsps. sugar

2 egg yolks beaten

4 tsps. baking powder

2 egg whites beaten

1/2 tsp. salt

2 cups milk

Mix together all dry ingredients. Beat egg yolks & add to milk & melted margarine. Mix together well with dry ingredients. Beat egg whites until firm & fold into mixture. Fry on hot griddle. *Contributed by Tracy Loshack.*

## French Toast Pigs in a Blanket

10 slices of bread- remove crusts and roll flat
10 cooked breakfast sausages
3 eggs
1/2 cup milk
3 Tbsp. sugar

1 tsp. cinnamon
1 tsp. vanilla
1 Tbsp. flour
Maple Syrup

Cook sausages and set on paper towel to cool and drain. Mix eggs, milk, sugar, cinnamon, vanilla and flour. Roll 1 sausage tightly in each slice of bread. Dip each roll into batter until submersed. Fry in butter until golden brown on all sides. Serve with maple syrup. *Contributed by Brent Matsalla.*

## Lattice Egg Bake

5 eggs
1 cup milk
1/2 tsp salt

1/4 tsp pepper
1/4 cup chopped green onions
1/2 cup shredded cheese

Mix the above ingredients in a bowl & pour into pie crust and bake at 350 deg. for 40 mins. Remove from oven and lattice 7 strips of bacon over top return to oven at 400 deg. for 20 mins. *Contributed by Tracy Loshak.*

## Lodge Pancakes

3 egg yolk
1 1/2 cups buttermilk
3 Tbsp. melted butter
Mix together, then add
1 1/4 cups flour

1/2 tsp. baking soda
2 tsp. sugar
1 tsp. baking powder
1/2 tsp salt
3 egg whites

Mix all ingredients together. Fold in: 3 egg whites that have been whipped stiff. Fry in a pan with hot oil.

*Josie volunteered at the Gateway Lodge Auxiliary and they made these pancakes for the residents and they asked for the recipe. They are really light and fluffy. The residents enjoyed them, of course when they prepared this recipe it was 30 eggs. The auxiliary sold tickets for the spring Lodge Tea. *Contributed by Canora Gateway Lodge.*

## Omelette Muffins

Favorite omelette stuffings
4 beaten eggs
1/4 cup milk

1/2 tsp. baking powder
1/2 tsp. oil
Salt and pepper

Spray/butter muffin tins. Add your favorite Omelette stuffings: Onions, green onions, mushrooms, bacon, ham, etc. Top with your favorite grated cheese/s. Beat 4 eggs with milk. Add baking powder, salt and pepper and oil to the egg mixture. Mix well. Then add eggs to the toppings in the muffin tins and bake at 375 for 20-25 min. Makes 6 omelette muffins.

## Scrambled Eggs

6 eggs
1/2 cup milk
1/4 tsp. salt
1/8 tsp. pepper

Whisk ingredients until eggs are frothy, pour into medium heat frying pan and stir with spatula until fluffy and liquid is dissipated. *Contributed by Arayah Miller.*

## Slow Cooker Steel Cut Oatmeal

1 cup steel cut oats (not quick cooking and not regular oats)
1/2 cup Red River Cereal
5 cups water
1/2 tsp salt

1 tsp cinnamon (or more to taste)
1/4 cup coconut cane sugar (or more to taste)
1/3 cup raisins
1 – 2 apples diced (can leave the peel on for more fiber)
*Continued on next page...*

Put all ingredients in a slow cooker or crockpot, cover and cook for 1 ½ - 2 hours on high or approx. 4 hours on low or until the liquid has been absorbed and the oats are thoroughly cooked. Serve with milk of choice and sweeten to taste with sugar or maple syrup. Can top with chopped almonds or walnuts. Can be frozen. Prepare ingredients in the slow cooker the night before and then turn on upon waking for an easy morning. *Contributed by Shawna Sicotte.*

## Tips and Hints for Breakfast Ideas

Make bacon ahead with less mess by cooking it in the oven. Place 2 sheets of parchment paper between 2 large heavy baking or cookie sheets, place the bacon in layers between the parchment layers. The bacon will be crispier and you could remove from the oven and drain the fat throughout the baking. This is great for preparing bacon for a lot of people.

No time to prepare breakfast:
1. Make boiled eggs ahead of time and store in the shell in a separate open container in the fridge, ready for a quick breakfast on the go, or a quick snack.
2. Make waffles or pancakes in advance and freeze in a freezer bag, they are ready to thaw and heat or pop into a toaster.

For a Mexican twist, simmer eggs in salsa. Add ½ cup salsa in a saucepan and simmer. Crack eggs and prepare as you wish, serve.

## Appetizer Tips

Prepare most appetizers in advance, whenever possible to save the cooking and reheating to just before serving.

Plan color in your display of appetizers and add garnish such as parsley, or dried green onion.

Plan your appetizers per person depending on the serving of your main meal: less if you will serve a meal within the hour, and more if eating later. If you are only serving appetizers provide a variety.

Many dips develop the taste if prepared ahead to blend flavor.

Stack cake stands or raise dishes on boxes when displaying appetizers to be easily reached and short of space.

Serve appetizers or dips inside a hollowed out bread, bell peppers, or melons.

Appetizers should be bite size. But if you require a spoon to be used, put the appetizer in a small cup or shooter glass.

Identify separate signs for allergies, vegan or hot/spicy items so your guests are aware.

Roll up your appetizers using ham or a tortilla wrap, attach with a decorative pick or skewer to easily serve and keep in place.

## Alfredo Sauce

1/4 cup butter
1 cup heavy cream
1 clove garlic

1 1/2 cups grated Parmesan cheese
1/4 cup chopped fresh parsley

Melt butter in a saucepan on medium heat. Add cream and simmer for 5 minutes. Add crushed garlic and cheese and whisk fast. Add cheese and whisk quickly. Stir in parsley and serve. *Contributed by Brent Matsalla.*

## Beer Cheese Dip to serve with Pretzels

4 ounces shredded cheddar Jack
2 ounces of an amber ale
2 ounces cream cheese

1/4 tsp. paprika
Pinch of cayenne pepper if wanting it spicier

In a small saucepan, combine the above 5 ingredients. Stir until melted and smooth. Serve with the pretzels. The pretzels and cheese taste better the same day they were made. NOTE: to increase the amount of cheese sauce for a larger crowd, use the following proportions: Amber Ale - 1 part, Cream cheese - 1 part, Cheddar jack - 2 parts and increase paprika by 1/4 tsp.
NOTE: this cheese dip can be made with dairy free cheese as well.

## Cheddar Cheese and Nacho Cheese Sauce

1 cup milk
4 tsp. all-purpose flour
1/4 tsp. salt

1/2 cup shredded cheddar cheese
1/4 tsp. pepper
Taco seasoning for nacho cheese sauce

Mix 1/4 cup milk and flour in saucepan on medium heat stirring constantly with a whisk. Stir in remaining milk and salt. Bring mixture to boil, stirring constantly to avoid burning on bottom of saucepan. To thicken, reduce heat to low and simmer for a few minutes, continuing to stir. Remove from heat and stir in cheese and pepper. Add a bit of taco seasoning to make a nacho cheese dip. *Contributed by Brent Matsalla.*

## Chili Sauce

30 large ripe tomatoes (peeled and chopped)
8 medium onions
3 green peppers (seeded, diced and cut up)
2 red peppers (seeded, diced and cut up)
2 cups diced celery

3 cups vinegar
3 Tbsp. Pickling salt
2 1/2 cups brown sugar
6 Tbsp. whole mixed pickling spice (tied in cheese cloth bag)

Combine all ingredients bring to a good boil. Then simmer uncovered until thick about 3 hours. Remove pickling spice bag. Pour into hot sterilized jars and seal. Makes about 8 pints.

## Cranberry Sauce

3/4 cup sugar
1/2 cup orange juice
1/2 cup water
12 oz. fresh cranberries rinsed and cleaned

Pinch of salt
1 tsp. cinnamon
Grated rind of an orange

Combine and stir the sugar, orange juice, and water in a saucepan over medium heat. Add cranberries, salt, cinnamon and orange rind. Bring to a simmer over medium heat, stirring frequently. Continue cooking, for 10 minutes but don't let all cranberries to pop, keep some whole. You can also add a handful more cranberries near the end. Let cool 30 minutes. Cover and chill. You can make this recipe up to 3 days in advance. *Contributed by Brent Matsalla.*

## Guacamole

2 avocados, diced and mashed
1 lime squeezed for juice
1 tsp. salt
1/4 cup finely diced onion
3 Tbsp. chopped fresh cilantro
1 plum tomato, diced
1 tsp. minced garlic
1 pinch ground cayenne pepper or a dribble of hot sauce or diced pickled jalapenos

Mix ingredients and cover. Keep refrigerated. *Contributed by Brent Matsalla*

## Horseradish Sauce with Sour Cream

3 Tbsp. butter
3 Tbsp. flour
2 cups milk
1/2 cup sour cream

1/2 tsp. salt
1/2 tsp. pepper
1 1/4 cups horseradish

Melt butter over heat, stir in flour. Add milk slowly bring to a boil. Make sure it's smooth and thick. Stir in sour cream and remove from heat. Season with salt and pepper. Stir in horseradish. This makes 2 cups.

## Horseradish Sauce with Certo

1 cup grated horseradish
1/2 cup vinegar
3/4 cup sugar

1/2 bottle liquid Certo
Yellow food coloring

Combine horseradish and vinegar and blend. Add sugar and Certo. Bring to a rolling boil. Remove from heat and let stand 1 minute and seal in jars. Keep cool. *Contributed by Bernice Gulka.*

### Horseradish Sauce with Water

2 cups grated horseradish

Boil until syrupy:
1 cup sugar
1/2 cup vinegar
1/2 cup water

Cool and add horseradish and then about 3/4 cup sour cream. Mix. *Contributed by Marian Skoretz.*

### Joe's Dill Sauce

1/2 cup Miracle Whip
1/2 cup plain yogurt or sour cream
1 tsp. dried dill weed or 2-3 Tbsp. of fresh dill
1/2 tsp. salt
1/4 tsp. garlic power
1/4 tsp. black pepper
1/4 tsp. onion powder

*Dill sauce on zucchini patties.*

Mix and chill. It's great on anything potato including pierogies and a dip for raw veggies and potato chips. *Contributed by Brent Matsalla.*

### Orange Barbecue Sauce

1/2 cup barbecue sauce
1/2 cup marmalade or 1/4 cup orange juice and 1/4 cup honey

1 tsp. tabasco sauce

Baste on meat.

### Mushrooms Sauce

1 lb. white or brown mushrooms
2 cups whipping cream
1/4 cup margarine

1 pkg. onion soup mix
Garlic powder

Slice the mushrooms and sauté in margarine until there is liquid in the pan from the mushrooms. Add the cream and onion soup mix and a generous dose of garlic powder. Simmer until slightly thickened. These are a very good substitute for hard to come by morels! We made this for every Christmas meal we shared with Grandma! *Contributed by Gerald Kwasny.*

## No Dairy Mushroom Sauce

1 lb. sliced mushrooms
2 Tbsp. olive oil
1 thinly sliced shallot or onion
1 cup dry sherry, vermouth, or wine
1 cup chicken stock
1 Tbsp. soy sauce
2 tsp. cornstarch dissolved in 1 Tbsp. water
1/4 tsp. salt
1/2 tsp. pepper
Optional: fresh dill and green onion

Sauté mushrooms and onions in olive oil. Add sherry/vermouth/wine, chicken stock, soy sauce, salt and pepper. Add dissolved cornstarch and bring to a boil to thicken. *Contributed by Brent Matsalla.*

## Refried Bean Dip

1 small jar salsa
1 can refried beans
1 pkg. taco seasoning mix

1 - 250 gram tub of sour cream
Shredded cheddar cheese (approximately 1 cup)
1 -2 fresh, chopped tomatoes

Heat salsa, beans, and seasoning in a fry pan until bubbly. Pour into a 9" x 13" pan. Or a larger pie plate. Let cool. Add sour cream to cover (or if salsa is really spicy add more) sprinkle with cheddar cheese and add the chopped tomatoes last. You can add more cheese or sour cream depending on your choice. Also alternate: add green onion, diced peppers etc. Serve with plain taco chips. *Contributed by Theresa Mudry.*

## Salmon Dip

1 can salmon
1 pkg. cream cheese
1/4 cup mayonnaise

1 Tbsp. sour cream
2 shakes of dried green chives (optional)

Mix together with mixer or food processor Serve on crackers.

## Salsa

4 tomatoes diced
1 onion diced
2 large jalapenos diced

Parsley or Cilantro
Lime juice
Salt and pepper to taste

Combine and keep refrigerated in sealed container.

## Salted Caramel Sauce

| | |
|---|---|
| 1 cup granulated sugar | 2 Tbsp. salted butter or reg. butter with 1/4 |
| 1/3 cup water | tsp. salt |
| 3/4 cup heavy cream | 1 tsp. vanilla extract |

Add the sugar and water to a heavy bottomed much larger than necessary sauce pan. Make sure all sugar is wet. Cook over medium heat but DO NOT STIR! If you stir it will crystalize. You will need to stand by as the caramel will turn amber, then darker amber, very fast and you need to remove it from the heat immediately when it does turn amber color. SLOWLY add the cream to the amber sugar mixture. It will steam and foam up and try to kill you so be very careful. This is why you need the larger pot. It will also give off steam that can burn you. Add butter and vanilla and stir in until creamy. Refrigerate to thicken. Great on baked apples or pie as well as an ice cream topping along with some chopped nuts of choice. Keeps for 3 months kept refrigerated or 3 months frozen. *Contributed by Brent Matsalla.*

## Sweet and Sour Sauce #1 (for Meatballs)

| | |
|---|---|
| 1/2 cup brown sugar | 1 Tbsp. soya sauce |
| 1/2 cup vinegar | 3 Tbsp. corn starch |
| 1 beef Oxo cube with 1 cup water or 1 cup beef broth | 1 can pineapple chunks |

Bring to a boil and add cornstarch to thicken. Add any type of meatball and heat together in oven for at least 1/2 hour.

## Sweet and Sour Sauce #2 (for Meatballs)

| | |
|---|---|
| 1 cup white sugar | 1/2 cup ketchup |
| 1 cup water | 2 Tbsp. cornstarch |

Boil ingredients and thicken, pour over meatballs and bake for 30 minutes in moderate oven. *Contributed by Eleanor Hadubiak.*

## Vegetable Dip

| | |
|---|---|
| 1 cup mayonnaise | 1 1/2 Tbsp. dill weed |
| 1 cup sour cream | 1 tsp. Beau Monde spice |
| 1 Tbsp. onion powder | |

*Contributed by Mary Rieger.*

# Soups

## Beet Borscht (Ukrainian)

1 onion (diced)
3-4 celery stalks (diced)
2 large carrots (diced)
1 clove garlic (diced) or 1 tsp, of garlic powder
1-2 cups leek (halved and diced, optional)

1 tablespoon butter or coconut oil for sautéing
1 bunch of beets grated (about 3 cups)
1 large can of diced tomatoes
1 carton chicken broth
1/4 cup chopped fresh dill
2-3 Tbsp. chopped fresh parsley
2-3 potatoes (diced)
1 cup frozen peas
2-3 Tbsp. chicken bouillon powder
Salt and pepper to taste

Sauté onion, celery, garlic, and carrots in butter or coconut oil until clear and they start to brown slightly. Season with salt and pepper. Do not burn. Add the leek after the above has been sautéing for 5-10 minutes. Add grated beets, tomatoes, chicken broth, diced potatoes, chopped dill and parsley. Add a bit more seasoning with salt and pepper. Add water to desired consistency. I usually use the chicken broth carton and the empty tomato can to rinse them out. Add chicken bouillon to taste, it should taste just a wee bit salty after adding the bouillon. Bring to a very slow early boil and reduce heat to minimum so the soup just simmers slowly. Cover with lid. Do not bring to a hard boil it will ruin the fresh taste if you boil it vigorously. Simmer for at least an hour. Add frozen peas and simmer for 30 minutes more. You can add a bit of cream or a dollop of sour cream in each soup dish, depending on your taste and/or diet. Keep refrigerated, good for 3-4 days. Do not add the dairy to the whole pot as it won't keep in the fridge as long. Freezes well.

See *Easy Beet Preparation* under *Miscellaneous* to assist with this recipe.

## Bean Dough (Kesta) Soup

8 cups of chicken broth
1/2 cup dried bean variety
(split pea, green or red lentils)
1/2 cup green and yellow
beans cut into bite size pieces
*(any bean variety will work, if
you choice dried navy beans or
pinto beans soak overnight as
package indicates) I have used
canned bean varieties as well.
1/4 cup diced onion
2 stalks of celery
1-2 Tbsp. butter or margarine
Bay leaf
2 eggs, slightly beaten
3/4 cup flour (roughly)
Salt and pepper to taste
1/2 tsp. chicken base

Brown the onion and celery in the butter in a large soup pot. Add the dry beans or the soaked beans. Add the chicken broth and bay leaf. Bring to a boil and reduce heat for about 30 minutes.

Mix with a fork in a medium size bowl, the eggs, then salt, pepper and chicken base. Slowly, 1 tsp. at a time, add the flour to the egg mixture until it forms stiff but still soft dough.
Bring the broth and beans to a soft boil. Using 2 teaspoons, drop the 1/2 a tsp. of dough into the broth one piece at a time. Allowing it to cook and rise in the pot. I use one spoon to hold the dough and the other to remove the pieces into the broth. The spoon used for removal can be dipped into the broth to keep it from sticking occasionally, as the steam from the broth is rising and sticking. If the dough is not forming in the broth add more flour to your egg mixture. The dough pieces will triple in size so try to pinch off small amounts in order to make them bite size. After the dough is dropped into the broth, turn down the heat a bit not to over boil but cook the dough through. The dough pieces should float to the top when cooked. Then serve. Note: fresh beans from the garden are best but I use a frozen variety as well. *Contributed by Theresa Mudry.*

## Broccoli Soup

12 oz. Broccoli heads
1 quart (liter) chicken broth
Parmesan or cheddar cheese

2 Tbsp. cream
Salt and pepper to taste

Bring broth to boil, add broccoli, and cook until tender. Using slotted spoon place broccoli into processor, blend and return to pot, stir in cream add grated cheese for serving.

## Buckwheat (Kasha) Soup

3 cups cooked buckwheat
1 cup cooked rice
3/4 cup butter or margarine
Salt and pepper to taste

1-1/2 cups chicken stock (approximately, used to cover buckwheat)
1/2 cup half-and-half cream (approximately)
6 cups chicken stock

Mix the buckwheat and rice with the salt, pepper, and butter. Place in a buttered casserole dish and add the liquids to just cover the mixture. Bake at 350 for 40 minutes. Service with hot chicken stock. Sauerkraut, bacon and onion could be added as an alternative before baking. The hot casserole could be served as a side dish as well. This Kasha soup has a buttery nut taste.

## Cabbage and Kielbasa Soup

2 tsp. oil
1 cup onions, chopped
1 cup carrots, thinly sliced
1 cup potatoes, diced
1/4 lb. kielbasa sausage, sliced and quartered
1 -19 ounce can tomatoes, coarsely chopped
4 cups cabbage, shredded

2 1/2 cups beef stock (or water and beef bouillon)
1/4 cup parsley, chopped
1 Tbsp. sugar
1/2 tsp. paprika
1/2 tsp. pepper

In large heavy saucepan, heat oil over medium heat; cook onions, carrots, potatoes and kielbasa for 5 minutes or until onions are softened. Stir in tomatoes, cabbage, beef stock, parsley, sugar, paprika and pepper. Cover and bring to a boil. Reduce heat to medium-low; cover and simmer for 20 minutes or until vegetables are tender.

## Cabbage and Potato Borscht (no beets)

In a large soup pot, add 2 peeled potatoes to boil. When you are able to roughly mash the potato with a potato masher in the water. In the meantime, fry 1/2 head of cabbage, 1 medium onion and some celery. Add to the mashed potato. Add 1 can tomato soup with 1 can tomatoes or fresh tomatoes. Bring to a boil and then simmer until vegetables are cooked.

## Cabbage Soup with Caraway Seeds

1 medium head of green cabbage shredded
2 medium onions, chopped
4 Tbsp. butter
2 Tbsp. flour
2 tsp. salt
4 cups water

2 cups tomato juice
1/2 tsp. black pepper
2 Tbsp. sugar
1 tsp. caraway seeds
1/2 to 1 cup sour cream

*Continued on next page...*

Gently cook cabbage and onions in butter on low heat for 15 minutes. Sprinkle with flour and salt. Slowly add water and tomato juice, pepper, sugar and caraway seeds. Cook uncovered in low heat for about 1 hour. Service hot topped with sour cream. Can add one or two potatoes after the water and tomato juice. *Contributed by Mona Zarazun.*

## Carrot Soup

| | |
|---|---|
| 3 Tbsp. butter, onion and garlic | 2 stalks celery |
| Melt butter and heat onion and garlic. | 1 bay leaf |
| 5 cups water | 2 Tbsp. chicken in a mug |
| 2 1/2 cups carrots sliced | Salt to taste |
| 1/4 cup rice | |

Add remaining ingredients, boil then cool. Remove bay leaf and blend before serving.

## Cheddar, Cauliflower and Potato Soup

| | |
|---|---|
| 4 cups cauliflower chopped | 2/3 cup onion, chopped |
| 1 cup potato, diced | 3 Tbsp. flour |
| 1 container chicken broth | 3 cups milk |
| 3 Tbsp. butter | 2 1/2 cups shredded cheddar cheese |

Cook cauliflower and potato in broth until tender. Meanwhile in saucepan melt butter, sauté onion stir in flour and gradually whisk in milk. Cook stirring until thickened. Stir into cauliflower mixture. Remove from heat, add cheese stirring until cheese melts can add parmesan cheese to serve. *Contributed by Bernice Gulka.*

## French Onion Soup

| | |
|---|---|
| 3 Tbsp. butter or margarine | 1 Liter beef broth (or beef bouillon cubes |
| 3 large onions, sliced thin | dissolved in 1 L water) |
| 1 Tbsp. flour | 4 thick slices French or Italian bread |
| 1/2 tsp salt | 1/3 cup grated mozzarella cheese |
| Pepper, to taste | 1/3 cup grated Parmesan cheese |

In a heavy soup pot, melt the butter or margarine and brown the onions slowly, until golden. Sprinkle in the flour to coat onion evenly and cook a few minutes. Season with salt and pepper and add broth, stirring continually to blend well. Bring to a boil, the lower to simmer and cook, lightly covered, for 30 minutes. Toast bread and place in large ovenproof soup tureen or individual ovenproof bowls. Sprinkle bread with Parmesan cheese; pour soup over bread and top with grated Mozzarella cheese. Brown the cheese under the broiler and serve.
Grandma really enjoyed this soup! *Contributed by Twila Hadubiak.*

## Italian Wedding Soup

1 egg lightly beaten
1/2 cup dry bread crumbs
4 Tbsp. parmesan cheese
1 pkg. frozen, chopped, thawed, drained spinach

10 cups chicken broth
1 1/2 tsp. Italian seasoning
1 lb. ground beef
1/2 cup uncooked orzo pasta
Salt and pepper

In saucepan bring broth to a boil. Reduce heat and simmer. In a bowl, combine egg, 2 Tbsp. parmesan cheese, Italian seasoning and bread crumbs. Mix with ground beef, shape into 1" balls, brown and add to broth. Reduce heat and simmer. Add pasta, seasoning to broth when almost done add spinach and remaining parmesan cheese.

## Kapusta (Sauerkraut) Soup

1 cup diced onion
2 cloves crushed garlic
1 cup diced celery
1 cup leek, halved then diced (optional)
1 cup diced carrots
1/2 lb. bacon or smoked ham or back bacon or ham bone

1 qt. sauerkraut
2-3 cups chicken stock
4 bay leaves
1/4 cup fresh dill
2 cans of Habitant French Canadian Pea Soup
Salt and pepper to taste

Fry up the bacon using the soup pot. Just as the bacon is almost fully cooked, toss in the onion, garlic, celery and carrots and fry in the bacon fat until the onions are clear. Be careful not to burn the vegetables, so stir quite often and a lot. While you're frying the bacon and the vegetables, put the sauerkraut in a sieve and give it a nice cold water bath under a running tap. Add the washed and drained sauerkraut to the pot and keep frying it. Depending on how much bacon fat there was, you may want to add some butter. When the sauerkraut starts to brown a bit, add the chicken stock and bay leaves. Simmer it for about an hour covered with a lid. Add the Habitant Pea Soup and simmer another ½ to 1 hour. Serve with some half-and-half cream or a teaspoon dollop of sour cream.

## Kapusta Soup

Pork riblets – couple packs
1 big jar of sauerkraut
1 onion chopped
Whipping cream

Boil pork riblets for 2 hours, skimming off the junk off the top. Take the jar of sauerkraut, drain and boil in water until soft, which isn't very long, drain. Fry onion in butter, until soft. Add to sauerkraut. Make a paste with 1 1/2 Tbsp. of flour with butter. Place in strainer and add whipping cream to sauerkraut with broth from pork riblets. I clean the riblets off and add the meat to the soup, the best part, in my opinion. Enjoy!

Side note: this is the way my mom (Rosie) made it, without a recipe of course! She was quite sick already, but before she was too sick to tell me how she made it, I made sure I received the details, because it is a family favourite. *Contributed by Darla Wolkowski.*

## Kasha or Buckwheat Lazy Cabbage Rolls

2 cups of buckwheat
3 cups of chicken broth
1 diced onion
2 cups shredded cabbage or coleslaw mix
(you can also sub shredded kale, Swiss chard, or beet leaves)

1/2 cup butter or margarine
1/4 cup chopped fresh dill
3/4 cup milk (or substitute broth and more margarine/butter to top) almond milk works fine too.

Cook buckwheat on medium heat in broth like you would cook rice, but only to a thick lava-like consistency, stirring often so it doesn't burn on the bottom. While buckwheat is cooking, lightly fry (3 min or so, remember you are baking this as well) an onion and the cabbage/coleslaw with the butter or margarine. Add fresh dill and combine all ingredients into one pot. Add the milk, or you can substitute more broth and top with some more butter/margarine instead. Almond milk works fine. Bake at 350F until the top is nicely brown, for 1 -1 1/2 hours. Eat as soup by adding to warm chicken broth, or heat and serve with ketchup as a lazy cabbage roll side dish. The soup is wonderful paired with kale chips.

## Kutia (Traditional "Ukrainian Christmas" Wheat Soup)

2 cups wheat

1/3 cup honey

3 qt. water

1 cup poppy seeds

2/3 cup sugar

1/2 cup chopped nuts (optional)

Dry wheat in an oven set at 250 for 1 hour, stirring occasionally. Wash and soak in water overnight. Next morning, bring wheat to boil and simmer for 3-4 hours until kernels burst open. Scald poppy seeds and simmer for 3-5 min. Drain poppy seeds and grind twice using finest blade on food processor. Set aside. Combine honey and sugar in hot water. Set aside. Before serving add sweetened mix and poppy seeds to cooled boiled water.

## Lemon Rice Soup

To the chicken broth add:

2 grated carrots

1/2 cup rice

1/4 cup lemon rind (finely grated) using some juice also.

When heated through and rice cooked, add a 1/2 small container of cream. This makes 3 quarts of soup. *Contributed by Twila Hadubiak. (Josie loved this soup).*

## Potato Leek Soup

3-4 Rustic (or Yukon Gold) potatoes (peeled, cubed)

2-3 cups cleaned, chopped leek

1 small onion chopped

3 cloves of garlic, minced

4 Tbsp. butter or margarine

Salt and pepper to taste

5- 6 cups chicken broth or water with bouillon

1/2 head of cauliflower, chopped fine (optional)

1/2 cup cream (optional)

Sour cream, bacon bits and chives for garnish

Melt butter and cook the onion and leeks until coated in butter and onions are transparent. Add the potatoes and cauliflower, sauté about 5 minutes, then add the salt and pepper and the garlic, stir 1 minute. Add enough chicken broth to cover the vegetables and simmer the soup until the potatoes are tender. Optional: I have used leftover baked potatoes and diced the potato (with the skins) into the soup. This takes less time to cook. Another option: The soup broth will become creamy so adding cream may not be required. If you prefer to have a more chunky soup texture, a rough smash with a potato masher in the pot will crush most of the potatoes, or if you prefer, blend the entire soup. Serving the soup with sour cream, chives and bacon bits is the best. This was another favourite soup of Josie's. Brent introduced her to leeks on one of his visits and Eleanor started to grow them, so Josie enjoyed making this soup. *Contributed by Theresa Mudry.*

## Roasted Red Pepper and Sweet Potato Soup

| | |
|---|---|
| 3 sweet red peppers chopped roughly | 3 cloves garlic |
| 2 sweet potatoes peeled, diced | 2 Tbsp. olive oil |
| 1 medium onion | 1 tsp. Italian seasoning |

Put the above ingredients into an oven proof roaster at 425 for 1 hour or until the vegetables are soft. Slightly cool. The food process the vegetables to the consistency that you prefer. Some chucks or all puree. Add 1 liter of chicken or vegetable stock. Bring soup to a boil and simmer. Note you could serve with a yogurt dollop in your bowl. Other vegetables that could be interchanged: regular potatoes as well as sweet potatoes, some carrots could work as well. *Contributed by Theresa Mudry.*

## Russian (Doukhobor) Cabbage Borscht

1 clove garlic (diced) or 1 tsp of garlic powder
1-2 cups leek (halved and diced, optional)
1 tablespoon butter or coconut oil for sautéing
3 cups chopped cabbage
1 can of tomato soup or 1 can of tomato paste
1 can diced tomatoes
1 carton chicken broth
1/4 cup chopped fresh dill
2-3 Tbsp. chopped fresh parsley
2-3 potatoes (whole/peeled)
2-3 Tbsp. chicken bouillon powder
Salt and pepper to taste

1 onion (diced)
3-4 celery stalks (diced)
2 large carrots (diced)

Sauté onion, celery, garlic, and carrots in butter or coconut oil until clear and they start to brown slightly. Season with salt and pepper. Do not burn. Add the leek and cabbage after the above has been sautéing for 5-10 minutes and sauté for another 5-10 minutes until the cabbage begins to soften and cook. Add tomato soup, diced tomatoes, chicken broth, peeled potatoes whole, chopped dill and parsley. Add a bit more seasoning with salt and pepper. Add water to desired consistency. I usually use the chicken broth carton and the empty tomato can to rinse them out. Add chicken bouillon to taste, it should taste just a wee bit salty after adding the bouillon. Bring to a very slow early boil and reduce heat to minimum so the soup just simmers slowly. Cover with lid. Do not bring to a hard boil it will ruin the fresh taste if you boil it vigorously. Simmer for at least an hour. Take out the whole potatoes and mash them, then add back to the soup and simmer for 30 minutes more. You can add a bit of cream or a dollop of sour cream in each soup dish, depending on your taste and/or diet. Keep refrigerated, good for 3-4 days. Do not add the dairy to the whole pot as it won't keep in the fridge as long. Freezes well.

## Southwest Hamburger Soup

1 lb. ground beef or leftover meatloaf
1 Tbsp. Worcestershire sauce
1 Tbsp. A1 or HP steak sauce
1 tsp. garlic powder
1 1/2 tsp. cumin powder
1 1/2 tsp. ground ginger
1 Tbsp. parsley flakes
1 tsp. chili powder
1 cup diced onion
1 cup diced celery
1 cup diced carrot
1 cup diced peppers
1 cup sliced mushrooms
1/2 cup leek (optional)
2-4 bay leaves
1 can diced tomatoes
1 carton beef broth
1/2-1 cup pearl barley
Corn and beans can also be added but
optional
Salt and pepper to your taste
Butter for sautéing

Brown hamburger, Worcestershire, garlic, cumin, chili, salt and pepper. Or you can also use leftover hamburger or meatloaf. Drain fat and set aside. Sauté onion, celery, carrots, peppers, leek, and mushrooms. Salt and pepper to taste. Add broth, tomatoes, bay leaves, and barley. You can also add corn and beans if you like. *Contributed by Brent Matsalla.*

## Split Pea Soup

Boil ham bone in water with 2 tbsps. Pickling spices in a cheese cloth. Also add 1 small onion, 2 stalks celery and 2 carrots with 1 cup dried split peas for about 1-2 hours until bone is dry and vegetables are over cooked. Remove bone and any fat that doesn't belong in the soup. Blend. This can also be made with cauliflower.

## Zuppa Tuscan (Kale and Potato) Soup

1 medium onion, diced
1 clove garlic, minced
2 Tbsp. margarine or butter
1 stalk of celery diced
1/2 lb. bacon, diced
2 spicy sausage links or 1/2 lb. ground beef
Chicken broth
4 large potatoes, sliced raw
Beans could be added as well
Red pepper flakes
Kale
1/2 cup cream
Parmesan Cheese

In a large soup pot brown onion and garlic and celery in margarine or butter. Add the bacon pieces to fry crisp. Add and brown 2 spicy sausages (taken out of the casing) or use ground beef with a spice. Drain the fat from the meat. Add: chicken broth and sliced potatoes or if desired beans. Boil until potatoes are cooked. Add red pepper flakes. Add cream. Add cut up Kale. Cook to heat through. When serving sprinkle parmesan cheese on top of each bowl. *Contributed by Theresa Mudry and daughter Mandelle Waddell.*

## Tips for Soups

- Chop all vegetables in spoon sizes to be eaten easily.

- Double your recipe and save another meal, most soups can be frozen.

- Consider each vegetable ingredient has a specific cook time. Such as: potato cooks longer than a tiny pea so add the pea at the end of your soup cooking time.

- Use salt sparingly and add additional salt if needed at the end. Too much salt, usually you could add a small cooked potato or some rice to absorb the salt added.

- Simmer is the best way to prepare a good soup.

- Add noodles as the final addition and cook tenderly. The noodles take on the flavor of the broth.

- Warm your milk or cream before adding to your soup to prevent curdling. You can even remove the soup from the heat and stir in your warm milk.

# Seasonings & Spice Mixes

## BBQ Rub

1/2 cup brown sugar
2 Tbsp. paprika
1 Tbsp. smoked paprika
1 Tbsp. black pepper
1 Tbsp. kosher salt

1 Tbsp. garlic powder
1 Tbsp. onion powder
1 tsp. mustard powder
1/4 tsp. cayenne pepper

Mix and store in airtight container until ready to use. *Contributed by Brent Matsalla.*


## Blackened Cajun Spice

3 Tbsp. smoked paprika
2 tsp. onion powder
1 tsp. garlic powder
1 tsp. thyme
1 tsp. oregano
1 tsp. cayenne (+ or -)
1 tsp. pepper
1 1/2 tsp. salt

Mix and store in airtight container. Good on all meats and fish/sea food. Also great on grilled vegetables. You can also use this for dips, chili, eggs, and soups. *Contributed by Brent Matsalla.*


## Burrito Seasoning

1/2 tsp. chili powder
1/2 tsp. paprika
1/4 tsp. garlic powder
2 tsp. ground cumin
1/4 tsp. black pepper
1 tsp. salt

Mix together. Equivalent to 1 store-bought package. *Contributed by Brent Matsalla.*

## Cajun Spice Rub

2 tsp. salt
2 tsp. garlic powder
2 1/2 tsp. paprika
1 tsp. ground black pepper
1 tsp. onion powder

1 tsp. cayenne pepper
1 1/4 tsp. dried oregano
1 1/4 tsp. dried thyme
1/2 tsp. red pepper flakes

Mix and store in airtight container. Also great on corn and potato hash browns. *Contributed by Brent Matsalla.*


## Fajita Seasoning

1 Tbsp. cornstarch
2 tsp. chili powder
1 tsp. paprika
1 tsp. salt
1 tsp. white sugar

1/2 tsp. onion powder
1/2 tsp. garlic powder
1/2 tsp. ground cumin
1/4 tsp. cayenne pepper

Mix together and store in airtight container or Ziploc bag. Makes 4 servings. *Contributed by Brent Matsalla.*


## Greek Souvlaki Seasoning

2 Tbsp. paprika
2 Tbsp. oregano
2 tsp. thyme
1 tsp. garlic powder
1 tsp. ground cumin
1/2 tsp. cinnamon

1 tsp. salt
1 tsp. freshly ground pepper
1 tsp. dried mint or 2 Tbsp. fresh chopped mint leaves
Lemon juice
Olive oil

Blend spices (makes 1/4 cup). Use 1 Tbsp. seasoning mix to 2 Tbsp. lemon juice and 2 Tbsp. olive oil. Combine in Ziploc bag and add choice of cubed chicken, pork, or lamb for skewers. Refrigerate for 2 hours, mixing every half hour. Do not cut your cubes too thin or soak in marinade too long or you won't be able to skewer them without them falling apart. Soak skewers in hot water for half an hour before skewering. Grill skewers until meat is cooked. *Contributed by Brent Matsalla.*

## Jamaican Jerk Seasoning

2 tsp. cayenne pepper
2 tsp. salt
2 tsp. pepper
2 tsp. brown sugar
1/2 tsp. hot pepper flakes
1/2 tsp. cinnamon
1/2 tsp. nutmeg
1/2 tsp. clove
1/4 tsp. cumin
1 tsp. allspice
1 tsp. parsley
1 Tbsp. onion powder | 1 tsp. paprika
1 Tbsp. garlic powder | 2 tsp. thyme

Mix and store in airtight container. Great on meats, seafood, corn and grilled vegetables. *Contributed by Brent Matsalla.*

## Taco Seasoning

1 Tbsp. chili powder
1/4 tsp. garlic powder
1/4 tsp. onion powder
1/4 tsp. dried oregano
1/4 tsp. crushed red pepper flakes

1 1/2 tsp. ground cumin
1/2 tsp. paprika
1 tsp. sea salt
1 tsp. black pepper

Mix together and store in airtight container or Ziploc bag. Makes 10 servings. *Contributed by Brent Matsalla.*

## Vanilla Sugar Spice

2 cups raw organic sugar (or regular will work as well larger granular appears more elegant)
1 vanilla bean or 2 tsp. of pure vanilla extract

If using the vanilla bean - slice the bean and loosen the seeds in the bean - cut the bean into smaller pieces. Place the sugar and the vanilla bean pieces, with seeds into a jar with a cover. Shake the jar daily for up to 14 days. You will know the vanilla bean is completely extracted when the sugar has changed color. If you are using the liquid vanilla extract the method is quicker, mix the sugar and extract together in a sealable bag. Knead the sugar until the vanilla is evenly distributed. Then place on a cookie sheet to dry for 30 minutes. This sugar can be used from an airtight container. Add to fresh fruit, flavor a cup of coffee or hot chocolate, cookie or pie topping; even biscuits coming out of the oven. Great wrapped with a bow as a gift. *Contributed by Theresa Mudry.*

# Salads

## Creamy Bacon and Pea Salad

12 strips thick cut bacon, cooked and chopped finely
4 cups frozen sweet peas, thawed
1/2 cup shredded mild cheddar cheese
1/2 medium red onion, diced finely

Dressing:
1/2 cup sour cream
1/3 cup real mayonnaise
1 Tbsp. granulated sugar
2 tsp. white vinegar
Salt and pepper to taste

Whisk together all ingredients for the dressing in a large serving bowl until smooth and combined. Add chopped bacon, peas, cheddar cheese, and diced onions and mix. Chill for 3 hours before serving. *Contributed by Brent Matsalla.*

## Coleslaw Dressing

1 egg or 2 yolks
1/4 cup sugar (or less)
1 tsp. salt
2 tsp. cornstarch

1 tsp. dry or prepared mustard
1/3 cup vinegar
1/3 cup water
1 Tbsp. butter

Beat egg or yolks, stir in sugar, salt, cornstarch, and mustard. Gradually blend in vinegar and water. Cook in double boiler stirring constantly until thickened about 5-7 minutes add butter. Makes about 1 1/4 cups. Could use hot or cold over cabbage. Leftover or make ahead can store in fridge. *Contributed by Eleanor Hadubiak.*

## Coleslaw

2 or 3 heads of cabbage
2 sweet onions
2 or 3 carrots shredded or more
1/4 cup sugar sprinkle on vegetables and mix well
Brine:
1 cup vinegar
2/3 cup sugar
1 Tbsp. prepared mustard
1 tsp. salt
1 tsp. celery seed

Boil all the brine ingredients and then add 1 cup oil, boil for 1 minute longer. Put in jars and keep in fridge for weeks.

Another brine recipe:
1 cup vinegar

1 cup white sugar
1 cup Mazola oil

Boil for 5 minutes, pour over vegetables and seal in jars will keep in fridge for weeks. *Contributed by Rosie Wolkowski.*

## Cucumber Salad

8 or 10 cups cucumbers sliced with some peeled and some not
2 onions sliced (1 cup on average)

1 red and 1 green pepper, cut in pieces
As much celery as you like

Mix 3 Tbsp. pickling salt through the prepared vegetables, let sit in fridge for 1/2 hour then drain thoroughly.

In meantime mix:
2 cups sugar

1 cup vinegar
1 tsp. celery seed

Stir well until sugar dissolves but do not cook. Put drained vegetables in jar and pour the mix over cucumbers. Can be used in 8 hours from the fridge and will keep in fridge for up to 2 months. *Contributed by Olga Fullawka.*

## Cucumber Salad (refrigerated) with Mayo

3 cups mayo
1 cup sugar
1/2 cup vinegar

Salt and pepper to taste
Add slices of onion and cucumber.

Beat together all ingredients except cucumbers. Add cucumbers, then mix well together.

## Cucumber Sour Cream Salad

1 cup sour cream
3 Tbsp. chopped onion
2 Tbsp. dill
2 Tbsp. vinegar

1 Tbsp. sugar
1 tsp. salt
4 medium cucumbers sliced (about 5 cups)

Beat together all ingredients except cucumbers. Add cucumbers, then mix well together.

## Dill Pickle Pasta Salad

1/2 lb. dry shell pasta or approx. 3 cups
3/4 cup sliced pickles
2/3 cup cheddar cheese diced
3 Tbsp. finely diced white onion
3-4 Tbsp. fresh dill
1/2 cup pickle juice

Dressing:
2/3 cup mayonnaise
1/3 cup sour cream
1/8 tsp. cayenne pepper
4 Tbsp. pickle juice
Salt & pepper to taste

Boil pasta to package directions. Run under cold water to stop cooking. Toss cold pasta with about 1/2 cup of pickle juice and set aside for about 5 minutes. Drain & discard pickle juice. Combine all dressing ingredients in a small bowl and mix well. Toss all ingredients in a large bowl. Refrigerate at least 1 hour before serving. *Contributed by Brent Matsalla.*

## Dreamsicle Salad

1 - 3 oz. pkg. sugar free orange Jell-O
1 - 3 oz. pkg. sugar free instant vanilla
pudding

1 - 10 oz. can mandarin oranges, drained
1 - 8 oz. tub fat free frozen whipped topping,
thawed

Dissolve Jell-O in 1 cup boiling water. Add 1/2 cup cold water; let set in fridge for 20 minutes. With mixer or whisk, add dry vanilla pudding mix and beat until smooth. Fold in oranges and whipped topping (by hand). Refrigerate. Try strawberry Jell-O with strawberries, peach Jell-O with (no sugar added) peaches, etc. *Contributed by Brent Matsalla.*

## Fall Apple Salad

1 can (20 ounces) crushed pineapple,
undrained
2/3 cup sugar
1 pkg. (3 ounces) cream cheese, softened
1 cup diced unpeeled apples

1/2 to 1 cup chopped nuts
1 cup chopped celery
1 cup whipped topping
Lettuce leaves to serve

In a saucepan, combine pineapple and sugar; bring to a boil and boil for 3 minutes. Add gelatin; stir until dissolved. Add cream cheese; stir until mixture is thoroughly combined. Cool. Fold in apples, nuts, celery and whipped topping. Pour into a 9" x 9" pan. Chill until firm. Cut into squares and serve on lettuce leaves.

## Hickory Sticks Salad

1 can or 1 cup flaked turkey or leftover
turkey and chicken pieces
1 pkg. Hickory sticks
1/2 cup celery diced

1/2 cup shredded carrots
1 small onion diced small
1 cup cheddar cheese

Add miracle whip to ingredients to combine and dampen.

## Jelled Ginger Apple Salad

Soften 1 pkg. unflavored gelatin in 1/2 cup
ginger ale dissolved over hot water.
Add in 3/4 cup salad dressing

1/4 tsp salt
3/4 cup sour cream

Blend well chill until partially set fold in stiffly beaten egg whites. Pour into mold add 3/4 cup chopped walnuts. Dissolve 2-3 oz. pkg. lemon Jell-O in 3 cups hot ginger ale. Chill until partially set. Fold in 1 cup whole cranberry sauce, and 2 or 3 finely chopped apples. Pour over first layer.

## Jellied Vegetable Salad

| | |
|---|---|
| 1 pkg. lemon or lime Jell-O | 1 1/2 cups boiling water |
| 1 Tbsp. chopped onion (can be green onion) | 1/2 cup green pepper (optional) |
| Pinch of salt | 1 large carrot, shredded |
| 1 tsp. vinegar | 1/2 cup to 3/4 cup miracle whip |

Dissolve Jell-O in water and add vinegar and salt. Let set partially, then whip in salad dressing (miracle whip) and fold in vegetables.

## Jell-O Three Layer Salad

First layer:
1 pkg. lime Jell-O powder
1 cup well drained crushed pineapple
1 cup boiling water
Pour into 9" x 13" pan, partially set before pouring over second layer.

Second layer:
1 pkg. lemon Jell-O powder
1 cup cottage cheese (put through a sieve)
1 cup boiling water
1 cup whipping cream.

Let Jell-O cool and set slightly, cream the cheese whip the cream, add to Jell-O and pour over the slightly set first layer.

Third layer:
1 pkg. Cherry Jell-O powder

1 3/4 cups boiling water

When partially set, add well drained fruit. (any fruit but fruit cocktail in a can works well) pour over partially set 2nd layer and set in fridge to firm all layers.

## Lettuce and Radish Basic Salad with Dressing

| | |
|---|---|
| 4 cups torn leaf or iceberg lettuce | 1/8 cup sugar |
| 2 sliced green onions | 1/8 cup vinegar |
| 4 or more radishes | 1/4 cup half-and-half cream or sour cream |

Place vegetables in a large bowl. In a small bowl, stir the sugar, vinegar and cream until smooth. Just before serving pour over lettuce, toss lightly.

## Onion Salad

1/2 cup water
1/2 cup vinegar
3/4 cup sugar
2 tsp. salt
2 cups sliced onion (6 to 8 medium size)

Boil water, vinegar and sugar. Pour over sliced onions and let cool. (3 to 4 hours) Drain well.

Combine sauce:
2 Tbsp. mayonnaise
2 Tbsp. sour cream

3 tsp. celery seed
Salt and pepper

Add to drained onions and refrigerate. *Contributed by Elsie Obodiak.*


## Refrigerator Cucumber Salad

16 large cucumbers, peeled
3 medium onions
1 Tbsp. salt

Mix in:
3 cups Hellman's mayonnaise
1 cup sugar (or less)
1/2 cup vinegar
1 tsp. pepper
1 tsp. celery seed

Shred or finely cut cucumbers and onions in food processor. Add salt and let stand overnight. Drain very well in a colander for 2 - 3 hours. Store in sealable container in fridge up to 4 months.


## Saskatchewan Wedding Jell-O layered "Salad"

*1st layer* – Dissolve 1 cup boiling water and 1 package lime Jell-O. Add 1 cup (well drained) crushed pineapple. Pour into 9" x 13" pan and let set in fridge.

*2nd layer* – Dissolve 1 cup boiling water and 1 package lemon Jell-O. Cool slightly. Whip 1 cup whipping cream. Add 1 cup cottage cheese. Mix with partially set Jell-O. Pour over 1st layer and let set.

*3rd layers* – Dissolve 1/2 cup boiling water and 1 package cherry Jell-O. Cool slightly. Add can of well drained fruit cocktail or can of mandarin oranges. Pour over 2nd layer and let set. *Contributed by Sammy Breker.*

*Baba Josie's Kitchen*

77

## Sauerkraut Salad

1-28 oz. tin of rinsed sauerkraut       1 cup of sugar
1 medium onion sliced                   1/2 tsp. salt
1 carrot coarsely grated                1/2 cup salad oil
1 cup celery chopped                    1/2 cup vinegar
1 green pepper (optional)

Boil brine of sugar, salt, salad oil and vinegar. Pour over vegetables.

## Spinach Make Ahead

Large bunch spinach leaves                      1/2 cup sour cream
1/2 cup Swiss cheese, created or cubed          3 Tbsp. milk
1/2 cup cheddar cheese, shredded or cubed       2 tsp. lemon juice
2 cups mushrooms sliced                         2 tsp. granulated sugar
4 hardboiled eggs, sliced                       1/4 cup green onion, sliced thin
1 cup mayo                                      4 bacon slices, cooked and crumbled

Arrange torn up clean spinach leaves in bottom of medium size glass bowl, put cheese on top. Spread mushrooms over cheese. Cover with sliced eggs. In a small bowl cream together mayo, sour cream, milk, lemon juice and sugar. Stir in onion. Spread over top of salad right to the sides of bowl. Cover. Chill overnight and serve sprinkled with bacon on top. Substitute could be romaine lettuce instead of spinach.

## Spinach Salad

1 package baby spinach leaves - washed and      Dressing:
stems removed                                   1 small cup container of strawberry yogurt
8-10 fresh mushrooms – washed and sliced        2 Tbsp. of red wine vinegar
8-10 fresh strawberries – washed and sliced     2 Tbsp. of lemon juice
1/2 purple onion or a regular sweet onion –     1 Tbsp. of dried basil
sliced and quartered                            Salt and pepper to taste
1/2 lb. of bacon – fried, and chopped or
crumbled
3 hard-boiled eggs - sliced

Try different fruits and different flavors of yogurt to change it up every now and then. Blueberries are great too! You can also add toasted walnuts or pine nuts too. *Contributed by Brent Matsalla.*

## Taco Salad

1 lb. ground beef
1 can kidney beans (drained)
Dash tabasco sauce
1 1/2 heads of lettuce finely chopped

1 medium onion finely chopped
4 tomatoes finely chopped
1 1/2 cups grated cheese
Bag of flavored taco chips

Dressing: 1 bottle of green goddess dressing or 1 small bottle creamy cucumber dressing. Brown hamburger, add beans, tabasco sauce, let simmer, then cool, prepare the rest of ingredients and add together with dressing of choice.

## Wheat Salad

8 oz. cream cheese
2 Tbsp. lemon juice
1 large pkg. vanilla instant pudding

2 cups cooked wheat
1 large cool whip
1 can crushed pineapple drained

Mix together cream cheese, lemon juice, pudding and fold into cool whip. Add to wheat and pineapple.

## Canned Fruit – Syrup

**Thin syrup -** use 1 cup sugar to 2 cups water
**Medium syrup -** use 1 cup sugar to 1 cup water
**Thick syrup -** use 2 cups sugar to 1 cup water

**Boil the sugar and water in a covered saucepan for 5 minutes generally speaking, allow 1 cup syrup to each pint jar.**

## Tips for Sauces and Dips

**Sauces and dips are a great way to get more vegetables into our diets. It could be made healthy by controlling the additives. Make it green or black for Hallowe'en, red for Christmas. Giving permission to eat with our clean fingers can be more interesting, just remember if you have a double dipper in your family, individual bowls are still interesting.**

# Main Courses

## Baked Fried Chicken

1/2 tsp. salt
1 tsp. seasoning salt
3/4 tsp. pepper
1 cup flour
2 tsp. paprika

In separate bowls for coating:
2 eggs, beaten
Milk
Breadcrumbs

Preheat the oven to 400. Cut ½ stick of butter into pieces and place in a 9" x 13" pan. Melt butter in the pre-heat. Spread butter on bottom of pan, make sure there are no dry areas. Mix dry ingredients, beat eggs in separate bowl along with separate bowls for flour/spice mix and breadcrumbs. Dip chicken pieces in milk, shake excess milk off. Dip into flour/spice mix, then dip in egg, and roll in breadcrumbs. Cook for 20 min. turning part way through. *Contributed by Brent Matsalla.*

## Barley and Mushroom Casserole

1 can pieces and stems drained
4 Tbsp. or more butter
1 large onion chopped

1 cup pearl barley uncooked
2 cups chicken broth

Sauté onions and mushrooms. Add uncooked barley and brown lightly. Pour into greased casserole. Add 1 cup broth season to task with salt and pepper. Cover and bake at 350 for 25 minutes. Uncover the casserole and add the 2nd cup of broth. Continue cooking until barley is cooked, if necessary an additional cup of broth may be required if all liquid is absorbed. *Contributed by Albina Hrychenko.*

## Beef and Vegetable Casserole

4 or 5 potatoes
5 or 6 carrots
1 lb. hamburger
1 onion

Salt and pepper to taste
1 Tbsp. vinegar
1 can mushroom soup
1 can creamed corn

Cut and peel potatoes and carrots into bite size pieces, put in casserole. Fry hamburger and onion until brown, add salt and pepper and vinegar. Add the soup and corn last to the casserole dish. Cook at 350 for 45 min. *Contributed by Rosie Wolkowski.*

## Beef Tacos

1 lb ground beef
1 pkg. taco seasoning
1 pkg. soft tortilla shells
1 cup shredded lettuce
1 cup shredded marble cheese
1 small tomato
Sour cream
Salsa

Brown ground beef in a frying pan. Drain. Add in package of taco seasoning with 2/3 cup water. Boil, stirring occasionally. Set taco shell on plate, fill with favourite toppings. Kyler goes for meat, cheese, and lettuce. Delicious! *Contributed by Kyler Eikelenboom.*

## Best Ever Meatloaf

2 eggs
2/3 cup milk
2 tsp salt
1/4 tsp pepper
3 slices fresh bread, crumbled
1 onion, chopped

1/2 cup shredded raw carrots
1 cup shredded cheddar cheese
1 1/2 lb. ground beef
1/4 cup brown sugar
1/4 cup ketchup
1 Tbsp. prepared mustard

Beat eggs lightly with fork. Add milk, salt, pepper, and bread. Beat again then add onion, carrots, cheese and beef, mix well. Pack into 9" x 5" loaf pan. Combine brown sugar, ketchup and mustard. Spread over loaf. Bake at 350° for 1 hour, let stand 10 minutes. *Contributed by Twila Hadubiak.*

## Bread Meat Tarts

Sliced bread
1 lb. lean ground beef
1 can mushroom soup
1 Tbsp. Worcestershire sauce
1/2 tsp salt

1/4 tsp. pepper
1 egg beaten
Dash of garlic powder
1/2 cup finely chopped onion

Cut crust off bread, butter one side of the bread, place buttered side into the muffin tin and press firmly. Fry onion and ground beef until browned and drain excess fat. Cool. Add all other ingredients to the meat. Mix and add to muffin tins and bake. Bake in 350 oven for 25-30 min.
Note: can add fresh mushrooms to the meat mixture and mozzarella cheese on top before baking.

## Canned Chicken

Chicken, cut into serving size pieces
2 Tbsp. pickling salt

1 gallon cold water

Cut chicken into serving sized pieces. Soak chicken overnight in a brine made of 2 Tbsp. pickling salt to 1 gallon cold water. The next morning drain off brine and pat dry. Pack pieces into sterilized quart jars. Wipe tops clean. Place on sterilized lids. Process in canner in hot water bath for 3 hours, timing from when the water begins to boil. Check to make sure jars are sealed before storing in a cool dark place. *Contributed by Eleanor Hadubiak.*

## Chicken in Onion Soup

1/2 cup honey
1/4 cup soya sauce
2 Tbsp. catsup

Dash of garlic powder
1 pkg. onion soup mix

Bake or boil chicken pieces. Drain and add sauce then bake 1/2 hour or so for sauce to coat.

## Chicken Cordon Bleu

Chicken breasts (cut in half and cut a pocket into the center)
1 slice of ham for each chicken breast
1 slice of Swiss cheese for each chicken breast
Flour

Bread crumbs
1/2 tsp. salt
1/4 tsp. pepper
4 eggs
2 Tbsp. water
Oil

Make a pocket in each half of chicken breast. This is easier to do when the meat is slightly frozen. Roll a slice of cheese and ham together and insert into the pocket. Refrigerate for 30 min. Combine flour, salt and pepper. Beat the eggs separately with the water. Coat the breasts with flour and dip in egg, then coat in bread crumbs, form into round mounds. Refrigerate for 1 hour. Brown each chicken breast in hot oil on both sides, use a paper towel to remove excess oil. Place on to baking dish and bake about 1/2 hour at 300. Freeze well.

## Chicken and Mushroom Soup Casserole

6 chicken breasts
1 pkg. Swiss cheese slices
1 pkg. stove top stuffing

1 can cream of mushroom soup or celery soup
3/4 cup milk
2 Tbsp. margarine

Grease a 9" x 13" pan. Place chicken in the pan. Place cheese slices over chicken, dilute soup with the milk and 1/2 the seasoning from the stove top stuffing. Pour over chicken and cheese and bake until chicken is tender at 350, about 1 hour. Sprinkle over the crumbs and stuffing mix with the other 1/2 of the seasoning. *Contributed by Mary Rieger.*

## Chicken - like Schneider's Coating

4 cups bread crumbs
1 Tbsp. paprika
1 tsp pepper

1 Tbsp. salt (or less to taste)
1 Tbsp. celery salt
1 Tbsp. Italian seasoning

Mix bread crumbs and herbs and spices together and store in airtight container in fridge.
Moisten chicken pieces with water and press chicken pieces on both side in coating mix.
Arrange skin up on non-stick pan. Bake at 375 for 45 minutes. Chicken will look dry at first but then coating starts to work and it will be crisp and perfect.

## Chicken Salad

8 cups chicken (cubed and cooked) could use leftover chicken or cans of chicken.
2 lbs. green grapes
2 cans water chestnuts
2 Tbsp. soya sauce

2 cups sliced almonds
2 cups cut up celery
3 cups mayonnaise
1 tsp. curry powder

Mix together well, will keep in fridge for 1 week. (serves 16). *Contributed by Bernice Gulka.*

## Chicken Velvet Soup (creamed Chicken)

6 Tbsp. butter or margarine
1/3 cup all-purpose flour
1/2 cup milk

1/2 cup light cream
3 cups chicken broth

1 cup finely chopped cooked chicken or can of pieces of chicken. (add dash of pepper) Melt butter in saucepan. Blend in flour, add milk, cream and broth. Cook and stir until mixture thickens and comes to a boil. Reduce heat. Stir in chicken. Heat until it just starts to boil. Garnish with parsley.

## Cream Chicken

4 chicken breasts or chicken pieces
1 can Campbell's mushroom soup
1 can half-and-half cream
1 medium onion diced
2 stalks diced celery
1 clove garlic
1 Tbsp. finely chopped fresh parsley
8 mushrooms sliced (optional)
1/4 cup fresh chopped dill
Salt and pepper to taste

Preheat the oven to 350. Heat 2 Tbsp. oil in frying pan with crushed garlic clove, onions and celery. Season with salt and pepper and fry until browned. In separate soup pot or roaster, combine soup, cream, parsley, mushrooms and dill. Heat and stir until smooth. Add chicken, onion, garlic and celery to mushroom sauce. Bake covered for 1 hour.

## Deep Fried Pierogies with Hamburger Filling

1 1/2 cups mashed potatoes         1 egg
1 cup rice                         3 Tbsp. flour

So it would be easy to handle; mix hamburger meat which is fried with onions. Make like pierogies and deep fry.

## Easy Pasta Alla-Checca

1 lb. pasta noodles (spaghetti, fettucine, or linguine)     Salt and pepper to taste
Handful cherry tomatoes                                      2-3 Babybel mozzarella cheese
Handful of fresh basil                                       1/4 cup olive oil
3 cloves minced garlic                                       Parmesan cheese

Mince garlic, cut up cherry tomatoes and basil. Set aside in bowl along with 1/4 cup of olive oil with salt and pepper. Cover with plastic wrap and let sit at room temperature for a couple hours or overnight. Cook pasta in salted water until al dente and drain. Break apart cheese and add to pasta. Pour the pasta into the garlic, tomato and basil mixture. Season to taste with salt and pepper and add more olive oil if needed. Serve topped with parmesan and fresh basil. *Contributed by Jill Mudry.*

## Famous Spiced Fried Chicken

3 lbs. frying chicken (cut up)
1 egg beaten with 1 Tbsp. water
2 cups cracker crumbs

A good pinch of each: dried parsley, sage, rosemary, thyme, oregano, paprika, chili powder, celery salt, onion salt, garlic salt and black pepper.
1/2 lb. butter or bacon fat

Place chicken pieces in pressure cooker with sufficient water and cook for 20 minutes. Remove chicken pieces drain and allow to cool slightly. Mix eggs and water in shallow bowl, blend cracker crumbs with herbs and spices. Dip chicken pieces in egg then roll in cracker crumbs. Melt butter or fat in heavy skillet to fry chicken - turning only once.

## Fish Batter

2 cups flour
1 beaten egg
1/4 tsp. baking powder

Fish seasoning
1/2 tsp. salt

Milk to make a batter to coat the fish fillets.

## Fish Fry

Fish fillets (we like fresh walleye or Grandma's favorite, Northern Pike)
Milk
Flour, seasoned with salt & pepper, seasoning salt and garlic powder

Eggs, slightly beaten
Corn Flakes, crushed
Oil for deep frying

Heat oil for deep frying, just enough to cover the fillets. Have bowls or deep plates for 1) milk 2) flour mixture 3) beaten eggs 4) Corn Flakes. Dip fillets in milk. Drain slightly then coat with the flour mixture. Place the fillet in the lightly beaten egg to coat, then cover with the crushed Corn Flakes. Drop the fillets in the heated oil and cook until golden brown and the fillet is stiff. Remove from the oil, drain on paper towel, and sprinkle with seasoning salt and garlic powder. *Contributed by Gerald Kwasny.*

## Gnocchi

Gnocchi in mushroom cream sauce.

Gnocchi in tomato roasted pepper sauce.

1 cup finely mashed or riced potatoes
1 egg, beaten

1 cup flour (approx.) to make a light dough with more flour to cover work surface
Salt to add to boiling water

If making fresh mashed potatoes, allow them to cool before adding the beaten egg. Gradually add flour while mixing until a dough forms and is no longer too sticky. Roll pieces of dough into a 3/4" rope. Cut into 1" pieces and mash slightly with fork to leave a dent. Boil water with salt and add gnocchi pieces. When they float to the top, they're done. Remove from boiling water and add to your sauce of choice. Great with onions and butter, pesto sauce, mushroom sauce, Alfredo sauce, cheese sauce, etc. You can also add basil or dill to the dough. *Contributed by Brent Matsalla.*

## Hamburger Casserole

1 lb. ground beef
2 cups chopped onion and celery
1 can cream of mushroom soup
1 can tomato soup

1 1/4 cups water
1 tsp. chili powder
2 cups Chow Mein noodles

Brown gr. beef, add onion and celery cook until soft, mix other ingredients and bake at 350 for 45 min.

## Head Cheese

3 or 4 pig's feet
3 or 4 pork hocks
1 Tbsp. salt or more

2 bay leaves
6 to 8 cloves of garlic
1 tsp. whole pickling spice

Soak feet and hocks overnight. Wash and scrub feet well. Put meat in a fairly deep pot and cover with cold water. Bring to a boil. Remove all scum while meat is boiling. Add salt and spices. Turn down heat to simmer slowly. Cover and simmer slowly for 4 to 5 hours until meat falls away from the bones freely. Can be transferred to a slow cooker and simmered longer.
*Continued on next page…*

Remove meat from bones and cut into small pieces. Place in glass pans. More crushed garlic may be sprinkled over meat. Strain stock and pour over top of the meat and stir. When cooled, cover and place in fridge to set. If too much water is used, you can add gelatin to make it gel. Slow simmering keeps broth clear, otherwise it will be gray in color.

## Honey Garlic Chicken

6 bone in chicken pieces (breast, legs or thigh)
1/2 cup brown sugar
2 tsp. dry mustard

4 minced garlic cloves
2 Tbsp. soya sauce
1/2 to 3/4 cup liquid honey

Place chicken skin side down in baking pan. Evenly distribute ingredients over chicken in given order. Don't mix them together. Bake at 350 for 1 hour. Turning chicken every 15 minutes. Lift chicken from juice. Skim off fat if any. Service with rice and using sauce for dipping.

## Impossible Cheeseburger Pie

1 lb. ground beef
1 1/2 cups chopped onion
1 1/2 cups milk
3/4 cup Bisquick mix
3 eggs
1/4 tsp. salt and pepper

1 can tomato soup
2 cups celery
1 can mushrooms
1 pepper
1 pkg. mozzarella cheese (slices)
Sprinkle of chili and garlic powder

Heat the oven to 400F. Grease pie plate. Fry beef on stove until brown (add spices to meat). Sauté onion, celery, pepper until soft. Add to beef. Add soup and can of mushrooms. Pour into plate. Top with cheese. Bake 25-30 min. It is done when knife inserted into center comes out clean. *Contributed by Darla Wolkowski.*

## Kentucky Style Fried Chicken

3 lbs. fryer chicken (cut up)
Dip in spice mix of:
1 pkg. "Italian salad dressing" dry mix or 2 tsp. Italian spice

1/4 cup flour
1 tsp. salt

Then dip into mixture of:
3 eggs
2 tsp. melted margarine
2 tsp. lemon juice
Coat with batter:
3/4 cup milk

1 cup club soda or beer
1 cup pancake flour mix
1 tsp. paprika
1/2 tsp. sage
1/4 tsp. pepper

Fry in 1 cup oil and 1/2 cup margarine, ensure the temperature of the oil is at 350. Brown well on both sides for 10 or 15 min. Turn only once. Put in oven for 1/2 hour at 350.

## Kyshka Buckwheat Sausage

2 cups buckwheat (cleaned)
2-1/4 tsp. salt
1/4 + 1/2 cup fat
4 + 1 cups water

Minced garlic
1-3/4 tsp. pepper
Sausage casing

Bring to boil 4 cups of water and 2-1/4 tsp. salt. Add 2 cups clean buckwheat and cook for 1/4 hour. Add 1/4 cup fat which you may cut off a ham. Minced garlic and 1-3/4 tsp. pepper.
Mix well and cool. Spoon into clean casing and coat in an open pan where you have added 1/2 cup lard and 1 cup water. Prick sausage with a knife to release air but leave in the pan to ensure the casing doesn't burst.

## Lasagna

Sauce: 2 - 28 oz. cans tomatoes or 4 - 6 oz. cans of tomato paste
2 Tbsp. brown sugar
1 Tbsp. oregano
4 bay leaves
Salt and pepper to taste
2 cloves garlic

2 cups finely chopped onion
1/8 cup vegetable oil
1 or 2 lbs. ground beef
1/2 lb. shredded mozzarella cheese
3/4 lb. ricotta cheese or drained cottage cheese
Wide macaroni or lasagna noodles

In saucepan combine tomatoes, bay leaves, brown sugar, oregano, salt and pepper, onion and garlic in oil. Brown meat and combine with sauce simmer for 1 hour. Cool. Remove bay leaves.
Put layers alternating of macaroni pasta, meat and tomato mixture and cheese in a pan until done. Sprinkle with parmesan cheese and bake at 350 for 45 min. uncovered. This could make 2 casserole dishes 8" x 12".

## Lemon Chicken

2 skinned and boneless chicken breasts (cut up)
1 Tbsp. light soya sauce
1/4 tsp salt,
Dash of pepper
1 Tbsp. tapioca starch
1 cup flour
1/2 tsp. baking powder

1 egg beaten with dash of salt
1 cup water (1/4 cup for marinate, 3/4 cup. for sauce)
1 Tbsp. white vinegar
3 Tbsp. white sugar
1/4 tsp. lemon extract or lemon juice
6-8 slices of fresh lemons

Marinate chicken with soy sauce, salt, pepper for 1/2 hour at least. Prepare batter mix with flour, baking powder, egg and 1/4 cup of the water. Dip chicken into mixture and deep fry for 5-10 min. In hot oil until golden brown. While chicken is cooking, use a saucepan to prepare the lemon sauce using lemon extract, starch, lemon slices, 3/4 cup remaining water, vinegar and sugar. Bring to a boil. Continue to stir as it thickens. Pour lemon sauce over chicken and serve. *Contributed by Bev Zarazun.*

## Mediterranean Chicken Skillet

1/2 cup mayo
1 cup chicken broth or water with chicken base
Salt and pepper

2-5 chicken breast
1 cup rice
1/2 cup cheddar cheese, grated

Boil chicken breasts in broth for 15 minutes. Combine mayo, rice and seasoning and add to chicken. Cover and simmer, until chicken is tender. Top with grated cheese return to melt. *Contributed by Bernice Gulka.*

## Microwave Tuna Casserole with Zucchini

5 cups cooked egg noodles
2 cans tuna flaked and drained
1/2 cup chopped celery
1/3 cup sliced green onion
1 small zucchini sliced
1 cup cheddar cheese
1 medium tomato chopped

1/2 cup sour cream
1/2 cup mayonnaise
2 tsp. prepared mustard
1/2 tsp. salt
1/2 tsp. dried thyme
1/4 tsp. dill weed

In a large bowl combine noodles, tuna, celery and onion. In a small bowl combine the sour cream, mayo, and herbs. Add to large bowl mixture of tuna and noodles. Spoon half of the mixture into a 2 quart microwave safe bowl, topping with zucchini layer, repeat layers until complete. Microwave on high (uncovered) 6 - 8 minutes or until heated through. Sprinkle with cheese and tomato on top. Microwave uncovered 2 more minutes. Let stand for 3 minutes before serving. *Contributed by Mary Rieger.*

## Monte Cristo Sandwiches

Mix 1 egg with 1 Tbsp. water
12 slices of bread
6 slices ham
6 slices chicken
6 slices Swiss cheese
2 Tbsp. butter

Dip sandwiches in egg mixed with water then dip in 1 cup bread crumbs mixed with salt and pepper to taste. Brown the sandwich on a frying pan with 2 tbsp. butter until brown and cheese is melted.

## Mushroom and Sweet Pepper Vegetarian Lasagna

9 lasagna noodles
Sauce:
2 tsp. vegetable oil
1 large onion, chopped
1/2 lb. fresh sliced mushrooms
3 cloves of minced garlic
1/4 cup chopped fresh parsley

1 tsp. each dried basil and oregano
1/4 cup tomato paste
1 can undrained tomatoes
2 coarsely chopped sweet peppers, either red, yellow or green
Salt and pepper

Filling:
2 cups skim milk cottage cheese
1/3 cup grated parmesan cheese

1 tsp. dried oregano
3 cups shredded mozzarella cheese

Tomato Sauce: in a large skillet, heat oil and cook onion and mushrooms for 5 minutes, stirring often. Add garlic, parsley, basil oregano, tomato paste and tomatoes, mashing with potato masher to break up the tomatoes; simmer, uncovered, for 10 minutes. Add peppers and simmer for 10 minutes or until sauce is thickened. Season with salt and pepper. In a large pot of boiling water, cook noodles for 8 to 10 minutes until tender. Drain under cold running water and set aside in single layer.
Filling: combine cottage cheese, half of the parmesan, and the oregano; mix well. Assemble in a 9" x 13" baking dish, spread sauce over bottom. Top with layer of noodles. Cover with half the cheese mixture, then sprinkle with mozzarella cheese. Repeat layers. Top with parmesan. (Lasagna can be prepared to this point, covered and refrigerated for 1 day. Add 15 minutes for baking) Bake covered in 350 oven for 30 minutes. Uncover and bake for 10 to 15 minutes longer or until bubbly. Remove from oven and let cool 5 minutes before serving. *Contributed by Leslie Stanier.*

## Oriental Casserole

1 lb. ground beef
2 onions (chopped)
1 cup celery (chopped)
1/2 cup minute rice
1 can water

1 can Chinese vegetables
1/4 cup soya sauce
Salt and pepper to taste
3 Tbsp. butter

Brown beef, add other ingredients, put in a greased casserole dish. Sprinkle with dry uncooked stir fry rice noodles or Chow Mein noodles. Bake at 350 for 30 min. *Contributed by Lil Popoff.*

## Oven or Slow Cooker Ribs

Ribs (or roast)
1 cup ketchup
1/4 cup brown sugar
1/4 cup molasses
1 tsp. garlic powder
1 tsp. onion powder
1 tsp. chili powder
1 tsp. paprika

3 Tbsp. Worcestershire sauce
2 Tbsp. soy sauce
3 Tbsp. mustard
2 Tbsp. vinegar
1/2 onion chopped fine
1/2 cup beef broth
2 Tbsp. parsley flakes
Salt and pepper

Boil ribs with a couple bay leaves for an hour. Mix sauce. Add ribs and toss to cover them, then bake at 350 for 2 hours or 5 hours in crockpot or slow cooker. You can also use a roast if you brush it with vegetable oil, cover with Montreal Steak Spice and seer in a hot frying pan in hot oil. *Contributed by Brent Matsalla.*

## Pizza Buns

1 lb. sausage, bacon, and ham.
1 can mushrooms
1 pepper
1/2 lb. cheddar cheese

1/2 lb. mozzarella cheese (grated)
1 can tomato soup
4-5 Tbsp. Worcestershire sauce
1 Tbsp. soya sauce

Cut meats into small pieces with onion and fry until brown. Add mushrooms, pepper and cheeses. Add soup and heat through. Add last 2 sauces and cool. This will store in fridge for 1 month or could be frozen at this point. To use: put on pizza dough or on bun halves broiled in the oven. *Contributed by Eleanor Hadubiak.*

## Pot Roast Dinner

4 lbs. blade or cross rib roast
Salt and pepper
2 Tbsp. Worcestershire sauce
1 1/2 Tbsp. vinegar
1 cup ketchup
3 Tbsp. flour
1 Tbsp. brown sugar

1 tsp. Dry mustard
3 potatoes, peeled and quartered
3 green peppers quartered (optional)
2 onions, sliced
3 carrots, cut into ½" slices
2 stalks of celery, cut in ½" slices

Slowly brown the roast on both sides over hot stove, season with salt and pepper to taste. Mix together ketchup, flour, Worcestershire sauce, vinegar, brown sugar, mustard, salt and pepper. Place browned meat in the center of heavy duty foil. Top with half of the ketchup sauce. Arrange vegetables on top and add remaining sauce. Bring long ends of foil together and make a double fold, turn sides up and seal securely. Place double thickness of foil over grill. Bake packaged roast and vegetables over slow grill for 1 1/2 to 2 hours, or until meat is tender (check by unfolding and piercing meat with a fork; without letting source run out) pour sauce into gravy boat to serve.

## Ribs

1/4 cup cornstarch
2 cups catchup
1/2 cup brown sugar
1/2 cup white sugar

2 garlic cloves
Onion finely chopped
1/2 cup vinegar

Roll in cornstarch and fast-brown the ribs. Add ingredients to ribs and simmer 2 hours or in crock pot for 5 hours.

## Rum Runner Ribs

(These are worth the extra prep time!)
1/2 cup Chili sauce
1/2 cup ketchup
1/2 cup canned, crushed pineapple with juice
1/4 cup HP Sauce
1/4 cup brown sugar

1/4 cup finely chopped green onion
1/4 cup dark rum
1 tsp. lime zest
1 tsp. minced ginger
Pinch ground allspice
4 lbs. (2kg) parboiled* pork back ribs

Stir chili sauce with ketchup, pineapple, HP sauce and brown sugar. Bring to a boil in a saucepan over medium heat. Cook, stirring for 5 minutes. Remove from heat; stir in the green onion, rum, lime zest, ginger and allspice until well combined. Cool slightly. Preheat the grill to medium-high. Toss ribs with half of the sauce mixture; grill, turning and basting often with remaining sauce, for 10-15 minutes or until glossy and well-marked. *To parboil ribs, cut each rack into 2-3 bone portions. Place in a large pot with 1 sliced lime and enough equal parts of water and chicken broth to cover ribs. Bring to a boil; reduce heat and simmer, covered, for 45 minutes. Discard lime slices. Cool ribs in cooking broth for 1 hour. Drain well. Grill as directed or wrap lightly and reserve for up to 24 hours in the refrigerator before grilling. *Contributed by Twila Hadubiak.*

## Sweet & Sour Ribs

1 lb. pork ribs
1 small bottle ketchup
1 tsp vinegar

1 cup brown sugar
Pinch of garlic powder

Boil ribs for approximately 1-1/2 hours. Mix all other ingredients together in a bowl. Drain ribs & put into a roaster & cover with sauce. Cook at 300 deg. for approx. 1-1/2 hours. Serve with rice. *Contributed by Tracy Loshack.*

## Sandy's Goulash

1 medium size onion diced
Salt and pepper
Sprinkle of Italian seasoning
1 lb. hamburger fried and drained of fat
1 Tbsp. Worcestershire sauce
1 Tbsp. soy sauce
1 can diced tomatoes
1 pkg. elbow macaroni
2 cups of shredded mozzarella or the more-stringy Bocconcini cheese balls

Fry (brown) hamburger, salt, pepper, and Italian seasoning. Drain fat. Add tomatoes to the hamburger in frying pan and simmer for 10 min. on medium heat. Cook macaroni to instructions on package. Mix all ingredients together and add the cheese. Bake in the oven until cheese melts and starts to brown. *Contributed by Sandra Pridge.*

## Sesame Pork Tenderloin Marinate

2 pork tenderloins (1 lb. each)
1/2 cup soya sauce
3 Tbsp. olive oil
1/2 tsp ground ginger or 2 tsp. minced fresh ginger root

1 to 3 garlic cloves, minced
1/2 cup honey
1/4 cup brown sugar, packed
1/3 cup sesame seeds, toasted

Place pork in larger re-sealable plastic bag. Add soya sauce, oil, ginger and garlic. Seal and turn to coat. Refrigerate for 4 hours or overnight. Drain and discard marinate, place pork on greased rack in foil lined roasting pan. Combine honey and brown sugar, spoon over top of pork, sprinkle with sesame seeds and bake uncovered at 375 for 35 to 40 min. Let stand 5 minutes before serving. *Contributed by Bev Zarazun.*

## Shishliki

2 lbs. lamb
1 sliced lemon
1 Tbsp. lemon juice
Salt
Pepper
1 large onion, sliced

Cut lamb into small cubes but big enough not to fall through the grill. Add cubed lamb to a bowl and season generously with salt and pepper. Add lemon juice. Mix until lamb is nicely coated. Layer in a sealable container with lemon and onion slices. Cover and refrigerate for 3–7 days, turning the lamb once a day. Put lamb onto skewers and grill.
Alternate: Not big on lamb? Try chicken instead.

## Southern Fried Chicken

4 cups vegetable oil
1 chicken fryer cut up
4 egg whites
1 1/2 cups biscuit mix

1 tsp. baking powder
1/2 tsp. of each: cinnamon, ginger, and seasoning salt
Pinch cayenne pepper

Heat oil to 360. Dry chicken pieces. Beat egg whites until frothy. Place spices and biscuit mix in separate bowl mix together. Divide the mixture in 1/2 in bowl and 1/2 in bag to toss on chicken. Roll chicken in bowl mixture then in egg whites, then shake in bag one piece at a time. Fry chicken for 12-18 minutes. *Contributed by Bev Zarazun.*

## Special Bun Sandwich

1 bun                              Margarine
1 cheese slice

Slice the bun open. Spread the bottom bun with margarine. Place cheese slice on top of margarine. Close bun and enjoy Kyler's specialty. *Contributed by Kyler Eikelenboom.*

## Stew

1 lb. meat cut in cubes            1 can golden mushroom soup
Vegetables of choice               1 can water
Salt and pepper                    2 Tbsp. Minute Tapioca

Put in oven at 300 for 6 - 8 hours. "Important" do not lift the lid during the baking time. *Contributed by Mary Rieger.*

## Stir-fry Vegetable and Beef

1 lb. beef sliced thin or leftover steak    1 tsp. ginger
1/2 tsp. beef bouillon                      2 tomatoes cut in wedges
1/3 cup boiling water                       1 large pepper
1/4 cup soya sauce                          6 green onions cut in 1" lengths
1 Tbsp. cornstarch                          1/2 cup shredded carrots
2 Tbsp. oil                                 1/2 cup sliced celery

Heat oil in stir fry pan and cook sliced beef then remove from pan. Cook vegetables for 2 min. Starting with the harder vegetables first. Return meat to pan with vegetables. Mix remaining ingredients and add, toss to cook through.

## Stroganoff Meatballs

To make meat balls add:
2 lbs. ground beef
1 1/2 cups of breadcrumbs
1/4 cup milk

1/4 cup chopped onion
2 eggs
1 tsp. salt and pepper to taste

Make meatballs into desired size. Place on a cookie sheet or open roasting pan and bake at 375 for 25-30 min. Remove from oven drain and set aside

Sauce:
1/2 cup chopped onion
4 Tbsp. butter
2 Tbsp. flour

2 Tbsp. ketchup
1 - 10 oz. can consommé or 1 cup of water
and beef base, or beef broth
1 cup sour cream

Brown onion in butter, add flour, mix well. Add ketchup and consommé, cooking slowly until thickened, add sour cream and then meat balls. Place in casserole and heat in 300 oven until serving time.

## Stuffed Chicken Breast with Apricot Sauce

4 chicken breasts
4 thin slices of ham
Spinach leaves
1/4 cup feta cheese
1/4 cup apricot jam
Salt and pepper to taste

Put chicken breasts between plastic wrap and pound flat. Put a slice of ham on each breast, cover with spinach leaves and top with feta. Close the chicken breast and secure with toothpicks or tie shut with butcher's string. Bake for 45-60 min. at 350 F. Microwave apricot jam for 45 seconds until thinned. Remove toothpicks or string and top breasts with the heated apricot jam. Option: Instead of apricot sauce you can use hollandaise sauce. *Contributed by Sandra Pridge.*

## Tangy Meat Loaf

| | |
|---|---|
| 1 1/2 lb. lean ground beef | 1 tsp. Worcestershire sauce |
| 1/2 cup cheddar cheese, grated | 1/2 tsp. pepper |
| 1/4 cup rolled oats | 1 egg |
| 2 onions, finely chopped | 1/3 + 1/4 cup ketchup, divided |
| 1 tsp. salt | 2 Tbsp. brown sugar |

Mix together and blend in 1/3 cup ketchup and egg. Press into a 9" x 5" x 3" loaf pan. Top with 1/4 cup ketchup and brown sugar. Bake at 350 deg. For 1 hour.
Also good with scalloped potatoes! Optional: Dairy Free Cheese instead of the cheddar cheese. *Contributed by Jamie Lynn Rawson.*


## Topping for Buns

| | |
|---|---|
| 1/2 cup grated cheese | 1/2 can tomato soup |
| 2 Tbsp. chopped onion | Dash of cayenne, paprika, and pepper |
| 1 green or red pepper (optional) | 2 Tbsp. Worcestershire sauce |
| 6 slices of fried crispy chopped bacon | |

Mix together, put on bun halves, and broil for 5 minutes. *Contributed by Theresa Mudry.*


## Turkey Casserole Leftovers

| | |
|---|---|
| 2 Tbsp. butter | 2 eggs, well beaten |
| 2 Tbsp. chopped onion | (Optional) 1/2 cup chopped celery |
| 3 cups cooked rice | 1 tsp. salt |
| 1 1/2-2 cups cooked turkey, chopped | Fresh ground pepper |
| 1 cup turkey gravy | 1 cup shredded mozzarella cheese |

Sauté butter and onion. Add remaining ingredients, mix, pour into casserole pan and top with cheese. Bake at 350 degrees. *Contributed by Jenelle and Mark Breker.*


## Turkey Noodle Bake

| | |
|---|---|
| 1-10 oz. can of cream of mushroom soup, undiluted | 1 small onion chopped |
| 1/2 cup milk | 8 oz. medium noodles (uncooked - wide variety) |
| 1 cup chopped cooked turkey | 1 cup water |
| 1 cup shredded cheddar cheese | 1/4 cup bread crumbs |

*Continued on next page...*

In a 2 quart casserole stir together: soup & milk. Add turkey, cheese and onion. Mix well. Stir in uncooked noodles coating with soup mixture. Pour water over mixture. Top with bread crumbs. Bake covered in preheated 350 oven for 50 minutes or until noodles are tender. *Contributed by Eleanor Hadubiak.*

## Turkey and Mushroom Croustades

24 slices of bread with cut off crusts. Butter each side and press into muffin tins and bake at 350 for 10 min. or until golden brown.

Filling:
1 onion chopped
1 can mushrooms (drained - pieces and stems)
1 tin flakes of turkey or leftover turkey
3 Tbsp. flour

1 cup milk
Salt and pepper to taste
1 tsp. lemon juice
1/2 cup butter

Melt butter and sauté onions and mushrooms. Stir in turkey. Sprinkle with flour and blend. Add milk gradually and mix. Remove from heat - stir in salt, pepper and lemon juice. Fill each croustade with filling. Cover each with shredded cheese if desired. Bake at 350 for approximately 10 min. Alternate: add fresh mushrooms or broccoli pieces. This recipe freezes well. *Contributed by Bev Zarazun.*

## Turkey Potato Patties

1 egg
1 1/2 cups diced, cooked turkey
1 cup cold mashed potatoes
1/4 cup dry bread crumbs

Green onion, parsley, black pepper and salt to taste
2 tsp. Dijon mustard
1/4 tsp. thyme
1/4 tsp. sage

Form into patties and brown on lightly oiled pan. Makes about 8 patties.

## Zucchini Patties #1

2 cups frozen zucchini drained well.
4 eggs beaten
1/4 cup flour
1 tsp. salt

1 tsp. baking powder
1 medium onion chopped fine
1/2 green pepper chopped fine (optional)
1 cup crushed soda crackers

Make into patties and fry in frying pan.

## Zucchini Patties #2 (Taste like Potato Pancakes)

1 cup flour
2 tsp. baking powder
1/2 tsp. salt
1/4 cup oil or margarine
1 cup grated cheese
1/2 cup chopped or grated onion
3 cups grated zucchini
2 eggs, well beaten
2 or 3 cloves of garlic, crushed

Sift first three ingredients, cut in margarine. Mix in remaining ingredients. Heat vegetable oil in skillet or frying pan. Place mixture by tablespoons in hot oil and fry until golden brown. Turn gently and serve with sour cream, cottage cheese or ketchup. *Contributed by Eleanor Hadubiak.*

## Tips for Spicing and Seasoning

Apple dumplings - sprinkle with cinnamon, sugar and butter
Beef stew - use a small quantity of pickling spice.
Boiled eggs - add celery salt and paprika
Canned corn - add chili powder, salt, pepper and a lump of butter
Corn-on-the-cob - use paprika as well as salt and pepper
Cottage cheese - mix 2 tbsp. caraway seeds into each cup of cheese. Season with salt and pepper, eaten with rye bread is a continental supper
Sweet potatoes - mash them and blend with cinnamon, and paprika
Tomato juice - improved with a pinch of marjoram.

- If you are blending spices, remember to taste your spices mixed before you incorporate them into a recipe. This will determine the heat level of your dish as well.
- To help fresh herbs stay fresh, wrap in a paper towel and a plastic wrap or bag. Store in the fridge. Mark the bag or write on the outside of the paper towel the type of herb it is so you don't have to open each one.
- Freeze herbs in ice cube trays for serving size use. Either alone or in oil. Once frozen, place in a freezer-safe clear container or bag, either mark the bag or the container because all green herbs look similar.
- Dried herbs (see recipe to use microwave) Store dried herbs, away from heat, avoid moisture and direct sunlight in order to last longer.

## Baked Beans

2 cans pork and beans any flavor
5 slices bacon chopped
3/4 cup diced onion
3/4 cup diced celery
1 Tbsp. Worcestershire sauce
2 Tbsp. soy sauce
1 cup ketchup
3 Tbsp. mustard
1 Tbsp. brown sugar
1/4 cup molasses
1 Tbsp. dried parsley

Brown bacon, onion, celery. Add other ingredients and stir well. Cover and put in oven at 300 for 2 hours. Remove lid and stir. Bake for another 3-4 hours, stirring every hour or so until top is darkened. You may need to add more water if beans are too thick as there should be some liquid. *Contributed by Brent Matsalla.*

## Baked Cinnamon Macaroni

4 eggs beaten
3/4 cup cream
3/4 cup milk
Beat together with the eggs

Cinnamon
1 Tbsp. sugar or to taste
Salt to taste

Sprinkle cinnamon into milk egg mixture and beat. Add Cinnamon to desired taste. Put mixture into cooked macaroni. Bake at 350 for 1/2 hour or more. Use an 8" x 8" pan. *Contributed by Eleanor Ludba.*

## Baked Macaroni (without Eggs)

3 cups cooked macaroni
1/2 cup margarine
6 Tbsp. flour

2 cups milk
1 tsp. salt
3 cups grated cheddar cheese (1 cup reserved for on top of macaroni)

Heat milk; melt butter in frying pan add flour and mix. Add hot milk and cook until thickened add 2 cups of cheese add macaroni. Place in baking dish add cheese and crushed cornflakes on top (if desired).

## Baked Macaroni

2 cups noodles or macaroni, cooked and strained
1/4 cup butter
1 cup milk or half-and-half cream
1/2 tsp. salt
1/2 tsp. pepper
1/2 cup grated cheddar cheese
1 Tbsp. sugar
4 eggs, beaten
1 tsp. baking powder

Mix all together. Bake in a 6"x10" Pyrex pan at 300 F until done, about 3/4 hour. *Contributed by Eleanor Hadubiak.*

## Beet Leaf and Rice Casserole

10 cups rice
1 medium onion
1 lb. bacon
1 Tbsp. fresh dill
20-24 beet leaves (approximately)
1/2 cup butter
1/2 cup heavy cream (whipping)
Salt and pepper to taste

Prepare rice. Dice bacon and fry until crisp. Drain on paper towel. Sauce diced onion in the butter until soft. Add to the rice with the bacon and dill. Season. Starting with the rice mixture, alternate with a layer of beet leaves, making 3 or 4 layers and ending with the rice mixture on top. Drizzle cream over top of casserole. Bake at 350 for 45 to 50 minutes. Cover with foil for first 30 minutes. Options: cook rice in chicken broth instead of water. Substitute Swiss chard for the beet leaves. Omit bacon for a vegetarian casserole. You can use beet leaves that were frozen. Filling can be used as cabbage roll filling. *Contributed by Theresa Mudry.*

### Brine for Marinating Vegetables

Use all variety of harder vegetables: carrots, cauliflower, celery, peppers, onion, or zucchini

| | |
|---|---|
| 8 cups water | 8 tsp. pickling salt |
| 4 cups sugar | 1/4 cup oil |
| 4 cups vinegar | 2 cloves garlic |

Bring to a boil and cool before pouring over cut up vegetables. This makes about 6 quarts.

### Broccoli Casserole

Boil Broccoli in a bit of water just to steam it. Drain water. Add a chunk of margarine and a chunk of cheese whiz and simmer to melt. Then add broken cheese crackers. Bake 1/2 hour in moderate oven.

### Cabbage Roll (Holubshi) Filling

1/2 cup margarine/butter
1 medium onion
2 cups rice uncooked or combination of buckwheat and rice
Salt and pepper

Prepare the cabbage leaves (sweet or sour method) cut and prepare the leaves to fit the size of your palm, roughly. Cut the tough spine of the leaf away as much as you can to easily roll the leaf around the filling. Cook the rice or substitute with buckwheat and rice mixture. (Prepare the same way). Melt the butter and onions. When the rice is cooked add the onion mixture and salt and pepper to taste. Let it cool to warm. Place about 1 Tbsp. of rice mixture on a leaf (if the leaf is smaller or larger adjust accordingly). Fold in sides towards the center. Starting at the outer edge. Roll to secure the bundle. Place each roll side by side in a roaster or in a large freezer Ziploc to freeze for later use. When ready to serve add as many rolls as you require. Add some hot water (to cover the bottom of the pan) and tomato soup to the sweet rolls, and water and more butter and onions to the sour. For the sour cabbage rolls foil lining assists for a burnt edge on the cabbage. Bake at 325 or until a fork twists in the cabbage roll breaks it easily. Approximately 11/2 hours.

## Cabbage Rolls with Sour Leaves

Cut out core from cabbage head quite deep to ensure leaf layers are exposed. Put cabbage into an x-large Ziploc bag or freezable plastic dish. Put pickling salt in middle of the core hole. Pour vinegar over the salt and continue until the vinegar seeps into the bag. Freeze for 3-7 days depending on size of cabbage head and sourness. Remove and separate the leaves. Remove the spine of each cabbage leaf, cut up the leaves into the size for cabbage rolls and prepare the filling, or freeze the cut up leaves in a Ziploc bag to make cabbage rolls later. Smaller pieces of the cabbage can be frozen for use in the Lazy Cabbage roll recipe. *Contributed by Theresa Mudry.*

## Cabbage Rolls (Holubshi) with Sweet Leaves

Cut out core from cabbage head quite deep to ensure layers are exposed. Put pickling salt in middle of the hole. Then put in hot water let sit for 3 or 4 days and take leaves apart.

## Carrot Casserole

| | |
|---|---|
| 6 Tbsp. butter or margarine | 10 oz. can of cream of celery or mushroom soup |
| 1/2 cup chopped onions | 5 cups chopped (par-cooked) carrots |
| 3/4 cup shredded cheddar cheese | 1 pkg. Stove Top Stuffing (chicken) |

Fry onions in butter. Remove from heat. Add soup and cheese, mixing well. Set aside. Put carrots in a 9" x 13" glass dish. Spread onion, soup and cheese mixture on top of carrots. Mix stuffing according to directions and place on top of mixture in dish. Bake uncovered at 350° for 20-25 minutes. *Contributed by Twila Hadubiak.*

## Coconut Ginger Turmeric Rice

1 cup Basmati or Jasmine rice (but any rice will do)
1 cup coconut milk + 1 cup water (or 2 cups coconut water)
1 Tbsp. chicken base soup mix
1 tsp. ground ginger
1 tsp. turmeric
1 tsp. parsley flakes
1 Tbsp. coconut oil

Rinse rice and place in rice cooker or a saucepan. Add other ingredients and cook as you would any rice. Makes 4 servings of beautiful bright yellow rice. *Contributed by Brent Matsalla.*

## Cornmeal (Nachinka)

1/4 lb. butter
1 cup cornmeal
1 quart warm milk
4 well-beaten eggs

1 small onion
1 tsp. sugar
1 tsp. salt
1 tsp. baking powder
Dash of ground allspice

Fry the chopped onion in butter until it is golden brown. Turn the heat to low. Add the cornmeal into the butter and mix well. Add the sugar, salt, dash of allspice and the warm milk. Stir slowly until the cornmeal begins to thicken. Remove from heat. Add the well-beaten eggs and baking powder. Mix well together and place in a Pyrex pan and bake in a 325 F oven for 1 hour. *Contributed by Eleanor Hadubiak.*

## Cooked Beans

3 1/2 to 4 cups prepared beans
Medium onion diced
2 stalks of celery diced
Large tin of canned tomatoes
1 green or red pepper diced

1/2 tsp. garlic salt
1/4 tsp. tabasco sauce (optional or add more)
Medium size tin of pineapple tidbits
1/2 lb. fried bacon or side pork

Put in a large casserole or crockpot and bake at 300 for 2 hours.

## Creamed Carrot

| | |
|---|---|
| Small roaster of cut up carrots | 1/2 cup butter |
| 1 cup whipping cream | 1/4 cup brown sugar |

Mix well and bake at 350 for 30 min. Stir and bake 15 minutes longer. Cool. Fill containers with mixture evenly and freeze. *Contributed by Marian Skoretz.*

## Fried Mushrooms

Wash mushrooms, drain. Dip each mushroom in seasoned flour (salt and pepper). Then in a slightly beaten egg diluted with 1 Tbsp. water, then in bread crumbs. Pan-fry in hot margarine until golden brown. Arrange in a shallow baking dish without crowding them. Sprinkle lightly with salt and pepper. Place in moderate oven 350 for 5 minutes. Serve.

## Fried Rice

| | |
|---|---|
| 2 cups long rice (uncooked) | 1 can of pieces and stems mushrooms and |
| 1 pkg. onion soup mix | the juice |
| 3 Tbsp. oil | 1 medium onion, diced |
| 1/4 cup soya sauce or alternative | 1 small pepper, diced (optional) |
| 3 cups boiling water | 3 celery stalks, diced |

Mix together in a large casserole dish. Bake at 350 for 1 hour. Half way through baking mix as the vegetables rise to the top. *Contributed by Mary Bugera.*

## German Potato Dumplings - Knadels (Knoedels)

| | |
|---|---|
| 5 cups mashed potatoes | 1 diced onion |
| 2 large eggs | 1/4 lb. margarine |
| 1 tsp. salt | 2 1/2 cups flour |
| 1/4 tsp. pepper | |

Mix together the potatoes, eggs, salt and pepper. Add flour and knead well. Mixture should be sticky but not wet. Flour bread board and continue to knead dough adding more flour if needed. Roll pieces of dough into thin log. Cut dough into pieces the size of a finger. Drop pieces into slow boiling water with salt and oil added to the water. Let cook for about 10 minutes or until the fingers rise to the top of the pot. Remove and drain. Serve with sautéed onions and margarine. Freezes well. *Contributed by Mary Reiger and Lindsay Striowski.*

## Home Baked Beans

7 cups water
1 lb. dried navy beans (can use white beans, lima beans and dried kidney beans)
1 pkg. bacon just chopped
1 chopped onion
1 bay leaf
1/4 cup catsup

3 Tbsp. molasses
1 1/2 tsp. Worcestershire sauce
1 tsp. dry mustard
1/2 tsp. ginger
1/2 tsp. salt
1/4 cup brown sugar

Bring water to boil. Add beans and boil for 2 mins. Cover, remove from heat and let stand overnight. In the morning add bay leaf to beans, bring to a boil, cover and simmer about 40 minutes. Brown the chopped bacon, add onion. Drain off fat. Drain beans, reserving 2 cups of the liquid that the beans cooked in. To this liquid add remaining ingredients. Mix with beans, bacon & onion. Bake at 400 for 1 hour or so in slow cooker until beans are soft. *Contributed by Bev Zarazun.*

## Lazy Cabbage Rolls (Meatless)

4 cups cooked rice
2-3 cups sauerkraut dry
6 slices bacon, cooked coarsely chopped (optional)
1 small onion, minced fine
2 cloves garlic, minced (optional)

1/4 cup butter or margarine
Salt and pepper to taste
2-1/2 cups of half-and-half cream to cover rice and sauerkraut in casserole or a mixture of half cream and half chicken broth. (Amounts are approximate)

Place all ingredients in a buttered casserole dish, ensuring the liquid covers the rice mixture. Bake at 350 until the top edges begin to brown and the liquid is absorbed approximately 30- 40 minutes.
Substitute could be to use all chicken broth as well. Rice can be substituted with buckwheat as well.
See recipe: *Cabbage Rolls (Holubshi) with Sour Leaves* for making a sauerkraut alternative.

## Macaroni Salad

Boiled elbow macaroni
Eggs
Celery
Cucumbers

Potatoes (optional)
Whipping or heavy farm cream
Creamy salad dressing

Add a little bit of mayonnaise, little oil, and salt and pepper to taste.

## Marinated Mushrooms

3 cans whole mushrooms          1 Tbsp. oregano
1/2 cup vinegar                 2 Tbsp. parsley flakes
1/4 cup oil                     1 1/2 - 2 cloves garlic
1/2 tsp salt

Mix vinegar, oil and spices in a quart jar. Drain water from mushrooms and add them with the garlic to the jar. Cover with the lid and leave on the counter for 24 hours, shaking the jar occasionally. Store in fridge. Eat raw. *Contributed by Devon Dziaduck.*


## Nalysnyky (Ukrainian Cottage Cheese Pancakes)

3 eggs                          1/2 tsp. salt
1/2 cup milk                    3/4 cup flour
1/2 cup water                   3/4 tsp. baking powder

Beat eggs, add water, milk, salt, flour and baking powder. Mix until smooth. The batter will be quite thin. Preheat frying pan to 300 and grease lightly with vegetable oil. Fry as you would pancakes until they are yellowish. Stack on a plate.

Filling:                        1/4 cup cream
2 cups cottage cheese           1/2 tsp. salt
1 egg                           1/4 cup melted butter

Add beaten egg, cream and salt to the cottage cheese and mix. Spread 1 Tbsp. filling on each pancake and roll. Dip in melted butter and place in buttered casserole dish. Bake at 350 for 20 min. Serve hot, topped with sour cream and chopped green onion.


## Onion Rings

Mix same amount of beer and flour. Salt and pepper to taste. Let stand 3 hours. Cut large onions into rings and coat with batter. Deep fry.


## Pearl Barley Casserole

Fry 1 cup pearl barley in 1/2 cup margarine. Add 3/4 cup slivered almonds, 1 onion chopped, and season with dry parsley. Add salt and pepper to taste. Then add 3 1/2 cups chicken broth or chicken in a mug mixed with water. Add 1 can mushrooms. Bake uncovered for 1 hour or more.

## Perashke Dough (Russian)

| | |
|---|---|
| 1/2 or 1/3 cup butter | 1 tsp. baking soda |
| 4 cups sour cream | 1 tsp. salt |
| 4 egg yolks | 6 cups flour |
| 1 tsp. baking powder | |

Mix butter and flour as for pies and then add other ingredients. Roll out dough and fill with mushrooms, cabbage, onion and fried ground beef. For a sweet filling add fruit. This recipe is similar to Mexican empanadas. *Contributed by Stefka Zarazun.*

## Pierogi Casserole

| | |
|---|---|
| 16-20 regular size frozen pierogies | 1/2 cup diced cooked ham |
| 1 medium onion chopped | 1/4 cup shredded cheddar cheese |
| 1/4 cup milk | 10 oz. can cream of mushroom soup |
| 1 Tbsp. margarine | |

In a small skillet melt margarine and sauté onion for 5 minutes. In a medium size casserole dish, combine frozen pierogies, onion and ham. Combine milk and mushroom soup and pour over casserole. Top with cheese. Bake for 35 minutes at 350. Serve.

## Pot Barley Risotto

1 cup pot barley
2 Portobello mushrooms
1 medium onion chopped
3 cloves of garlic, crushed
1 cup of toasted sliced or slivered almonds
4 dried whole shitake mushrooms
1 1/2 cups of boiling water
2/3 cup fried bacon crumbled
3 cups chicken stock

Soak the shitake mushrooms in 1 1/2 cups of boiling water for one hour.
Fry onion in about 2 Tbsp. of butter, once transparent add pot barley, fry for another 3-5 minutes. Drain mushrooms and slowly add liquid to pot barley, cook for about 10 minutes. Place this in a casserole dish.

Cook the Portello mushrooms in a pan, until done, add garlic. And now add the mushrooms to the casserole with pot barley mixture. Take the shitake mushrooms and slice, add to casserole.
Add remaining ingredients and bake for 1 1/2 hours to 2 hours or until liquid is absorbed. Bake at 350 uncovered.
Enjoy! I also add brown mushrooms too, in my opinion never too many mushrooms! *Contributed by Darla Wolkowski.*

## Potato Pancakes #1

4 cups grated potatoes
1/4 cup milk
1 big clove garlic
2 eggs

Seasoning salt and garlic salt (if needed)
1 tsp. salt
2 tsp. baking powder
2 Tbsp. grated onion
Approx. 1 cup of flour

Mix all together. Drop by spoonful on greased frying pan. Fry until brown on each side. Serve with sour cream. *Contributed by Bernice Gulka.*


## Potato Pancakes #2

4 large potatoes (russet are good or use older potatoes because they become starchy and this is the best quality to use)
1 yellow onion (more or less 1/2 cup)
2 cloves of garlic
1 egg

Salt
Pepper
Garlic salt
1/4 tsp. baking powder
1/4 cup flour (more or less to blend the mixture into a texture to stick together)

Grate, shred or food process the potatoes, garlic and onions into a fine porridge like consistency. If there is a lot of liquid strain some out. Depending on the potato starch you may need to add more flour, or 1 more egg. Heat vegetable frying oil in a medium skillets. In batches, drop heaping scoops of potato mixture into the skillet. Press to flatten cook about 3 minutes on each side, until browned and crisp. Drain on paper towel. Taste and adjust the seasoning if required. Serve with sour cream and chives. Some people enjoyed them with applesauce. Leftover potato pancakes can be heated for breakfast in cream and chives. *Contributed by Theresa Mudry.*


## Potato Puff

2 cups cold mashed potatoes
2 Tbsp. cream
2 eggs

1 cup milk
Salt and pepper to taste

Mix all ingredients together well. Pour into a greased 2 quart casserole. Bake at 350 for 30 to 60 min.

## Potato Skins

| | |
|---|---|
| 6 small to medium sized baking potatoes | 4 ounces grated cheddar cheese |
| Extra virgin olive oil | 1/2 cup sour cream |
| Kosher salt | 2 green onions, thinly sliced, including the |
| Freshly ground pepper | greens of the onions |
| 6 strips of bacon | 1 diced pepper (optional) |

Scrub the potatoes clean then pierce with fork and baste with oil, then bake at 400 for 1 hour or potatoes give a little when pressed. Cook the bacon while potatoes are baking and set on paper towel to de-grease before crumbling. Cut baked potatoes in half and scoop out the insides, leaving about 1/4" of potato on the skin. Increase the heat of the oven to 450 and brush potatoes with olive oil then sprinkle with salt. Place on a baking rack in a roasting pan. Bake on each side for 10 min. then flip over and bake another 10 min. Add the filling and return to oven and broil for another 2 min. or until the cheese bubbles. Top with sour cream and/or salsa and green onions. *Contributed by Brent Matsalla.*

## Smashed Potatoes

Boil potatoes until tender. Put boiled potatoes on a parchment paper covered cookie sheet and smash them down with a fork or masher. Melt 1/2 cup butter and pour over potatoes. Season to your liking (I use French fry seasoning, dill and parsley) and bake at 350 for 15-20 min. or until edges are crispy. *Contributed by Brent Matsalla.*

## Spanakopita (Greek Spinach Pie) with Tzatziki Sauce

3 Tbsp. olive oil
1 large onion, chopped
1 bunch green onions, chopped
2 cloves garlic, minced
2 lbs. spinach, rinsed and chopped
3 Tbsp. chopped fresh parsley
2 eggs, lightly beaten
1/2 cup ricotta cheese
1 cup crumbled feta cheese
1 box phyllo (Filo) dough sheets
1/4 cup olive oil

*Spanakopita with tzatziki sauce and barbequed souvlaki pork skewers and Greek salad*

*Continued on next page...*

Tzatziki Sauce:

1 (8 ounce) containers plain yogurt          Salt and pepper to taste
2 cucumbers - peeled, seeded and diced       1/4 cup fresh chopped dill
2 Tbsp. olive oil                            1 tsp. garlic powder
1/2 lemon juiced

Preheat the oven to 350. Lightly oil a 9" x 9" square baking pan. Heat 3 Tbsp. olive oil in a large skillet over medium heat. Sauté onion, green onions and garlic, until soft and lightly browned. Stir in spinach and parsley, and continue to sauté until spinach is limp, about 2 minutes. Remove from heat and set aside to cool. In a medium bowl, mix together eggs, ricotta, and feta. Stir in spinach mixture. Lay 1 sheet of phyllo dough in prepared baking pan, and brush lightly with olive oil. Lay another sheet of phyllo dough on top, brush with olive oil. The sheets of dough dry out very fast, you have to cover the pile of sheets with a damp towel in-between making each pie. Spread spinach and cheese mixture onto phyllo sheet and fold into burrito size. Brush with oil and place on parchment paper lined cookie sheet. Bake in preheated oven for 30 to 40 minutes, until golden brown. Mix Tzatziki sauce ingredients and chill. Cut into squares and serve while hot. Top with Tzatziki sauce. *Contributed by Brent Matsalla.*

## Turnip Fluff

1 medium turnip          1 cup milk
2 eggs                   1 Tbsp. flour
2 Tbsp. brown sugar      Salt and pepper to taste
Pinch of ground cinnamon

Cook turnip and mash well. Mix all ingredients (except cinnamon and brown sugar) and place in greased oven dish. Sprinkle with cinnamon and brown sugar. Bake slowly at 275 for 30 minutes. *Contributed by Mona Zarazun.*

## Twila's Beans

2 cans beans and maple sauce     1 pkg. bacon (cooked and cut into small
2 cans beans and tomato sauce    pieces)
1 can pork and beans             1/2 cup hickory BBQ sauce
1 can tidbits of pineapple       1/2 cup molasses
1 red pepper                     3 Tbsp. Worcestershire sauce
1/2 of white onion               Salt and pepper to taste

Put into crockpot on slow for 5-6 hours. *Contributed by Twila Hadubiak.*

## Wedge Potatoes

Cut potatoes in pieces
Mix 1/3 cup flour
1/3 cup parmesan cheese

1 tsp. paprika
Dash of salt and pepper to taste

Dip potatoes in milk, roll in flour mixture put on a cookie sheet (greased or parchment lined). Sprinkle with melted butter and crushed garlic. Bake at 400 for 40 - 45 min. *Contributed by Ernie and Shirley Zarazun.*

## Zucchini Bake

3 cups zucchini, shredded
1 large onion, shredded
1/2 cup oil
3/4 cup grated cheese
3 eggs, beaten
2 or 3 cloves garlic, crushed
Salt and pepper

Biscuit Mix:
1 cup flour
3 Tbsp. butter
2 tsp. baking powder
Rub biscuit mix like for a pie crust

In a large bowl, shred zucchini and onion and cheese. Beat eggs and add oil, garlic, salt and pepper. Pour over the first ingredients and stir well, adding the biscuit mix in. Pour into a large 6" x 10" or 9" square Pyrex pan, sprayed with pam. Bake 45 to 60 minutes in a 350 degree oven. *Contributed by Eleanor Hadubiak.*

## Zucchini Casserole

4 cups zucchini
1 cup onions (coarsely chopped)
2 tsp. oil
1/2 tsp. salt
1/4 tsp. garlic powder
1/2 tsp. oregano
2 Tbsp. chopped parsley or 1 tsp. dried
1/2 tsp. pepper
1/2 tsp. basil
2 tomatoes chopped
2 eggs well beaten
2 1/2 cups mozzarella cheese

Sauté zucchini in oil until soft, add spices and tomatoes. Blend eggs and cheese and stir in. Bake at 375 for 18-20 min. *Contributed by Linda Matsalla.*

## Tips for Serving Side Dishes

If you are preparing a large meal and the sides are ready early, take a cooler with a lid, place a hot heating pad or a hot wet towel into the cooler. Place the side dishes into the cooler and they will be kept warm until the main course is ready.

When preparing dressing or stuffing, make sure your bread cubes are really dry. This will help to make the stuffing not soggy. Remember to add stock and seasoning for flavor to your liquids if cooking the dressing separately.

To match side dishes to your main course dishes:
1. Check what is seasonal at the market, and check what is older in your fridge.
2. Think color contrasts to interest the eye pallet.
3. Keep in mind the time to prepare, can you prepare before your main dish or during
4. Select heavy or light sides. Example: deep fried dishes would accommodate a light side.
5. Combine seasoning for your side dishes to blend with your main dish. Example: use lemon juice on your fish, add a splash of lemon to your carrots.

# Cakes

# Chart for Oven Temperatures

| 250-350 | 350-400 | 400-450 |
|---|---|---|
| Sponge cake (no shortening) Angel cake Pound cake Rich fruit cake Macaroons | Sheet cake Loaf cake Gingerbread Layer cakes Small cake Cupcakes Drop cookies | Plain cookies |

## Angel Food Cake Dessert #1

1 angel food cake mix (dry)
1 - 14 oz. crushed pineapple, drained OR use 1 pkg. cooked lemon or lime pie filling (cooled)

Beat the two ingredients together and pour into a 9" x 13" pan. Bake at 350 for 45 minutes. Serve with whipped cream. *Contributed by Theresa Mudry.*

## Angel Food Cake Dessert #2

Use a cooled baked angel food cake cut the cake into layers.
Mix lemon pie filling and dream whip put between layers and on top. (could use other pie fillings too)

## Apple Cake

3 Tbsp. butter
1/2 cup sugar
1/4 cup Splenda
1 egg beaten
1/2 tsp. salt
1 tsp. cinnamon

1/2 tsp. cloves
1 tsp. baking soda
1 cup flour
3 cups diced apple, with peel on
1 tsp. finely grated lemon peel
1/2 cup almonds or walnuts to decorate top of cake

Cream butter and sugar then add beaten egg. Stir together dry ingredients and add. Stir apple into the dough mixture. Grease an 8" x 8" pan. Bake at 360 for 40 to 45 minutes.

## Apple Streusel Coffee Cake

2 1/4 cups flour
3/4 cup sugar
3/4 cup butter
1/2 tsp. baking soda
1/2 tsp. baking powder

1 beaten egg
3/4 cup buttermilk or sour milk
1 can pie filling
1/3 cup raisins (optional)

Combine flour and sugar in large bowl, cut in butter until mixture is crumbly, set aside 1/2 cup of this mixture for a crumb topping. To remainder add baking powder and baking soda. Combine egg and buttermilk, add to dry ingredients, and stir until moistened. Spread two thirds of the batter over the bottom (as well as part way up the sides of a greased 9" spring form pan) Combine pie filling and raisins (or omit) spoon over batter. Drop spoonful of remaining batter over the filling. Sprinkle with reserved crumbs mixture. Bake at 350 oven for 50-55 minutes. Use any type of pie filling. *Contributed by Cynthia Fullawka.*

## Bachelor Cake

1 cup butter
1 cup sugar
2 eggs well beaten
3 Tbsp. hot coffee

3 tsp. cocoa
1/2 tsp. vanilla
1/2 cup peanut butter

Mix well, then line a layer of graham wafers on the bottom of the pan. Spread mixture. Refrigerate to set.

## Black Forest Dessert

1 Duncan Hines Chocolate cake mix
1 small instant chocolate pudding
4 eggs
1/2 cup oil

1 1/2 cups warm water
1 pkg. Mini marshmallows
1 can cherry pie filling

Stir together the cake mix and chocolate pudding, and then make a well. In the well, put the eggs, oil and water; beat well. Grease a 9" x 13" pan and layer the bottom of the pan with marshmallows. Pour the prepared batter on top and the spread a can of cherry pie filling on top of the batter. Bake at 350 for 45 minutes. As this bakes, the marshmallows come to the top and cherries go to the bottom. Freezes well.

## Best Blueberry Muffins

2-1/2 cups flour, plus 1 Tbsp. for dusting blueberries
1 Tbsp. baking powder
1/2 tsp. baking soda
1/2 tsp. salt
1 tsp. cinnamon
1/2 cup butter or margarine, melted
1 cup sugar
2 large eggs
1-1/2 cups plain yogurt
1 tsp. vanilla extract
2 Tbsp. lemon juice
1/2 cup blueberry pie filling
1 cup fresh or frozen blueberries

Preheat the oven to 400. Butter 18 muffin tins or use liners. Toss berries with flour and set aside. Whisk: flour, baking soda, baking powder, salt, and cinnamon and set aside. In mixing bowl mix until smooth: yogurt, eggs, lemon juice, melted butter, pie filling, and vanilla. Add dry ingredients to wet a little at a time but do not overmix. Fold in blueberries. Spoon into muffin tins. Optional: sprinkle muffin tops with sugar. Bake at 400 for 20-30 min. or until golden brown or if a skewer inserted into center comes out dry. Can cover with tin foil if getting too brown. *Contributed by Brent Matsalla.*

## Blueberry Cream Muffins

4 eggs
2 cups sugar
1 cup oil
1 tsp. vanilla
4 cups flour

1 tsp. salt
1 tsp. baking soda
2 tsp. baking powder
2 cups sour cream
2 cups berries

Beat eggs, add sugar, oil and vanilla. Combine dry ingredients. Add alternating with sour cream. Add berries last to the mixture. Bake at 350 until slightly brown. *Contributed by Albina Hrychenko.*

## Bran Muffin Mix

1 cup wheat germ
4 cups flour
3 cups natural bran
2 cups all bran cereal
2 cups white sugar
1/2 cup molasses
3 Tbsp. baking soda

1 quart buttermilk or sour milk with 2 Tbsp. vinegar
1 1/2 cups oil
4 eggs
1 - 2 cups raisins or 1/2 nuts and 1/2 dried cranberries
2 tsp. cinnamon
2 tsp. allspice

Mix together and this will keep from 6 to 8 weeks in the fridge to make fresh as needed. *Contributed by Mona Zarazun.*

## Cake Mix Dessert

Any type of cake mix. Omit water and add 1 can of cherries. Bake in a 9" x 13" pan. When cool cover with cream cheese icing.


## Cake Mix Poppy Seed Cake

1 pkg. white cake mix
1 pkg. vanilla instant pudding
1/2 cup poppy seed

4 eggs
1 cup water
1/2 cup oil

Beat eggs and oil together. Mix poppy seed in water. Blend poppy seed with cake mix and pudding. Mix into egg oil mixture. Bake according to cake mix instructions. *Contributed by Theresa Mudry.*


## Camden's Favorite Chocolate Cupcakes

2 cups sugar
1 3/4 cups flour
1 cup cocoa
2 tsp. brown sugar
1 tsp. baking powder
1/2 tsp. salt

Combine the above ingredients in a large bowl and add 2 eggs, 1 cup buttermilk or sour milk, 1 cup strong coffee, ½ cup vegetable oil, 1 tsp. vanilla. Beat for 2 minutes then pour into a greased and floured pan and bake at 350 deg. For 40 min or spoon into individual cupcakes. *Contributed by Camden Ledding.*


## Carrot Bar Cake

3 cups grated carrots
2 cups flour
2 cups sugar (1 white and 1 brown)
1 tsp. salt
2 tsp. cinnamon
2 tsp. baking soda
4 eggs
1 cup oil
1 cup chopped walnuts (optional)

Topping to spread on cooled cake:
1/4 lb. soft butter
1 lb. icing sugar
2 tsp. vanilla
1 cup chopped nuts
1 8oz. pkg. cream cheese

Beat together and put into a large greased cookie sheet to bake at 360. Cool.

## Carrot Cake

In a medium saucepan put:

| | |
|---|---|
| 1 1/2 cups sugar | 4 Tbsp. butter |
| 1 1/3 cups water | 1 tsp. cloves |
| 1 cup raisins | 2 large finely grated carrots |

Simmer all the ingredients together for five minutes. Then cover and rest for 12 hours. This is very important. Next day add 1 cup chopped nuts.

| | |
|---|---|
| 2 1/2 cups flour | 1 tsp. baking soda |
| 2 tsp. baking powder | 1/2 tsp. salt |

Bake in two greased pans or one Bundt pan at 275 for 2 hours. The carrots disappear and no one even knows they are added.

## Carrot Orange Cake

| | |
|---|---|
| 3 1/2 cups sifted flour | 3/4 cup packed brown sugar |
| 2 tsp. baking powder | 3 eggs |
| 1 tsp. baking soda | 3/4 cup orange juice |
| 1/2 tsp. salt | 1 Tbsp. orange rind |
| 1 tsp. cinnamon | 2 cups shredded carrots |
| 1/2 tsp. nutmeg | 1 cup walnuts |
| 1/2 cup soft margarine | |

Grease and flour a Bundt pan. Sift flour, baking powder, baking soda and salt with spices. Beat butter, sugar and eggs. Bake for 45 minutes at 350. Cool. Spread cream cheese icing: 1 pkg. cream cheese softened, 1/2 cup icing sugar, and 1 tsp. vanilla.

## Cheese Cake

| | |
|---|---|
| Graham crust: | 1/2 cup soft margarine |
| 1 1/2 cups crumbs | 1/2 cup sugar |

Mix thoroughly and press into an 8" x 8" or an 8" x 10" pan. Bake for 15 minutes.

Beat together the following:

| | |
|---|---|
| 8 oz. pkg. cream cheese | 1/2 cup sugar |

Then whip 3 pkgs. dream whip with 1/4 tsp. almond flavoring. Blend into the cream cheese mixture. Put fruit on top. Could be frozen before the fruit is added. *Contributed by Kathy K.*

## Cheesecake Cupcakes

24-36 paper muffin cups
1 pkg. vanilla wafers
3 - 8 oz. pkg. cream cheese

1 cup sugar
4 eggs
2 tsp. lemon juice

In a muffin tin, arrange vanilla wafers in bottom of each baking cup flat side down. Cream together all ingredients until smooth, fill each cup 3/4 full. Bake at 350 for 18 minutes. Can be frozen at this point when cooled. When serving add any pie filling on top. *Contributed by Bev Zarazun.*


## Cheesecake with Cottage Cheese

2 pkgs. lemon Jell-O powder
1 cup boiling water
1 cup cottage cheese

3/4 cup sugar (omit this if using sweeten whip cream)
1 tsp. vanilla

Cream cheese and sugar and vanilla, mix cream mixture with Jell-O powder. Dissolve Jell-O in boiling water and chill. Whip 2 cups cream, add 1 cup drained pineapple. Mix with the rest of ingredients. Line pan with crushed graham wafers mixed with 1/2 cup butter. Press into the pan. Add Jell-O cheese and cream mixture on top of the crumbs. Use some crushed graham wafers for the topping. Chill. *Contributed by Linda Matsalla.*


## Chocolate Carrot Cake #1

2 cups flour
1 tsp. salt
1 1/2 cups sugar
1 tsp. cinnamon
1 cup cooking oil
1 tsp. vanilla
1/2 cup orange juice or orange liqueur
4 lg. eggs
1/4 cup cocoa
2 cups shredded carrots
2 tsp. baking soda
1 1/3 cups shredded coconut

In a large bowl, with a mixer on low speed, beat flour, sugar, oil, orange juice, cocoa, baking soda, salt, cinnamon, vanilla, and eggs just until blended; Constantly scraping bowl. Increase speed to high, beat for 2 minutes. Stir in carrots and coconut. Spoon the batter into a greased Bundt pan or tube pan. Bake for 50 – 55 minutes at 350 deg. Cool cake in the pan for 10 minutes. Remove cake from pan and cool completely on rack. In a small bowl, mix 2 cups icing sugar and 2 Tbsp. Orange juice or orange liqueur until spreading consistency. Drizzle over top of cake to allow to run down the sides. *Contributed by Jim Matsalla.*

## Chocolate Carrot Cake #2

| | |
|---|---|
| 3 1/4 cups flour | 1 1/2 cups vegetable oil |
| 2 1/2 cups sugar | 1 cup apple sauce |
| 3/4 cup cocoa | 3 cups shredded carrots |
| 1 Tbsp. baking soda | 2 cups chopped walnuts |
| 2 tsp. cinnamon | Cocoa cream cheese frosting |
| 4 eggs | |

In a large bowl stir together flour, sugar, and cocoa, baking soda, cinnamon and salt. In small bowl, beat eggs until light; stir in oil and apple sauce. Add egg mixture, carrots and walnuts to flour mixture. Stir until flour is moistened. Pour batter into well-greased 12"x9" cake pan. Bake at 350 for 60 - 65 minutes. Cool in the pan for 10 minutes. Remove from pan, cool completely on wire rack. Frost top and sides with cocoa cream cheese frosting. Chill to set.

**Cocoa Cream Cheese Frosting for Chocolate Carrot Cake:**

In large mixer bowl, beat 3/4 of pkg. of cream cheese, softened, 1/4 cup butter, softened and 2 tsp. vanilla until smooth. Gradually beat in 3 Tbsp. cocoa and 2 3/4 cups icing sugar until smooth.

## Chocolate Cheesecake Cupcakes

| | |
|---|---|
| 12 vanilla wafers and baking cups | 2 Tbsp. flour |
| 1 pkg. 8 oz. cream cheese | 1 tsp. vanilla |
| 1/2 cup sugar | 4 squares 4 oz. semi-sweet chocolate |
| 2 eggs | 3/4 cup coconut or chopped pecans |

Place a vanilla wafer, flat side down in each baking cup. Beat cheese until smooth. Gradually beat in sugar and continue beating until light and fluffy, add eggs one at a time. Beating well. Blend in flour and vanilla then chocolate. Spoon into cups filling 3/4 full. Sprinkle with coconut or pecans. Bake at 325 for 30 minutes. *Contributed by Bev Zarazun.*

## Chocolate Cheesecake

| | |
|---|---|
| 1 pkg. of Duncan Hines deluxe deep chocolate cake mix | 1/2 cup sugar |
| 4 eggs | 1 1/2 cups milk |
| 1 Tbsp. oil | 1 tsp. vanilla |
| 2 pkgs. 8 oz. each cream cheese, softened | 1 envelope whipped topping |

Preheat the oven to 300. Measure 1 cup of dry cake mix; set aside. Stir together remaining dry cake mix, 1 egg and oil in a large bowl (mixture is crumbly) Press this crust mixture lightly into bottom and up the sides of a greased 9" x 13" x 2" pan. Blend cream cheese and sugar in same bowl. Add 3 eggs and reserved cake mix, beat 1 minute at medium speed. Gradually add milk and vanilla at low speed. Pour into crumb crust. Bake at 300 for 55-60 minutes. Cool spread whipped topping over cheesecake, sprinkle top with shaved chocolate. Chill 1 hour before serving. Store in refrigerator. Baked cheesecake can be frozen. *Contributed by Bev Zarazun.*

## Chocolate Chiffon Cake

1 3/4 cups sifted flour (3 times)  
3/4 cup sugar  
1/2 tsp salt

3 Tbsp. cocoa  
3 tsp. baking powder

Mix all dry ingredients and sift together.

8 egg whites (equaling 1 cup)  
1/2 tsp cream of tartar  
3/4 cup sugar

8 egg yolks  
3/4 cup cold water  
1 tsp. vanilla  
1/2 cup vegetable oil

Mix like all chiffon cakes. *Contributed by Chris Loshack.*


## Chocolate Fudge Cake

2 cups brown sugar  
2 cups flour  
1 cup melted margarine  
4 Tbsp. cocoa  
1/2 tsp. baking powder

2 tsp. vanilla  
2 eggs  
2 cups coconut  
1 can condensed milk

Mix first 7 ingredients together and spread in a greased 9" x 13" pan. Mix coconut and condensed milk, spread over chocolate layer. Bake at 350 for 30 minutes until lightly brown. *Contributed by Eleanor Ludba.*


## Chocolate Oatmeal Cake

1/2 cup rolled oats  
4 Tbsp. cocoa  
1 cup boiling water

2 eggs  
1/2 cup oil  
1 1/2 cups brown sugar

Mix oats, cocoa and water and let stand while you combine and beat eggs, oil and sugar.

Combine:  
1 cup flour  
1 tsp. baking powder

1 tsp. baking soda  
Pinch of salt

Add flour mixture to egg mixture. Then add oatmeal mixture. Bake at 350 in a 9" x 13" greased pan for 30 minutes.

## Chocolate Sheet Cake

Place together in a bowl:
    500 ml butter                           500 ml sugar

Put into sauce pan, bring to boil, pour over above and beat well:
    125 m butter                           250 ml water
    125 ml cocoa

Add to above and beat well.
    125 ml sour milk                    5 ml baking soda
    2 eggs                              2 ml salt
    5 ml vanilla

Pour into a greased cookie sheet with high sides (11" x 17") Bake for 20 min at 350.

Heat in sauce pan:
    60 ml butter                           40 ml milk
    30 ml cocoa

Stir into above:
    375 ml icing sugar                  2 ml vanilla

Pour immediately over hot cake. Spread slowly and icing will form when cooled.


## Chocolate Zucchini Cake

1/2 cup margarine
1/2 cup oil
2 eggs
2 cups grated zucchini
1/2 cup buttermilk or sour milk
1 3/4 cups sugar
1 tsp. vanilla
2 1/2 cups flour
1/3 cup and 1 tsp. cocoa powder
1/2 tsp. salt
1 tsp. baking powder
1 tsp. baking soda

Mix together bake on a large greased cookie sheet, sprinkle with chocolate chips and nuts (if desired). Bake at 350 for approximately 30 minutes. Cool in the pan 10 minutes before cutting.

## Christmas Cake

3 lbs. raisins

1 lb. currants

2 pkg. glazed fruit

2 pkg. baking cherries

1 lb. nuts (1/2 walnuts and 1/2 almonds)

1 lb. sugar

12 eggs

2 3/4 cups flour

2 tsp. flavoring (1 vanilla and 1 almond)

1 1/4 cups flour (to coat for fruit)

1 lb. butter

1 tsp. baking soda

1 tsp. salt

1/2 cup fruit juice

Bake for 4 1/2 hours in small size pans, 4 1/2 to 5 hours for medium size pans, or 5 to 5 1/2 hours large pans. Makes 2.

## Cinnamon Crumb Cake

Cake:

2 1/4 cups all-purpose flour

2 1/4 tsp. baking powder

1/2 tsp. salt

1 1/4 cups sugar

1/2 cup butter or margarine, softened

3 eggs

2 tsp. vanilla

3/4 cup whole milk

Topping:

2 cups all-purpose flour

1/2 cup sugar

1/2 cup packed light brown sugar

1 1/2 tsp. cinnamon

1 cup butter or margarine, softened

Preheat the oven to 350 grease a 9" x 13" baking pan; lightly dust with flour. Prepare the topping. In medium bowl, mix flour, sugars and cinnamon. Work in the butter until evenly distributed; set aside. Prepare cake; combine flour, baking powder and salt; set aside. In larger bowl, with mixer at low speed, beat sugar with butter until blended, scraping bowl often. Increase speed to medium beat until creamy, about 3 minutes, occasionally scraping bowl. Reduce speed to low; add eggs, one at a time, beating well after each addition. Beat in vanilla. Alternately add flour mixture and milk, beginning and ending with flour mixture; beat just until smooth. Spoon batter into the pan; spread evenly. With your hand, press topping into marble size chunks; evenly placing over batter. Bake for 35 to 40 minutes or until toothpick inserted in center of cake comes out clean. Cool completely in the pan on wire rack. To serve, warm for breakfast, or bite size pieces cold.

## Cinnamon Roll Cake

3 cups flour
1/4 tsp. salt
1 cup sugar
4 tsp. baking powder
1 Tbsp. cinnamon

1 1/2 cup milk
2 eggs
2 tsp. vanilla
1/2 cup butter, melted

Topping:
1 cup butter, softened
1 cup brown sugar

2 Tbsp. flour
2 Tbsp. cinnamon

Mix everything together except for the butter. Slowly stir in the melted butter and pour into a greased 9" x 13" pan. For the topping, mix all the ingredients together until well combined. Drop evenly over the batter and swirl with a knife. Bake at 350 for 28-32 minutes.

Glaze:
2 cups powdered sugar
5 Tbsp. milk
1 tsp. vanilla

1 Tbsp. Cinnamon
Thicken with flour if needed.

While warm drizzle the glaze over the cake. *Contributed by Brent Matsalla.*

## Coconut Rhubarb Spice Cake

1/2 cup shortening
1 1/2 cups packed brown sugar
1 egg
1 1/4 tsp. vanilla
2 cups all-purpose flour
1 1/2 tsp. cinnamon
1 tsp. baking soda
1/4 tsp. salt
1/4 tsp. all spice
1/4 tsp. cloves
1 1/2 cups buttermilk
2 cups finely chopped fresh or frozen rhubarb, thawed

Topping:

1/2 cup chopped pecans
1 tsp. cinnamon

*Continued on next page...*

In a large mixing bowl, cream shortening and brown sugar until light and fluffy. Add egg and vanilla beat well. Combine the flour, cinnamon, baking soda, salt, all spice and cloves; add to the creamed mixture alternately with buttermilk. Fold in the rhubarb. The batter is thick. Pour into a greased 13"x 9" baking dish. Combine the topping ingredients; sprinkle over the top. Bake at 350 for 40 - 45 minutes or until a toothpick is inserted near the center and it comes out clean. Cool on a wire rack. Note: if using frozen rhubarb, measure rhubarb while still frozen, then thaw completely. Drain in a colander, but do not press liquid out.

## Cream Cheese Cake

Wafer Crust:

| | |
|---|---|
| 8 graham wafers | Soften gelatin in water then set in a pan of |
| 1 heaping Tbsp. melted butter | hot water and stir until dissolved |
| 1/4 cup brown sugar | 1 envelope dream whip |
| Bake and cool. | 1/2 cup milk |
| 1 envelope gelatin (Knox) in 2 Tbsp. water | 1/2 tsp. vanilla |

Blend:

| | |
|---|---|
| 1/3 cup milk | 1 pkg. 8 oz. cream cheese |
| 1/2 cup icing sugar | 2 Tbsp. lemon juice |

Prepare dream whip, blend milk with cream cheese, icing sugar, lemon juice and gelatin. Add dream whip and blend until blended smooth. Pour into prepared wafer crust and chill until set. Cover with cherry pie filling.

## Cream of Wheat Cake

| | |
|---|---|
| 2 cups milk | Beat in 3/4 cup margarine |
| 1/2 cup cream of wheat | 1/2 cup sugar |
| Boil the milk and cream of wheat together until thick. | 1 tsp. vanilla |

Cream until smooth, add 1 cup coconut and 8 - 10 chopped cherries. Put a layer of wafers on bottom of 9" x 13" pan, spread with the cream of wheat filling, then top with wafers again. Top with cream cheese icing, let stand overnight to set before serving.

## Crumb Cake

| | |
|---|---|
| 1 1/2 cups brown sugar | 1/2 tsp. salt |
| 1 1/2 cups all-purpose flour | 1 tsp. baking powder |
| 2 tsp. cinnamon | 2 eggs |
| 1 tsp. nutmeg | 2/3 cup sour milk |
| 1/2 tsp. cloves | 1/2 tsp. baking soda |
| 1/2 cup butter (may use half butter and half shortening) | 1 cup raisins |

Preheat the oven to 350 degrees. Grease and line bottom of 6" x 10" pan with greased wax paper. Sift, then measure flour, add salt and spices, sift together 3 times. Add the brown sugar. Cut in butter until the mixture is fine. Reserve 3/4 cup crumbs for the topping. To remainder of the crumbs add the baking powder and raisins. Beat eggs until light. Add the sour milk with the baking soda dissolved in it. Make a well in the dry ingredients and add the egg-milk mixture, mixing until smooth. Pour batter into prepared pan and sprinkle with the reserved crumb mixture. Bake for 45 minutes.

## Cupcakes

| | |
|---|---|
| 1 cup sugar | 1 cup cream (if sour add 1 tsp. soda) |
| 2 eggs (beat together) | |

Add:

| | |
|---|---|
| 2 cups flour | Pinch of salt |
| 2 tsp. baking powder | 1 tsp. vanilla |

## Double-Lemon Poppy Seed Cake

| | |
|---|---|
| 1 pkg. (2 layer size) lemon cake mix | 1/2 cup cream cheese spread |
| 1 pkg. (85 g) lemon Jell-O powder | 2 Tbsp. butter, softened |
| 1 1/4 cups of water | 1 cup icing sugar, sifted |
| 1/2 cup oil | 2 Tbsp. shredded peel |
| 4 eggs | 1 Tbsp. juice from 1 lemon, divided |
| 1/4 cup poppy seed | |

Heat the oven to 350. Beat first 5 ingredients in large bowl with mixer until well blended. Stir in poppy seed. Pour into well-greased and lightly floured a Bundt pan. Bake for 50 minutes to 1 hour or until toothpick inserted near center comes out clean. Cool in the pan 30 minutes. Loosen cake from sides of pan with knife. Invert cake onto wire rack; gently remove pan; cool cake completely. Beat cream cheese and butter with mixer on low speed until well blended. Gradually beat in sugar and lemon juice. Spread over top of cake and garnish with the peel.

## Dump Cake

1 can pie filling (cherry, blueberry, strawberry work well)

1 can crushed pineapple (drained)

1 box cake mix (any flavor)

1 1/4 stick of margarine (sliced thin)

1/2 cup chopped walnuts

1/2 to 3/4 cup flaked coconut

Spread pie filling into a 9" x 13" pan. Scatter the pineapple over it. Sprinkle cake mix in a layer over the filling. Drop slices of margarine over the cake mix. Scatter nuts and coconut on top (do not stir). Bake at 350 for 40 minutes or until cake is done and lightly browned. Serve plain or with ice cream or whipped cream.

## Earthquake Cake

Spray 9" x 13" pan with cooking spray.

Lightly toast:

1 cup coconut

1 cup chopped pecans

Spread on bottom of pan and add 1 German chocolate cake mix (make as directed on pkg.)

Melt together:

1/2 cup margarine

8 oz. pkg. cream cheese

Add 1 1/2 - 2 cups icing sugar and pour this cream cheese and sugar mixture over unbaked cake. Bake at 350 for 40 - 45 minutes or until cake is done. Serve with ice cream. *Contributed by Devon Dziaduck.*

## Elvis Presley Cake

1 White or yellow cake mix

8 oz. can crushed pineapple

1 cup sugar

1/2 tsp. vanilla extract

8 oz. pkg. Cream Cheese

1/2 cup butter softened

3 cups icing sugar

1/2 tsp. vanilla extract

3 cups crushed pecans

Bake the cake mix to pkg. directions. Cool cake and poke holes in it. In a pan, boil crushed pineapple with juice and a cup of sugar and 1/2 a tsp. of vanilla extract. Then pour over cooled cake. Mix cream cheese with butter and icing sugar. Add vanilla and crushed pecans. Mix well and top the cake. Add another cup of pecans to top. Let sit for at least 6 hours or best, overnight. Keep refrigerated.

## Fruit Cake

1/2 lb. glazed cherries

1 lb. raisins

1 lb. currants

1/2 lb. cherries

1 can crushed pineapple

1/2 lb. chopped mixed peel

1/2 cup orange marmalade

12 eggs

1/2 cup honey

4 cups flour

1 tsp. baking soda

1 tsp. salt

1 tsp. cinnamon

1/2 tsp. nutmeg

*Contributed by Evelyn Kowalchuk.*

## Layered Lemon Dessert

2 cups flour
1 cup margarine
2 - 8 oz. pkg. cream cheese, softened
1 cup icing sugar

1 cup whipping cream
2 pkgs. lemon pie filling
Cool whip

Cut flour and margarine together as you would for pie crust until crumbly. Press into a 9" x 13" pan. Bake at 350 for 12 minutes. Beat cheese and sugar together well. Beat cream until stiff. Fold into cream cheese mixture. Spread over cooled crust. Prepare pie fillings according to directions on package. Cool, stirring often. Pour over cheese layer. Cover with cool whip spread over the filling. Can top with slivered almonds or pecans.

## Lazy Man's Black Forest Cake

1 chocolate cake mix (double layer)
1 bag small marshmallows
1 can cherry pie filling (large can)

1 large package chocolate pudding (not instant pudding)
Whipped cream

Grease a 8" x 13" pan and put down a layer of marshmallows. Add mixed cake batter over marshmallows. Scoop cherry pie filling on top of cake. You may need to bake the cake 15 minutes longer than instructed on cake mix. If not done. Add cooked pudding on top of warm cake. When cool, add whipped cream. *Contributed by Eleanor Hadubiak.*

## Lemon Loaf

1/3 cup Mazola oil
3/4 cup sugar
2 eggs
Grated rind of 2 lemons
1/8 cup lemon juice
1-1/2 cups flour
1/2 tsp salt
1 tsp. baking powder
1/2 cup milk
1/8 or 1/4 cup sugar mixed with juice of 1/2 a lemon for glaze or cutting into the loaf before baking

*Continued on next page...*

Cream oil and sugar, add eggs and stir well. Add rind and lemon juice mix. Mix together the dry ingredients (flour, salt, baking powder) and alternately add milk while mixing. Mix the sugar and lemon to add

Into the unbaked loaf and spread with a knife to roughly blend the sugary lemon into the loaf. OR you would use this as a glaze for the baked loaf, and you would spread it over the baked loaf on top and let cool.

To prepare your loaf pan, spray with cooking spray, put parchment paper on bottom and sides. By spraying with cooking spray the parchment will stick to the sides and assist in easy removal of the loaf from the pan. Bake at 350 for 50 - 60 min. *Contributed by Theresa Mudry.*


## Lemon Poppy Seed Zucchini Loaf

| | |
|---|---|
| 2 cups grated zucchini | 1 1/2 tsp. baking powder |
| 1 lemon, the juice and grated rind | 3/4 tsp. baking soda |
| 4 eggs | 1 tsp. salt |
| 1 1/2 cups oil | 1 tsp. lemon extract |
| 1 1/2 cups white sugar | 1 pkg. instant lemon pudding mix |
| 1 1/2 cups milk | 1/2 cup dry poppy seed |
| 4 cups flour | |

Mix dry ingredients together. Add liquids. Bake in 3 greased loaf pans at 350 for 1 hour and 10 minutes.


## Lemon Rhubarb Loaf

| | |
|---|---|
| 2 cups flour | 1/2 cup brown sugar |
| 2 tsp. baking powder | 1 Tbsp. cornstarch |
| 1/4 tsp. salt | 1/2 cup butter |
| 1/3 cup milk | 1 cup sugar |
| 1/3 cup real lemon Juice | 3 eggs |
| 1 1/2 cups thawed well drained slices of frozen rhubarb | 1 tsp. vanilla |

Glaze:

| | |
|---|---|
| 1 1/4 cups sugar | 2 Tbsp. softened butter |
| 2 Tbsp. lemon juice | |

Butter a loaf pan, line bottom with wax paper (or parchment). Preheat the oven to 350. Stir flour, baking powder and salt together. Stir in milk with lemon juice. Let stand 5 minutes. Combine rhubarb with 1/2 cup brown sugar and cornstarch in a food processor; pulse until combined but still chunky. Cook on high in microwave, stopping twice to stir, for 2 to 4 minutes. Cool. Beat butter with sugar until creamy. Beat in eggs, on at a time. Add vanilla. Alternately add in flour and milk in 2 additions. Spoon 1/3 of batter into loaf pan. Top with 1/2 rhubarb mixture. Repeat. Top with remaining batter. Swirl a knife through the batter and smooth the top. Bake for 60 minutes or until toothpick inserted in center comes out with just a few crumbs attached. Cool in the pan on a rack. Glaze the loaf. Stir sugar with lemon juice and butter until smooth. Drizzle over the cooked loaf.

## Lemon/Orange/Grapefruit Cranberry Muffins

2 cups all-purpose flour
1 1/4 cups white sugar
1 Tbsp. baking powder
1/2 tsp. salt
1/4 cup lemon, orange, or grapefruit juice
Grate the rind of fruit of choice

3/4 cup milk
2 eggs
1/2 cup vegetable oil
1 cup fresh or frozen cranberries, halved
1/3 cup toasted slivered almonds

Preheat the oven to 400. Grease 12 muffin tins or use paper liners. Combine flour, sugar, baking powder, and salt. Mix fruit juice and grated rind with milk in a measuring cup, to the sour milk; beat eggs, oil, and milk mixture in a bowl. Stir eggs into flour mixture and fold-in cranberries. Fill prepared muffin cups two-thirds full; top with almonds. Bake for 18 to 20 minutes or until a toothpick inserted into the center, comes out clean. Cool for 5 minutes before removing from pan to cool on a wire rack.

## Lemon Slice

1 cup all-purpose flour
1/2 cup butter
1 tsp. baking powder
1/2 tsp. salt

1 egg
1 Tbsp. milk
1 tsp. vanilla
Lemon pie filling

Preheat the oven to 350. Grease an 8" x 8" pan. Sift, then measure flour, add salt and baking powder. Sift into bowl. Cut the butter into the flour as for pastry. Beat egg slightly, add milk and vanilla. Add the egg-milk to the flour mixture, stirring until just blended. Press the soft dough into prepared pan. Cover with cooled lemon pie filling.

## Mandarin Orange Cake

2 cups flour
2 cups sugar
2 tsp. baking soda
Dash of salt

2 eggs
2 tsp. vanilla
2 cans (11 1/4 oz.) mandarin oranges (with juice)

Combine flour, baking soda and salt together. Beat eggs, gradually adding sugar and vanilla to egg mixture, then dry ingredients and mix until combined. Add oranges and juice from the can.
Back at 350 for 1 hour in a 9" x 13" pan.

Frosting:
1 cup brown sugar
1 cup whipping cream

1 tsp. vanilla.
Beat until stiff.

## Maple Walnut Chiffon Cake

2 cups pastry flour or 1 2/3 cups all-purpose flour

3 tsp. baking powder

1 tsp. salt

1 1/2 cups sugar

1/2 cup oil

5 egg yolks

3/4 cup lukewarm water

1 tsp. vanilla

1/2 tsp. maple flavoring

1/2 cup chopped walnuts

## Marble Chiffon Cake

1 square cooking chocolate

2 Tbsp. hot water

3 Tbsp. sugar

1/4 tsp. baking soda

1 1/2 cups flour (sifted)

1 cup sugar

2 tsp. baking powder

1 tsp. salt

3/8 cup of oil

6 unbeaten egg yolks

1/2 cup water

1 1/2 tsp. vanilla

1 cup egg whites (6-7)

1/2 tsp cream of tartar

Melt the chocolate, add hot water, sugar, baking soda and mix. Sift together flour, sugar, baking powder and salt. Make a well and add all, egg yolks, water and vanilla. Beat until smooth. Beat egg whites with cream of tartar until forms peaks. Pour egg yolk mixture into white's mixture gradually. Divide batter add chocolate mixture to 1/2 of batter. Pour plain and chocolate batter alternating into a tube pan.

## Milk Chocolate Cake

1/2 cup butter

1 1/2 cups sugar

2 eggs, unbeaten

2 cups sifted cake flour

1/2 tsp. salt

1 cup sour milk or buttermilk

1 tsp. vanilla

2 squares bitter chocolate

1 tsp. baking soda

1 Tbsp. vinegar

Cream butter and sugar, gradually add on egg, beat, add second egg, and continue beating. Alternating add flour and salt sifted together and sour milk with vanilla added. Melt chocolate over hot water in a double boiler. Add and beat thoroughly dissolve soda in vinegar and add last. Grease a 9"x 9" pan and bake at 350.

## Orange Date Cake

1/3 cup butter

1 cup sugar

1 egg

2 cups flour

1 tsp. baking soda

1 tsp baking powder

1/2 cup chopped dates

1 cup sour cream

1/2 cup chopped raisins

1/2 cup chopped nuts

Grated rind of 1 orange.

Cream butter, sugar, add the egg. Blend flour, baking soda, baking powder, then add the dates, raisins, nuts and grated orange. Mix with egg mixture and sour cream. Grease a 9"x 9" pan. Bake at 350 until browned approximately 40 minutes.

## Orange Zucchini Cake

| | |
|---|---|
| 1 cup flour | 1/2 cup vegetable oil |
| 1 tsp. baking powder | 2 eggs |
| 1/2 tsp. baking soda | 1/2 cup all bran cereal |
| 1/4 tsp. salt | 1 1/2 tsp. grated orange peel |
| 1 tsp. cinnamon | 1 tsp. vanilla |
| 1/2 tsp. nutmeg | 1 cup grated zucchini |
| 3/4 cup sugar | 1/2 cup chopped nuts |

Combine dry ingredients and set aside. Beat sugar, oil and eggs well, stir in cereal, orange peel, nuts and vanilla. Add zucchini and dry ingredients. Bake at 350 for 35 minutes in a 9" x 9" pan. *Contributed by Marian Skoretz.*

## Pineapple Cheesecake with Cottage Cheese OR Cream Cheese

Crust:

| | |
|---|---|
| 1 1/3 cups Oreo or graham crumbs | 1/4 cup sugar |
| 1/3 cup melted margarine | |

Mix together, spread into 9" x 13" pan. Save some for topping. Bake at 325 for 8 to 10 minutes then cool.

| | |
|---|---|
| 2 pkgs. lemon Jell-O | 1 tsp. vanilla |
| 1 cup boiling water | 2 cups whipping cream |
| 1 cup cottage cheese (dry) OR use 1 - 8 oz. pkg. of cream cheese | 1 cup crushed pineapple |
| 3/4 cup sugar | |

Dissolve Jell-O in boiling water. Mix Jell-O with cottage or cream cheese and sugar. Chill. Add vanilla to cream and whip. Fold in 1 cup drained crushed pineapple. Mix with other ingredients. Store in fridge or freeze.

## Pineapple Delight

| | |
|---|---|
| 1/2 cup butter | 2 cups cake flour |
| 1 cup sugar | 3/4 cup milk |
| 3 egg yolks | 2 tsp. baking powder |
| 1/4 tsp. salt | 1 tsp. vanilla |

Sift flour once and measure, add salt and baking powder. Cream butter and sugar very well, add eggs and milk to flour mixture with vanilla. Bake in moderate oven for 30 minutes.

| | |
|---|---|
| Filling: Boil together in double boiler | 1/2 cup sugar |
| 1 can crushed pineapple | Rind and juice of 1 lemon |
| 2 Tbsp. cornstarch | 1/2 tsp. vanilla |

Keep stirring until thick, then spread on baked batter.
Frosting: Beat very stiff 3 egg whites, fold in 8 Tbsp. icing sugar and 1 tsp. vanilla. Bake in oven until brown. *Contributed by Ann Belitsky.*

## Poppy Chiffon Cake

1/2 cup poppy seed
2 cups flour
3 tsp. baking powder
1 1/2 cups sugar
1 tsp. salt

1/2 cup salad oil
7 unbeaten egg yolks
2 tsp. vanilla
1/4 tsp. soda
7 eggs whites
1/2 tsp. cream of tartar

Soak poppy seed in a cup of water for 2 hours. Sift flour, baking powder, sugar and salt. Form a well and add: oil, poppy seed with the water, egg yolks, vanilla and soda. Beat until smooth. In another bowl mix 7 egg whites and 1/2 tsp. cream of tartar, beat until very stiff, pour yolk mixture into whites and fold.

## Poppy Seed Cake

1/4 cup poppy seeds
1/4 cup milk
1 lemon supreme cake mix
1-3 oz. pkg. instant banana pudding

4 eggs
1/2 cup salad oil
1 cup warm water

Spice mixture:
1 Tbsp. cocoa
1 Tbsp. cinnamon
1 Tbsp. white sugar

Glaze:
3 Tbsp. lemon juice
6 Tbsp. white sugar

Soak poppy seeds in milk overnight. Mix together cake mix, pudding, eggs, salad oil and water. Add poppy seed mixture. Grease and flour a Bundt pan or 9" x 13" pan. Pour in a layer of cake mixture, then add spice mixture and swirl. Repeat until all is used. Bake at 350 for 40 minutes. Turn cake out while still warm and cover in glaze. *From Zarazun Reunion.*

## Poppy Seed Chiffon Cake (Nellie's)

Soak overnight:
1/2 cup of poppy seed in 1/2 cup of water

1 1/2 cups sugar
2 cups flour
3 tsp. baking powder
1 tsp. salt

1 tsp. vanilla
1/2 cup oil
5 egg yolks

Make a well with above 5 dry ingredients and add 1/2 cup oil, poppy seed, vanilla, and egg yolks, (If it is too thick add another egg yolk. Beat very well.)

12 egg whites

1/2 tsp. cream of tartar

Beat egg whites with cream of tartar. Do not under beat. Fold together. Bake at 300 deg. F. in a round pan for 1 hr. or a rectangular pan for 45 minutes. *Contributed by Linda Matsalla.*

## Poppy Seed Plain Cake

1/2 cup poppy seed
1 cup milk
3/4 cup butter
1 1/2 cup sugar

2 cups flour
2 tsp. baking powder
4 egg whites (well beaten)
1 tsp. flavoring

Soak poppy seed in milk for 2 hours. Cream butter, sugar, then add milk and poppy seed. Add the dry ingredients and fold into egg whites.

## Pumpkin Cake

2 cups flour
1 tsp. baking powder
1 tsp. baking soda
1 tsp. cinnamon
1/2 tsp. salt

4 eggs
2 cups sugar
1 cup oil
1 cup cooked pumpkin

Beat eggs, and gradually add the sugar and continue beating until light and fluffy. Stir the oil and pumpkin into egg mixture, then add the dry ingredients.
Pour into a greased 9" x 13" pan. Bake at 350 for 25-30 minutes.

## Pumpkin Pie Cheesecake

3 Tbsp. butter, melted
250 g. cream cheese; softened
1 can sweetened condensed milk
540 ml. can of pure pumpkin

2 tsp. pumpkin pie spice
1/2 tsp. salt
1 tsp. vanilla
2 eggs; beaten

Preheat the oven to 350. Grease a 9" pie plate. Combine crumbs and butter; press firmly on bottom of pie plate. In large bowl, at medium speed, beat cream cheese until fluffy. Gradually beat in sweetened condensed milk until smooth. Add pumpkin, spice, salt and vanilla; mix well. Stir in eggs. Pour mixture into prepared crust. Bake for 50-55 minutes, or until center is set. Cool in the pan on wire rack. Refrigerate 2 hours before serving.

## Pumpkin Jelly Roll

3 eggs
3/4 cup sugar
2/3 cup cooked pumpkin
3/4 cup flour

1 tsp. baking powder
1 tsp. cinnamon
1/2 tsp. salt
1/2 tsp. nutmeg

Mix together. Pour into cookie sheet that is lined with parchment paper. Suggested fillings below:

Cream cheese filling:
8 oz. pkg. cream cheese
1 cup icing sugar

2 tsp. margarine
1/2 tsp. vanilla

Gingersnap filling:
1 cup whipped cream (could be 1 envelope of dream whip)      1/2 cup gingersnap crumbs
*Contributed by Twila Hadubiak*

## Pumpkin Muffins

4 eggs
2 cups brown sugar
1 1/2 cups oil
1 1/2 cups cooked pumpkin
3 cups flour
1 tsp. cinnamon

2 tsp. baking soda
2 tsp. baking powder
1 tsp. salt
1 cup raisins
1 cup butterscotch or caramel chips

Beat eggs, brown sugar and oil. Add pumpkin. Blend the flour, cinnamon, baking soda, baking powder and salt.  Add the raisins and chips to the flour. Mix together with the egg mixture, don't over mix. Bake at 350 for 20-25 minutes. *Contributed by Frances Charuk.*

## Quaker Oatmeal Berry Muffins

3 cups or 1/2 a pkg. of the dry Quaker Oatmeal Muffin Mix
1 egg
1 unsweetened individual serving size apple sauce (any flavor in 1/2 cup measure)
1/3 cup water (approximately until mixture is thoroughly wet.)
1 cup fresh or frozen raspberries or blueberries

Mix together all ingredients in order but do not over mix. Ensure to add berries last. Bake at 400 for 18 to 20 minutes or as directed on pkg. *Contributed by Theresa Mudry.*

## Rachael's Best Ever Banana Muffins

| | |
|---|---|
| 1 cup flour | 1 egg |
| 1/2 cup rolled oats | 3/4 cup sugar |
| 1 tsp. baking powder | 1/3 cup melted shortening (margarine) |
| 1 tsp. baking soda | 1 1/2 cups mashed bananas (3 -4) |
| 1/2 tsp salt | 3/4 cup raisins, optional |

Combine oats, flour, baking powder, baking soda, and salt in a bowl. Beat egg, sugar, melted shortening, banana and raisins together thoroughly. Add banana mixture to dry ingredients. Stir just until moistened. Fill muffin tins 3/4 full. Bake at 375 for 20 – 25 minutes.
Options are dairy free butter, chia seeds, blueberry powder, and dairy free chocolate chips. *Contributed by Rachael Rawson.*

## Raspberry Delight

| | |
|---|---|
| 20 graham wafers | 1 pkg. frozen sweetened raspberries |
| 1/2 cup sugar | 20 marshmallows |
| 1/4 cup butter melted | 1/2 cup milk |
| 1 pkg. raspberry Jell-O powder | 1/2 pint Whipping cream (1 cup) |
| 1 cup boiling water | |

Crush wafers, stir in sugar and butter. Put 3/4 of crumbs into a buttered pan. Dissolve Jell-O into boiling water. Add frozen raspberries and stir until thawed. Allow to partly set, pour over the crumbs. Let set until firm. Melt marshmallows in milk. Soak until smooth. Whip cream into marshmallow mixture. Pour over Jell-O, sprinkle remaining crumbs on top.

## Rhubarb Cake

2 cups flour
1/2 cup butter
1/4 tsp. salt
1 tsp. baking powder
1 egg beaten

*Continued on next page…*

Mix with fork, save 1 cup for top of cake. Flatten the rest into 9" x 13" greased pan.

For the filling, mix the following in order:

| | |
|---|---|
| 1 1/2 cups sugar | 2 eggs, beaten |
| 1/2 cups flour | 4 cups rhubarb |
| | 1/2 cup melted butter |

Pour over mixture in a pan. Cover with 1 cup of crumbs. Sprinkle with Cinnamon and sugar mixture. Bake at 350 for 1 hour 5 to 10 minutes. This freezes well. *Contributed by Elsie Carsten.*

## Rhubarb Cake with Sour Milk and Cinnamon

| | |
|---|---|
| 1/2 cup shortening or oil or margarine | 1 tsp. soda |
| 1 1/4 cups sugar | 1 tsp. baking powder |
| 1 egg | 2 cups rhubarb |
| 1 cup sour milk | 1 tsp vanilla |
| 2 cups flour | 3/4 cup brown sugar |
| 1/2 tsp. salt | Cinnamon to taste |

Bake at 350 for 45-50 min. *Contributed by Tina Brezinski.*

## Rhubarb Matrimonial Cake

| | |
|---|---|
| 5 cups of rhubarb | 1/2 tsp. salt |
| 1 1/2 cups sugar | 2 eggs |
| 2 Tbsp. flour | |

Cook rhubarb and above ingredients, then add remaining ingredients below.

| | |
|---|---|
| 2 cups flour | 1 tsp. baking soda |
| 2 cups rolled oats | 1/2 tsp. salt |
| 1 cup shortening | 1 tsp. baking powder |
| 1 cup brown sugar | |

Bake for 30 minutes.

## Rhubarb Muffins

| | |
|---|---|
| 1/3 cup oil | 1/3 cup chopped walnuts |
| 1 cup brown sugar, packed | 1 2/3 cups flour |
| 1 egg | 3/4 tsp. baking powder |
| 1 1/4 tsp. vanilla | 3/4 tsp. baking soda |
| 2/3 cup sour milk (1 Tbsp. lemon juice to regular milk) | 1/4 tsp. salt |
| 1 1/3 cups rhubarb cut up into 1/4 in. cubes (if using frozen rhubarb, thaw completely and drain) | |

*Continued on next page…*

Beat oil and sugar together. In a bowl, beat the egg, add vanilla and sour milk, mix. Add rhubarb and walnuts. Stir. Add next 4 ingredients together in separate bowl and mix. Add to wet mixture. Stir to moisten only. Fill greased muffin cups almost full. Bake in 400 oven for 20 - 25 minutes until wooden toothpick inserted in center comes out clean. Let stand for 5 minutes. Remove from pan to rack to cool. This makes 1 dozen muffins.

## Rhubarb Strudel Cake

| | |
|---|---|
| 2 cups flour | 1 egg |
| 1/2 cup sugar | 1 1/2 tsp. baking powder |
| 1/2 tsp. salt | 4 cups sliced rhubarb |
| 1/4 cup butter | 3 heaping Tbsp. strawberry or raspberry |
| 1 cup milk | Jell-O powder |

Mix flour, sugar, salt, butter, milk and egg, beat until smooth. Pour into 9" x 13" pan. Top cake with rhubarb mixture and sprinkle Jell-O powder evenly over.

| | |
|---|---|
| Topping: | 1/2 cup rolled oats |
| 1/2 cup flour | 1 Tbsp. cinnamon |
| 3/4 cup sugar (brown or white) | 1/4 cup butter |

Crumble and sprinkle on top of rhubarb mixture. Bake at 350 for 40 minutes. *Contributed by Pat Dubasoff.*

## Rhubarb Torte

| | |
|---|---|
| 1 2/3 cups graham crumbs (reserve 1/3 cup for sprinkle on top) | 3 Tbsp. cornstarch |
| | 1 cup sugar |
| 1/4 cup brown sugar | 1 - 4 oz. pkg. vanilla instant pudding |
| 1/4 cup melted butter | 1/2 cup less milk than pkg. above asks for |
| 4 cups rhubarb | 1 pkg. whipped topping |
| 1/2 cup water | 1 1/2 cups miniature marshmallows |

Mix first three ingredients and press into a 9" x 13" pan. Bake at 375 for 6 - 8 minutes. Cook rhubarb in water until soft. Combine cornstarch with sugar and add to rhubarb. Cook 2 or 3 minutes until thickened. Spread mixture on the crust. Make instant pudding using 1/2 cup less milk that the pkg. asks for. Prepare whip topping. Mix pudding, whip topping with marshmallows and top rhubarb mixture. Sprinkle 1/3 cup graham crumbs on top. *Contributed by Pat Dubasoff.*

## Saskatoon Coffee Cake

Topping:
1/4 cup margarine
3/4 cup brown sugar
1/2 cup flour
1 tsp. cinnamon

Base:
1/2 cup margarine
1 cup sugar
2 eggs
1 tsp. vanilla
2 cups flour
1 tsp. baking powder
1 tsp. baking soda
1 cup sour cream.

Mix and pour the ingredients for the base into a greased 9" x 13" pan. Cover the base with 2 cups or more Saskatoon berries. Mix the ingredients for the topping. Cover the berries with the topping. Bake at 350 for 40 - 45 minutes. *Contributed by Linda Matsalla.*


## Skor Kahlua Trifle

1 - 9" x 13" chocolate cake
2-4 Skor bars (or Skor chips)
1/2 - 3/4 cups Kahlua liquor

1 -500 ml. large Nutri-Whip or equal size whipped topping or cream
4 pkgs. chocolate instant pudding (made up as directed on the pkg. instructions)

Chocolate Cake for Trifle
3 cups flour
2 cups sugar
1/2 cup cocoa
2 tsp. booking soda
2 tsp. vanilla

2 tsp. salt
2 cups water
1/2 cup oil
2 tsp. vinegar

Mix ingredients for the chocolate cake, Bake cake at 350 for 35-40 minutes. Cool and cut into cubes. Layer in a glass bowl. The cake pieces, liquor, pudding, whipped cream and then Skor chips. Repeat layers.

## Sour Cream Cake

2 eggs broken into a cup and fill the rest of the cup with sour cream.
1 cup sugar
1 1/4 cups flour
1 tsp. baking powder
1/2 tsp. baking soda
1 tsp. vanilla
1/8 tsp. salt

Mix sour cream with the baking soda and set aside. Mix eggs and sugar. Blend flour, baking powder, and salt together. Add to egg mixture and alter with sour cream mixture. Bake at 350 in a 9" x 9" pan for approximately 30 minutes until toothpick insert shows no crumbs. Alternative: add 1 cup of raspberries just before putting into the pan.

## Sour Cream Coffee Cake (Grandma Pat's)

Cake ingredients:
1 cup butter (plus a little extra to grease pan)
2 cups sugar
2 eggs

2 cups white flour (or I've used GF baking flours before with no issue)
1 tsp baking powder
1/8 tsp salt
1/2 tsp vanilla
1 cup sour cream

Topping ingredients:
1/2 cup chopped pecans (plus 8 whole for the bottom of pan)

2 tsp sugar
1 tsp cinnamon

Grease pan with some melted butter and space out the 8 pecans at the bottom of a Bundt pan. Cream butter and sugar in mixer/bowl, then beat in eggs. Mix together the flour, baking powder, salt... then gradually add to the butter/sugar mixture. Add sour cream & vanilla. Spoon half batter into the pan. Then sprinkle half the topping mix. Layer the rest of the batter and then the rest of the sugar. Bake for 55-60 min at 350. *Contributed by Adam and Mandelle Waddell.*

## Spice Chiffon Cake

2 cups flour
1 1/2 cups sugar
3 tsp. baking powder
1 tsp salt
1 tsp. cinnamon
1/2 tsp nutmeg
1/2 tsp. all spice

1/2 tsp. cloves
1/2 cup oil
1 cup egg whites (approx. 6-7)
3/4 cup cold water
1 cup egg whites
1/2 tsp. cream of tartar

## Strawberry Shortcake

1 lb. frozen strawberries

1/2 cup sugar

Shortcake:
1 cup sifted flour (add 1 Tbsp.)
2 Tbsp. sugar
1 1/2 tsp. baking powder
1/4 tsp. salt

1/4 cup shortening
1 egg, slightly beaten
3 Tbsp. milk
2 pkgs. whipped topping

Preheat the oven to 450. Into a large bowl, sift flour, sugar (2 Tbsp.), baking powder, and salt. With a pastry blender, cut in shortening until mixture resembles coarse cornmeal. Add egg, stirring with a fork until well combined. Add milk, stirring until dough cleans side of bowl. (you make need to add an extra tablespoon of milk). Turn out dough onto lightly floured surface; knead gently 8 - 10 times. Roll out 1/3" thick. Place dough in an ungreased cookie sheet. Bake for 8 - 10 minutes or until light golden. Immediately, spread some butter after removing from oven. Top shortcakes with whipped cream and strawberries mixed with the 1/2 cup sugar. Serve immediately.

## Sweet Cake Doughnuts

3 eggs
1 cup sour milk
1 cup sour cream
1 cup sugar
1 tsp. salt

1 heaping tsp. baking powder
1 heaping tsp. baking soda
5 cups flour
3/4 tsp. nutmeg

*Contributed by Sophie Yaworski.*

## Upside-Down Cake

In a round or square pan melt in oven;

| | |
|---|---|
| 1 cup brown sugar | 2 Tbsp. butter |

Lay slices of fruit at bottom of pan over the brown sugar and butter.
Mix in another bowl the following:

| | |
|---|---|
| 1/2 cup butter | 3/4 cup sugar |

Mix and then add:

| | |
|---|---|
| 2 eggs | 2 cups flour |
| 3/4 cup milk | 2 Tbsp. baking powder |
| 1/2 tsp. baking soda | |

Mix together and place on top of fruit and bake at 325 for about 1 1/2 hours. *Contributed by Linda Matsalla.*


## White Fruit Cake

| | |
|---|---|
| 2 cups all-purpose flour | 1/2 cup slivered almonds |
| 1 1/2 tsp. baking powder | 1 cup margarine (softened) |
| Grated peel of 1 lemon | 1 pkg. 8 oz. cream cheese (softened) |
| 1 cup red or green candied cherries | 1 1/2 cups granulated white sugar |
| 1 cup candied fruit or split 1/2 with raisins | 4 eggs |

Bake at 350 for about 1 hour and 15 minutes, at first, then reduce the heat to 325. Could bake in tube pan or Bundt. *Contributed by Mary Rieger.*


## Zucchini Almond Cake

| | |
|---|---|
| 3 cups flour | 1 tsp. almond extract |
| 2 tsp. baking powder | 3 cups grated peeled zucchini |
| 1 tsp. baking soda | 1 cup ground almonds |
| 1 tsp. salt | 1 1/2 cups icing sugar |
| 4 eggs | 2 Tbsp. milk |
| 3 cups sugar | 1/4 tsp. almond extract |
| 1 1/4 cups vegetable oil | 1/4 cup toasted sliced almonds |

Grease a 10" tube pan or a Bundt pan. Sift flour, baking powder, soda and salt. In large bowl, beat eggs until thick and light colored. Gradually add sugar, 1/4 cup at a time, beating well after each addition. Stir in oil and almond extract. Blend in dry ingredients, mixing until smooth. Stir in zucchini and almonds. Bake at 350 for 1 hour and 15 minutes. Stir together icing sugar, milk and almond extract until smooth. Spread over top of cooled cake. Let icing run down sides. Sprinkle with sliced almonds.

## Zucchini Chocolate Cake

| | |
|---|---|
| 1/2 cup margarine | 1/2 cup oil |
| 1 3/4 cups sugar | 2 cups shredded zucchini |
| 2 eggs | 1/2 cup sour milk or buttermilk |
| 1 tsp vanilla | 6 Tbsp. cocoa |
| 1/2 tsp. baking soda | 1/2 tsp. salt |
| 2 1/2 cups flour | 1/2 tsp. cloves or cinnamon |

Cream margarine, oil and sugar. Add eggs, milk and vanilla. Sift dry ingredients together and add to creamed mixture. Stir in zucchini. Spoon half of batter into a greased 9" x 13" pan.

Filling:

| | |
|---|---|
| 1 - 8 oz. cream cheese | 1/2 cup sugar |
| 1 egg | |

Combine above 3 ingredients and spoon onto batter in a pan and then put remaining batter over. Sprinkle on topping 1/2 cup chopped nuts, 1/2 cup chocolate chips. Bake at 325 for 40-45 minutes.


## Zucchini Roll

| | |
|---|---|
| 3 eggs | 1 tsp. baking soda |
| 1 tsp. vanilla | 1 tsp. ground cinnamon |
| 1 cup flour | 1/4 tsp. salt |
| 3/4 cup sugar | 1 cup shredded zucchini (peeled) |
| 1/2 cup baking cocoa | |

Bake and roll like any jelly roll. Cool and fill. *Contributed by Mary Rieger.*

Filling:

| | |
|---|---|
| 1 pkg. cream cheese (softened) | 2 tsp. vanilla |
| 1/4 cup softened butter or margarine | 1 cup confectioners' sugar |

Additional confectioners' sugar to sprinkle on top.

# Cookies

## Baba's Ginger Cookies

3/4 cup shortening (i use butter)
4 Tbsp. molasses
1 cup sugar
1 egg
2 tsp baking soda
1 tsp. ginger
1 tsp. cinnamon
2 cups flour

Cream shortening & sugar. Beat in eggs & molasses. Add soda, ginger, and cinnamon. Mix well. Roll in balls the size of walnuts. Dip in granulated sugar. Place on ungreased sheet & press down w/ fork. Bake at 350 for 8 min. (makes approx. 3 dozen). *Contributed by Mandelle Waddell.*

## BBQ Cookies (small batch of 6)

1/4 cup butter, softened
1/4 cup brown sugar lightly packed
2 Tbsp. granulated sugar
1 egg yolk.
1/2 tsp. vanilla
1/2 cup + 1 Tbsp. of all-purpose flour
1/4 tsp. baking soda
1/4 tsp. salt
1/4 cup chocolate chips and/or combination of toffee bits and chocolate sprinkles (to add with the batter, or could be added to decorate at time of baking with the kids)

Mix together the butter and sugars, add egg yolk and vanilla. Blend the flour, baking soda and salt into the butter mixture, refrigerate into 6 individual cookie balls. Preheat the BBQ grill to just above 350. Butter a small cookie sheet that will fit on the BBQ. Carefully add the chocolate chips or toffee bits to the individual cookie balls by gently pushing the decoration into each ball or rolling in the sprinkles or toffee bits. Place on the greased cookie sheet and store in the fridge to chill for 10-15 minutes or until the BBQ is ready. When the temperature is just above 350, without totally lifting the lid, place the cookie sheet on to the grill. Bake for 12 minutes, without opening the lid. The temperature should stay close to 350. Remember heat is lost when you lift the lid.

## Cake Box Cookies

1 box cake mix
2 eggs
1/2 cup oil

Mix a boxed cake mix (any flavour) with egg and oil. Make into balls and place on a parchment paper lined cookie sheet. Bake at 350 for 5-10 min. Options: Add chocolate chips, Reese's Pieces, chopped nuts, etc. to the cookie dough. Option: These make great ice cream sandwiches. Soften some ice cream by stirring, place on cookie and top with caramel sauce and a top cookie layer. Put sandwiches back in freezer for 2 hours before serving. *Contributed by Brent Matsalla.*

## Cherry Winks

2/3 cup crushed cornflakes crumbs (for coating winks)
2 cups sifted flour
1 tsp. baking powder
1/2 tsp. baking soda
1/2 tsp. salt
3/4 cup soft butter
1 cup sugar

2 eggs
2 Tbsp. milk
1 tsp. vanilla
1 cup chopped nuts
1 cup dates (put into blender to break up)
3/4 cup maraschino cherries

Sift flour, baking powder, baking soda and salt. Set aside. Beat butter and sugar until light and fluffy. Add eggs, beat well. Stir in milk and vanilla. Add dry ingredients together with nuts, dates and cherries. Roll 1 Tbsp. size ball into the cornflake crumbs. Bake at 375 for 12 minutes. *Contributed by Debbie Gabora.*

## Chocolate and Creamy Peanut Butter Cookies

1 1/2 cups all-purpose flour
1/2 cup unsweetened cocoa powder
1/2 tsp. baking soda
1/2 cup butter (softened)
1/2 cup granulated sugar
1/2 cup brown sugar (packed)
3/4 cup peanut butter
1 egg
1 Tbsp. milk
1 tsp. vanilla
3/4 cup powdered sugar

Optional: Add a cup of mini chocolate chips and/or roll cookies in crushed peanuts. In medium bowl stir together flour, cocoa powder and baking soda; set aside. Mix butter, granulated sugar, brown sugar, and 1/4 cup of the peanut butter and use a mixer to mix well. Add egg, milk and vanilla and beat well. Beat in flour mixture. Shape this dough into 32 balls. For filling combine powdered sugar and remaining 1/2 cup peanut butter with a mixer until its smooth; you might have to knead it a couple of times if it crumbles. Shape this dough into 32 balls (these will be smaller). Flatten each chocolate dough ball and top with peanut butter dough ball. Shape chocolate ball around peanut butter ball and roll it all into one big ball. Flatten slightly with bottom of glass. Drop the flattened cookie into granulated sugar to coat just the one side. Bake in preheated oven at 350 for 8 minutes. *Contributed by Brent Matsalla.*

## Chocolate Chip Cookies

1 cup butter
3/4 cup brown sugar
1/4 cup white sugar
2 eggs

1 - 4 oz. pkg. of dry instant Jell-O pudding (any flavor)
2 cups flour
1 tsp. baking soda
2 cups chocolate chips (vary: 1/2 butterscotch chips)

Mix first 5 ingredients together. Add flour, baking soda and chips. mix. Drop cookie dough by tablespoon on a cookie sheet. Bake at 375 for 8 to 10 minutes. *Contributed by Eleanor Hadubiak.*

## Coconut Cookies

1/2 cup butter or margarine
3 egg yolks
1 cup flour
1 Tbsp. sugar

1 Tbsp. milk
1/2 tsp. baking powder
1/4 tsp. salt

Make a light dough mixing all above ingredients then roll out thin, cut into round cookies arrange on a cookie sheet to be ready to bake. Create the topping for the cookie.
*Continued on next page...*

Beat 3 egg whites until very stiff, and add
1 cup icing sugar

2 cups coconut
1 Tbsp. melted butter or margarine

Place 1 tsp. full on top of each cookie. Bake slowly and not too long. They should not get brown just golden. *Contributed by Mina Ozerney.*

## Cracker Jack Cookies

1 cup butter
1 cup br. sugar
1 cup sugar
2 eggs
2 tsp. vanilla
1 tsp. baking powder
1 tsp. baking soda
1 1/2 cups flour
2 cups oatmeal
1 cup coconut
2 cups Rice Krispies or organic quinoa puffs

Cream butter and sugars, beat in eggs and vanilla. Sift flour, baking powder and baking soda with the oatmeal. Mix well. Add remaining ingredients in order.
Drop by teaspoon full on greased baking sheet. Bake at 350 for 10 -12 minutes. Remove from baking sheet and let cool. Note: 1/2 cup raisins could be added.

## Dainty Shortbread

In small blending bowl mix:
1 cup butter
1/2 cup icing sugar
1 tsp. vanilla
Beat until fluffy.

Add:
1 1/2 cups flour
1/4 cup cornstarch

Beat for a bit until well blended. Drop by spoonful on silver (not a dark one) cookie sheet. Bake at 325 for approximately 20 minutes. *Contributed by Mary Anaka.*

## Dog Patch Biscuits

3 cups flour
3 tsp. baking powder
1 tsp. salt
1/2 tsp. nutmeg
1/2 cup white sugar

1 cup sour cream
3/4 cup buttermilk
1 level tsp. baking soda
1 egg

Mix together.

## Double Chocolate Chip Cookies

1 1/2 cup flour
3/4 cup packed brown sugar
1/2 cup butter softened
1/4 cup sugar
2 1/2 tsp. vanilla

1/2 tsp. baking soda
1/4 tsp. salt
1 egg
3/4 cup chocolate chips
3/4 cup white chocolate chips

Preheat the oven to 350. Into large bow measure all ingredients except the chocolate. With mixer on medium speed, beat ingredient until blended and smooth, stir in chips. Drop dough by rounded tablespoons 2" apart, onto ungreased large cookie sheet. Bake cookies for 10 to 12 minutes until done. Makes about 2 dozen.

## Get Up and Go Cookies

1/2 cup margarine
1 cup brown sugar
1/2 cup prune puree- you can mash your own or use baby food prunes
1 egg
1 cup applesauce

2 cups All Bran Cereal
1 1/2 cups flour - white, whole wheat or a mixture of both
1/2 tsp. baking soda
1 cup of raisins, chocolate chips, nuts or whatever you like in cookies.

In a big bowl cream margarine and sugar together. Mix the egg in well and then stir in prunes. Add the applesauce and stir. Add the dry ingredients and stir well. Add raisins, etc. Drop by spoonful onto cookie sheets. Bake in 350 oven for about 15 minutes. Cool on pan for a few minutes and remove with spatula and cool on racks. Star in covered containers. You can freeze as well. Prune puree: buy a can of prunes - take pits out. Mash the prunes with some of the juice or puree in food processor. This recipe is easy to change - if you want a harder cookie, add more flour or cook longer. You can soak the raisins in water or in the prune juice for softer cookies. You can try apricots or other dried fruits. Replace the flour with 1 1/2 cups whole wheat and 1/2 cup oatmeal flakes.

## Honey Drop Cookies

1/4 cup margarine
3/4 cup honey (liquid)
1 egg
1 3/4 cups sifted flour

1/2 tsp. baking soda
1/2 tsp. cinnamon
1/8 tsp. cloves
1 cup raisins or dry cranberries

Cream margarine and honey. Add egg, beat well. Combine dry ingredients and add to creamed mixture. Fold in raisins. Mix well. Drop by small spoonful greased cookie sheet bake at 350 for 10 to 15 minutes. Makes 4 dozen.

## Mini Chip Butter Crisps

2 1/4 cups all-purpose flour
1/2 tsp. salt
1 1/4 cups butter, softened

1 cup icing sugar
2 tsp. vanilla
1 1/2 cups (mini) chocolate chips

Stir together flour and salt. Cream butter, gradually beat in sugar and vanilla. Add dry ingredients to creamed mixture, slowly. Blend until smoothly combined. Stir in chocolate chips. Form dough into 1" balls. Place 1 dozen at a time on a cookie sheets, flatten to round shape. Approximately 2" apart with a bottom of a glass dipped in flour. Bake in 325 oven for 10 to 11 minutes. Cool. Makes 6 dozen. *Contributed by Tanis Hadubiak.*

## Oatmeal Cookies (Chewy)

1/2 cup honey
1/4 cup canola oil
1/4 cup smooth peanut butter
2 Tbsp. margarine, melted
1 Tbsp. vanilla
1 egg

1/2 cup whole wheat flour
1/2 cup all-purpose white flour
1/2 tsp. baking powder
1/4 tsp. baking soda
1 3/4 cups quick-cooking oats
2 squares baker's semi-sweet chocolate, chopped

Preheat the oven to 350. Beat first 6 ingredients, in large bowl with mixer until well blended. Mix flours, baking powder and soda. Gradually beat into honey mixture until well blended. Stir in oats and chocolate. Drop tsp. of dough, 2" apart, onto baking sheets. Bake 8 to 10 minutes or until golden brown. Cool on baking sheets 3 minutes before removing to wire racks. Cool completely.

## Oatmeal Chocolate Chip Cookies

1/2 cup brown sugar
1/2 cup butter
1/2 cup white sugar
1 egg
1 Tbsp. milk
1 tsp. vanilla

1/2 tsp. baking soda
1/2 tsp. baking powder
1 cup rolled oats
1 cup flour
1/2 tsp salt
1 cup chocolate chips

Cream together first 3 ingredients then add next 3 ingredients and mix. Add remaining ingredients and mix. Bake 12 minutes at 350 F. Makes 3 dozen. *Contributed by Eleanor Hadubiak.*

## Oatmeal Cookies

3/4 cup butter, softened
3/4 cup lightly packed brown sugar
1/2 cup granulated sugar
1 egg
2 Tbsp. water
2 tsp. vanilla

2/3 cups all-purpose flour
3/4 tsp. baking soda
1 tsp. cinnamon
1/2 tsp. nutmeg
3 cups oatmeal
1 cup chocolate chips or raisins

*Continued on next page...*

Cream butter, sugars, egg, water and vanilla together on medium speed with mixer until light and fluffy. Combine flour, soda and cinnamon. Add to creamed mixture, beating on low speed until blended. Stir in oats and raisins or chips. Drop dough by heaping tablespoons onto greased baking sheet. Press flat for crisp cookies; leave mounded for chewy cookies. Bake at 350 for 12 - 15 minutes or until edges are golden brown. Don't over-bake.

## Oatmeal Cookies (Very Crisp)

| | |
|---|---|
| 1 cup margarine | 1 tsp. baking soda |
| 1 cup sugar | 1 tsp. salt |
| 1 cup honey (liquid) | 1 cup raisins or dry cranberries |
| 2 eggs | 1 cup chopped nuts |
| 2 1/4 cups flour | 2 cups rolled oats |

Cream margarine, sugar and honey. Add egg, beat well. Combine dry ingredients and add to creamed mixture. Mix well. Fold in raisins, nuts and oats. Drop by small spoonful onto greased cookie sheet at 375 for 8 to 10 minutes. Makes 8 dozen.

## Oreo Style Cookies

| | |
|---|---|
| 2 boxes Duncan Hines chocolate cake mix | 4 eggs |
| 2/3 cup oil | |

Mix together well. Form ball and put in fridge to chill for a while. Grease cookie sheets and roll dough into marble sized balls. Bake at 350 for 10 minutes or until there are cracks in the cookie.

| | |
|---|---|
| Filling: | 1/2 tsp. vanilla |
| 4 oz. cream cheese | 1 3/4 cups icing sugar |
| 1/8 cup butter | |

Mix together to sandwich between 2 cooled cookies.

## Peanut Butter Cookies

| | |
|---|---|
| 1 cup margarine | 2 cups flour |
| 1 cup brown sugar | 1 cup oatmeal (or 1 1/2 cups flour and 1 1/2 |
| 1 cup white sugar | oatmeal) |
| 2 eggs | 1/2 tsp. salt |
| 1 cup peanut butter | 2 tsp. baking soda |

Cream together the first 3 ingredients. Then cream together the eggs and peanut butter, then add to margarine and sugars. Mix together the dry ingredients and add to creamed mixture. Bake at 350 for 12 minutes in ungreased cookie sheets. *Contributed by Theresa Mudry.*

## Peanut Butter Cookies (Crackle-top)

3/4 cup margarine
3/4 cup brown sugar, packed
3/4 cup honey (liquid)
1 egg
3/4 cup peanut butter

1 tsp. vanilla
2 1/2 cups flour
1/2 tsp. baking soda
1/2 tsp. salt
Granulated sugar to roll the cookie in.

Cream margarine, sugar and honey. Add egg, peanut butter and vanilla. Beat well. Combine dry ingredients and add to creamed mixture. Mix well. Chill 30 minutes. Form into small balls. Roll in sugar. Bake on an ungreased cookie sheet at 375 for 10 to 12 minutes. Makes 5 dozen.

## Philadelphia Cream Cheese Shortbread Cookies

1 cup butter
1/2 cup sugar
1 3/4 cups flour

1 - 3 oz. pkg. Philadelphia cream cheese
1/4 tsp. salt

Mix like all shortbread cookies.

## Rolo Cookies

1 cup margarine
1 cup brown sugar
1 cup white sugar

2 eggs
1 tsp. vanilla

Mix above ingredients.

Add:
2 1/2 cups flour
3/4 cup cocoa

1 tsp. baking soda
Mix with sugar and egg mixture.
4 pkgs. of regular size Rolo chocolates

Place 1 Rolo in the center of a cookie ball. Roll in additional white sugar. Place on a cookie sheet to bake leaving 2" between the cookies for room to spread. Bake at 375 for 7 minutes.
Cool on wire rack. Note: the batter will keep in the fridge to make a tray fresh for 3 days. *Contributed by Theresa Mudry.*

## Shortbread Cookies

1 lb. margarine or butter
1 cup icing sugar

3 cups flour (all-purpose)
2 tsp. almond flavoring

*Continued on next page...*

Chill dough, roll in balls and dip in unbeaten egg white, and roll in fine coconut or fine nuts. Make a hole by pushing a fingerprint in the middle and put a cherry or 1/2 tsp. of jam. Bake. Note: this could be rolled into balls or put in rolls in freezer. NOTE variation: the cookie shape could be cut into squares or rounds as well. *Contributed by Stefka Zarazun.*

## Shortbread in a Pan

250 grams 8 oz. butter
2 Tbsp. ground rice or rice flour

1/3 cup icing sugar
2 cups flour

Mix like all shortbread dough. Press mixture into 11" x 7" pan. Mark off in squares, or rectangles with an edge of a knife, and prick with fork. Bake in slow oven 35 to 40 minutes. Cut along knife, let stand 10 minutes. Leave on wire rack to cool. *Contributed by Mary Bugera.*

## Thick and Chewy Smarties Cookies

1/2 cup butter or margarine
1 cup packed brown sugar
3 eggs
1 tsp. vanilla

2 cups peanut butter
4 1/2 cups rolled oats mixed with 2 tsp. baking soda
1 cup smarties
1 cup chocolate chips

Beat sugar and butter in bowl, beat in eggs, vanilla and peanut butter. Blend well. Stir in oats mixture until stiff dough forms. Stir in smarties and chips. Shape into balls. Place 3" apart on a cookie sheet, flatten with fork. Bake at 350 for 8 - 10 minutes. *Contributed by Frances Charuk.*

## Thumbprint Cookies

1/2 cup butter or margarine
1/4 cup packed brown sugar
1 egg
1 tsp. vanilla
1 1/2 cups flour
1/4 tsp. salt
1 1/2 cups flaked coconut
Favourite jam, jelly or frosting

Soften butter, beat in brown sugar. Blend in egg and vanilla. Add flour, salt and coconut; mix well. Form dough into balls, making indentation in the top of each cookie with thumb. Arrange about 15 on a microwave safe platter at a time and microwave on HIGH for 2 -3 minutes when cool fill with jam or jelly. These cookies freeze well with the jam.

## Zucchini Granola Cookies

3/4 cup butter or margarine
1 cup brown sugar
1 egg
1 tsp. vanilla
Grated rind of 1 orange
3 cups grated zucchini

3 - 3 1/2 cups flour
1 tsp. baking soda
1 tsp. salt
3 cups granola cereal
1 cup chocolate chips

Cream butter and sugar, add egg and vanilla, orange rind and zucchini. Add granola and chocolate chips. This will be a sticky dough (don't add more flour). Drop by spoonful on a greased cookie sheet. Bake at 350 for 12 - 15 minutes. *Contributed by Olga Fullawka.*

## Tips for Picking the Best Fruit

**Apples**
- look for bright color and blemish free

**Avocados**
- look for a little bit of give
- look for dark colors
- if stem comes off easily, it's ripe
- if stem comes off and it's brown under, it's over-ripe

**Berries**
- pick ones with nice aroma from a distance
- over-ripe will be mushy

**Honey Dew Melons and Cantaloupe**
- look for give on the bottom, opposite the stem
- bottom should be slightly sticky
- stem should have nice aroma
- best melons have most intense color

**Nectarines and Peaches**
- look for blemish free
- look for a little give
- pick ones with nice aroma

**Oranges and Citrus Fruits**
- pick one that looks heavier than it should be

**Pears**
- look for a little give
- any spots turn brown when ripe

**Pineapples**
- pick ones with nice aroma
- try to pull out leaves at the top, if they come off easily, it's ripe

**Tomatoes**
- look for a little bit of give
- nice aroma

**Watermelons:**
- pick one that looks heavier than it should be
- knock to find the hollow sound
- look for the yellow spot, white spot is not ripe

# Pies

## Apple Pastries (Crab-apples)

| | |
|---|---|
| 4 cups flour | 1 cup soft margarine |
| 1/4 cup sugar | 4 egg yolks |
| 3/4 tsp. salt | 1/2 cup sour cream |

Mix dough and chill for 30 minutes. Lightly grease a large jelly roll pan. Roll half dough into oblong shape to cover. Fit into a pan, up sides and corners. Add filling.

| | |
|---|---|
| Filling: | 1/2 tsp. cinnamon |
| 1/2 cup fine bread crumbs | 6 cups coarsely chopped apples (could be 1/2 |
| 1 cup sugar | crabapples or all crabapples) |
| 2 Tbsp. cornstarch | |

Combine breadcrumbs, sugar, cornstarch and cinnamon and sprinkle over apples. Roll remaining pastry in a large piece, lay over apples. Add topping.

Topping:

| | |
|---|---|
| 1 egg white | 2 Tbsp. sugar |

Beat egg whites lightly with a fork, brush over pastry. Sprinkle with 2 Tbsp. sugar. Prick the dough. Bake at 450 until well browned, cut into squares. *Contributed by Eleanor Hadubiak.*

## Apple Pie Filling

12 cups diced apples
3/4 cup water (more or less)
1 cup brown sugar or coconut sugar (unless apples are really tart, add more)
3-4 Tbsp. cornstarch (more or less to thicken)
4-5 Tbsp. cinnamon or apple pie spice or pumpkin spice
4-5 Tbsp. butter
2 tsp. lemon juice

Crabapples or regular apples can be used or a combination of apples. Peel, core and slice apples and place with all ingredients into a Dutch oven pot. Heat and stir on the top of the stove until the liquid is thickened and the apples are coated. Freeze in 2 1/2 cup containers for apple crisps, pie or pastry filling.

## Apple Pie Filling with Pudding Powder

Dutch oven of apples cut up
Add 2 cups water
About 3 cups sugar (could be less)
Cook or bake until the apples change color.
Then add caramel or butterscotch pudding
powder (cooked type not instant)
1 Tbsp. cornstarch (to thicken)
Cook until thick and nice color.

## Apple Pie Topping

| | |
|---|---|
| 1/2 cup crushed almonds | 1/2 cup rolled oats |
| 1/2 cup flour | 1/2 cup brown sugar |
| 1/2 tsp. cinnamon | 3/4 cup melted butter |

Mix and sprinkle on top of one crust pie or tart and bake. *Contributed by Bernice Gulka.*

## Apples or Crab-apples Filling to Freeze for Pies

4 cups cut up apples
1 1/2 cups sugar
1-2 Tbsp. cornstarch

Cook until color changes. Cool and freeze.

## Apple Sauce for Apple Pie Filling to Can or Freeze

| | |
|---|---|
| 12 cups sliced apples | 1/4 tsp. nutmeg |
| 4 1/2 cups sugar | 1 tsp. salt |
| 1 1/2 cups cornstarch | 10 cups water |
| 2 tsp. cinnamon | |

Bring to a boil until thick add 2 tsp. lemon juice. Fill jars 1 1/2 cups sauce, then add apples to fill the jars but not to full. Process for 20 minutes to seal the 7-9 jars.

## Better Than Pumpkin Pie

2 -8 oz. cans pumpkin
385 ml evaporated milk
3/4 cup sugar
3 eggs

1 tsp. cinnamon or pumpkin pie spice
2 layer size spice cake mix
1/2 cup melted margarine
1/2 cup chopped nuts, if desired

Mix first 5 ingredients well. Pour into a greased 9" x 13" pan. Sprinkle dry cake mix over pumpkin mixture. Drizzle with margarine. Sprinkle chopped nuts on top. Bake at 350 for 1 hour.

## Butter Tarts Filling #1

2 eggs
1 cup brown sugar
Pinch of salt
1/4 tsp. nutmeg

4 Tbsp. butter or
1 Tbsp. butter and 1/2 cup cream
1 cup raisins (optional)

## Butter Tarts Filling #2

1 egg
1 cup brown sugar
2 Tbsp. butter
1 tsp. vinegar

1/4 tsp. vanilla
1/3 cup corn syrup
1/2 cup raisins or currants
Some nuts

## Carrot Pie Filling (like Pumpkin)

1 cup sugar (or less if desired)
1/2 tsp. salt
1 tsp. ginger
1 tsp. cinnamon
1/2 tsp. nutmeg

1/8 tsp. cloves
1 1/2 cups cooked mashed carrots
3 eggs beaten
1 1/2 cups milk or light cream
1 unbaked pie shell.

Mix together and fill the pie shell. Bake. *Contributed by Olga Fullawka.*

## Cream Cheese Pumpkin Pie Filling

4 oz. cream cheese (softened)
1 Tbsp. milk or half-and-half
1 Tbsp. sugar
1 1/2 cups cool whip (whipped topping)
1 ready crust graham cracker crust
1 cup milk or half-and-half

2 pkg. (4 serving size) vanilla instant pudding
1 can pure pumpkin
1 tsp. ground cinnamon
1/2 tsp. ginger
1/4 tsp. cloves

Mix cream cheese, milk and sugar in bowl. Stir in whipped topping, spread on crust. Mix 1 cup milk with pudding until blended. Stir in pumpkin and spices. Spread over cream cheese layer refrigerate 3 hours.

## Crumble Peach Pie

| | |
|---|---|
| 1 unbaked pie shell | Pinch of salt |
| 4 cups sliced peaches | 2 Tbsp. lemon juice |
| 1 cup sugar | 1/2 tsp cinnamon |
| 1/4 cup flour | |

Mix together and put into the unbaked pie shell. Topping: 1/2 cup butter, 3/4 cup flour, 1/2 cup brown sugar.


## Crustless Pumpkin Pie

| | |
|---|---|
| 1 can pure pumpkin (2 cups) | 1/4 tsp. allspice |
| 1 large can evaporated milk | 1/4 tsp. ginger |
| 2 eggs | 1/8 tsp. salt |
| 3/4 cup sugar | 1/2 cup graham cracker crumbs |
| 1 tsp. cinnamon | |

Combine first 4 ingredients. Beat until smooth, add spices and beat until well mixed. Stir in cracker crumbs. Pour into a greased pie plate. Bake at 325 for 50-55 minutes or until a knife comes out clean. Cool and serve with whipped cream.


## Custard Rhubarb Pie filling

| | |
|---|---|
| 2 1/2 cups rhubarb | 2 Tbsp. flour |
| 1 egg yolk and 1 whole egg | 1 Tbsp. butter |
| 1 cup sugar | |

Beat eggs to a thick froth. Add flour, sugar and butter mix. Add rhubarb but into a pie crust. Bake at 400 for 10 minutes then at 350 for 25-30 minutes. *Contributed by Albina Hrychenko.*


## French Apple Pie Filling

| | |
|---|---|
| 5-6 medium tart apples, peeled and sliced. | 1/2 cup brown sugar |
| 3/4 cup white sugar | 1/2 cup butter or margarine |
| 1 tsp. cinnamon | 1 unbaked 9" pie shell |
| 1 cup flour | |

Combine white and brown sugar with cinnamon and mix lightly with sliced apples. Fill unbaked pie shell with apples. Combine flour and brown sugar, cut in butter until coarse mixture. Sprinkle over apples. Bake at 425 for 50-60 minutes or until apples are tender. If top of pie starts to brown too quickly, cover with foil.

## German Kuchen

Base Ingredients:

| | |
|---|---|
| 2 cups flour | 4 Tbsp. sugar |
| 3 tsp. baking powder | 2 Tbsp. margarine |

Mix the above ingredients with fingers until fine crumbs. Add:

| | |
|---|---|
| 1 egg | Fruit |
| 1 cup cream | Sugar |

Pat into a greased pan with fingers. Put a layer of fruit, sprinkle sugar over the fruit. Batter Ingredients:

| | |
|---|---|
| 1/2 tsp. baking powder | 1 egg |
| 3/4 cup flour | Cream |
| 3/4 cup sugar | |

Add cream and make it thin enough to run off the spoon over the fruit.
Crumb Ingredients:

| | |
|---|---|
| 3/4 cup sugar | 2 Tbsp. margarine |
| 3/4 cup flour | Cream |
| 1/2 tsp. baking powder | |

Cream to make pea size crumbs. Put over the batter and bake at 375 deg. For 45 minutes. *Contributed by Jaedyn Matsalla.*

## Hawaiian Cream Pie

| | |
|---|---|
| 1 1/2 cups graham wafer crumbs | 1/3 cup margarine (melted) |
| 3 Tbsp. sugar | |

Combine together the above and press into the bottom of a 9" pie plate. Bake at 375 for 8 min. Cool.

| | |
|---|---|
| 1-85g pkg. of vanilla pudding using 1 1/2 cups of milk. | 1/4 tsp. ground ginger |
| 3/4 cup crushed pineapple (drained) | 2 cups mini marshmallows |
| 1 cup flaked coconut (3/4 for inside, 1/4 for topping) | 200 ml. heavy cream (whipped) |

Add pineapple, coconut, and ginger to pudding cover with wax paper and chill. Remove from refrigerator, mix well, fold in marshmallows and whipped cream. Pour into crumb crust sprinkle with 1/4 cup coconut and decorate with cherries.

## Hawaiian Haupia Chocolate Cream Pie

1 1/2 cup grounded graham crackers
1/3 cup sugar
6 Tbsp. melted butter
1/2 tsp. cinnamon
1 cup milk
1 can (14 oz.) coconut milk
1 cup sugar
3/4 cup water
1/2 cup cornstarch
1 1/4 cup semi-sweet chocolate chips
1 1/2 cup heavy cream
1/4 cup icing sugar
1 tsp. vanilla extract
1/4 cup toasted coconut

Mix graham crumbs, sugar, cinnamon and butter. Press into a greased pie plate and bake for 8 min. at 375 degrees. Combine milk, coconut milk and sugar in a sauce pan. Mix cornstarch with water and add to the sauce pan. Bring to a boil on medium heat stirring constantly. Turn to low and whisk for another 3 minutes until mixture is thick. Divide mixture in half. Melt chocolate chips in double boiler or microwave. Fold the melted chocolate to half the custard. Add the white custard to the pie shell. Top with chocolate custard. Combine icing sugar, vanilla to the heavy cream and whip until stiff peaks form. Toast coconut under the broiler for a few minutes. Top pie with whip cream and toasted coconut. Optional: Lay well-drained pineapple pieces or banana slices on bottom layer. *Contributed by Brent Matsalla.*

## Impossible Apple Pie

6 cups apples (sliced)          3/4 cup milk
1 1/4 tsp. cinnamon             1/2 cup Bisquick
1/4 tsp. ground nutmeg          2 eggs
1 cup sugar                     2 Tbsp. margarine

Heat the oven to 325, grease a pie plate. Then mix apples and spices, place in the greased plate. Beat remaining ingredients until smooth, in a blender for 1 minutes. Pour over apples, sprinkle with streusel.

Streusel:
Mix until crumbly: 1 cup Bisquick          1/3 cup packed brown sugar
3/4 cup chopped nuts                       3 Tbsp. margarine.

Bake until knife inserted in center comes out clean. 55-60 minutes.

## Impossible Pumpkin Pie with Flour

| | |
|---|---|
| 4 eggs | 2 tsp. vanilla |
| 1/2 cup margarine | 2 cups cooked mashed pumpkin |
| 2 cups milk or light cream | 1 1/2 tsp. cinnamon |
| 1/3 cup flour | 1/4 tsp. ginger |
| 1 cup sugar | 3/4 tsp. nutmeg |
| 1 cup fine coconut | |

Put in blender and beat before baking. Pour into greased pie plate.

## Jam Tarts

Make any dough for tart shells, then put some jam on the bottom, then mix up a white cake mix, and put a drop on top, then bake.

## Lemony Dessert Pie
Meringue:

| | |
|---|---|
| 3 egg whites | 1/3 cup sugar |
| 3/8 tsp. cream of tartar | 3/4 tsp. vanilla |

Beat egg whites with cream of tartar until they hold soft peaks, beat in sugar, 1 Tbsp. at a time, add vanilla and beat until shiny and very stiff. Divide into two 7½" pie plates and bake in preheated oven 250 for 1 hour. Turn oven off and leave for 2 hours in the oven or until dry.

| | |
|---|---|
| Lemon filling: | 6 Tbsp. butter |
| 2 whole eggs | 1/3 cup fresh lemon juice |
| 1 cup sugar | 1 1/2 tsp. grated lemon rind |

In a heavy saucepan or top of double boiler beat eggs and sugar together, then add butter, lemon juice and lemon rind, cook until the mixture coats the spoon. Do not allow to boil, then chill, covered in the refrigerator (this filling can be made a day or two ahead) 3 cups vanilla ice cream (softened) To assemble: Place meringue on serving platter and spread with 1 cup softened ice cream, freeze until ice cream is firm, spread with half the lemon butter, return to freezer until firm and spread with second layer of ice cream, refreeze spread with remaining lemon butter, refreeze, and so on. Top with 2nd meringue cover and freeze until ready to use. Take out of freezer 20 - 30 minutes before serving.

## Peanut Butter Cream Pie

1/3 cup butter, melted
1/4 cup brown sugar
1/4 cup unsweetened cocoa powder
1 1/4 cup Graham cracker crumbs
1/2 cup + 3 Tbsp. powdered sugar, divided
1/4 cup + 1/2 cup creamy peanut butter, divided
1 1/2 cups whip cream
1 tsp. vanilla extract
1 box instant vanilla pudding mix
1 1/2 cups milk

Mix butter, brown sugar, cocoa and Graham cracker crumbs. Press into a pie plate and chill. Mix 1/2 cup powdered sugar with 1/4 cup peanut butter until crumbles start to form. Add a few drops of water if the mix is too powdery. Add half the crumbles to the bottom of the pie shell and reserve other half for the topping. Add 3 Tbsp. powdered sugar and vanilla extract to whip cream and mix on high until soft peaks form. In a separate bowl, combine instant vanilla mix with milk and 1/2 cup peanut butter. Mix on medium until smooth. Fold in 1 cup of the premade whip cream and mix until blended nicely. Add the filling to the pie crust. Top with the remainder of whip cream and the rest of the peanut butter crumbles. Alternate: Top with Reese's Pieces, cut up Reese's Peanut Butter Cups, Reese's Mini Peanut Butter Cups, or drizzle with chocolate syrup. *Contributed by Brent Matsalla.*

## Pumpkin Pie Filling

2 cups pumpkin
2/3 cup brown sugar
2 tsp. cinnamon
1/2 tsp. ginger

1/2 tsp. salt
1 1/2 cups milk
2 eggs
1/2 cup of heavy cream

Pour into prepared pie shell. This makes 2 pies. *Contributed by Eleanor Hadubiak.*

## Pumpkin Pie - Microwave

1/2 cup butter placed in a 10" pie plate.
Microwave at high 1 minute until melted.

2 cups vanilla wafer crumbs
2 Tbsp. sugar

Add crumbs and sugar; mix well. Firmly press on bottom and up sides of dish. Microwave at high 2 minutes, rotating dish 1/2 way after 1 minute.

1 can 16 oz. pure mashed pumpkin
1 cup brown sugar (packed)
1 Tbsp. flour

1/2 tsp. salt
1 can -13 oz. evaporated milk
2 eggs, beaten

In 2 qt. casserole blend together the above items to make a pumpkin custard. Microwave at medium for 12-14 minutes. Stirring every 5 minutes until hot and thickened. Pour hot pumpkin custard filling into prepared pie shell. Microwave at medium 22 - 25 minutes. Rotating dish after 12 minutes. The pie is done when the edges are set and the center is still slightly soft. Let stand at room temp. About 15 to 20 minutes to set and Cool before serving. *Contributed by Bernice Gulka.*

## Raspberry Angel Pie

3 egg whites
1 tsp. vanilla
1/4 tsp. cream of tartar
Dash of salt
1 cup sugar

Heat the oven to 275. Grease a 9" pie plate. Combine egg whites, vanilla, cream of tartar and salt. Beat with beater until frothy. Start to add sugar 1 Tbsp. at a time, beating after each addition. Continue beating until stiff. Spoon this mixture into pie plate and shape into shell by pushing up sides and hollowing the center a bit with a spoon. Bake for 1 hour then turn oven off and leave the pie in the oven with the door closed for 45 minutes.

3 oz. raspberry Jell-O powder
1 1/4 cups boiling water

Raspberries (as desired)
1 cup whipping cream (not sweetened)

Put Jell-O powder in bowl. Add boiling water and mix until Jell-O powder dissolved. Chill, set bowl in ice water until mixture is consistency of egg whites. Mash raspberries slightly, whip cream stiffly and fold into Jell-O. Chill a few minutes (until mixture holds shape). Pile into meringue shell. Chill several hours. Garnish with more whipped cream and whole raspberries. (Serves 6)

## Rhubarb Caramel Pie Filling

2 cups diced rhubarb
1 Tbsp. butter
1 1/4 cups brown sugar
2 Tbsp. corn starch
1/4 cup cream
1/8 tsp. salt
1 pie shell baked
2 egg yolks

Melt butter and add the rhubarb. Add sugar and cook for 10 min. Combine corn starch with 1/4 cup sugar, cream, egg yolks, and salt and cook for 3 min. Cool and pour into pie shell. *Contributed by Eleanor Hadubiak.*

## Rhubarb Meringue Pie

Mix together for the crust:
1/2 cup butter or margarine

1 cup all-purpose flour
1 Tbsp. white or brown sugar

Bake on an ungreased pan at 350 for 10 minutes.
2nd layer is the filling:

3 egg yolks
1 cup sugar
2 Tbsp. flour

1/4 tsp. salt
1/2 cup light cream
2 1/2 cups rhubarb

Cook together first 5 ingredients and then add rhubarb last. Pour over hot crust and bake at 350 for 10 minutes.
3rd layer:

3 egg whites
1/4 tsp. cream of tartar
1/3 cup white sugar

1 tsp. vanilla
1/4 cup coconut

Beat egg whites until very stiff, add cream of tartar, then add sugar a little at a time, finally add vanilla and coconut to meringue mixture. Bake at 350 for 10 min. again until brown. Variation: add strawberry Jell-O to the filling portion for color and flavor. *Contributed by Mary Fedorchuk.*

## Rhubarb Pie Filling

4 cups rhubarb
1 cup sour cream
1 1/2 cups white sugar
1/3 cup flour

Topping:
1/2 cup brown sugar
1/4 cup butter
1/2 cup flour

Fill into a baked pie shell and then add topping. Put in oven for a while to brown topping. *Contributed by Pat Dubasoff.*

## Rhubarb Pie Filling (not custard)

3 cups rhubarb
Combine with:
3/4 cup sugar

1/4 cup flour
1/8 tsp. salt

Pour into an unbaked pie shell. Bake at 400 for 10 min then at 350 for 30 min. *Contributed by Olga Fullawka.*

## Saskatoon Filling for Pie or Tarts

3 cups Saskatoon berries (fresh or frozen)
1/2 cup sugar

2 Tbsp. cornstarch (use cold water to dissolve starch)
1/2 tsp. lemon

Cook together slowly Saskatoon berries and sugar then thicken with cornstarch. Cool.

## Saskatoon Pie

1 - 2 part pie crust (top and bottom)
4 cups Saskatoon berries
2 Tbsp. lemon juice

1/2 cup sugar (to taste)
2 Tbsp. quick-cooking tapioca

Place berries in a saucepan; pour water (about 2/3 cup) to below surface level of berries and add lemon juice. Bring to boil and simmer for 20 minutes. Add sugar and blend in tapioca. Stir until mixture is thickened (crush a few berries during simmering process to add flour and extra flavor) Allow Saskatoon mixture to cool and pour into pie shell. Cover with top crust and bake for a further 30 minutes. (you can add 1/4 tsp. cinnamon, 1/4 tsp. nutmeg, 1/4 tsp. salt and 1/2 tsp. butter) to the Saskatoon mixture.

## Special Fluff Pie

2 Tbsp. margarine or butter
1/4 cup corn syrup
1 pkg. (6 oz.) semi-sweet chocolate morsels
2 cups Rice Krispies cereal

1 can (17 oz.) apricot halves, well drained, reserving the liquid
1 pkg. (3 oz.) orange flavor gelatin (Jell-O powder)
1 pint (2 cups) whipping cream, chilled

*Continued on next page...*

Additional whipping cream, whipped (optional) Melt margarine, corn syrup, and chocolate morsels in medium size saucepan over low heat. Stirring constantly until smooth. Remove from heat. Add Rice Krispies cereal, stirring until well coated, with a back of spoon, press mixture evenly around side and bottom of buttered 8" or 9" pie pan to form crust. Chill. Reserve 8 apricot halves for top of pie. Cut remaining halves into small pieces for filling set aside. Place Jell-O powder in small mixing bowl. Measure 1 cup of the reserved liquid from the fruit in a small saucepan. Heat until boiling. Add hot syrup to Jell-O, stir until dissolved. Chill until gelatin is consistency of unbeaten egg whites. Meanwhile, place whipping cream in large mixing bowl. Beat until stiff peaks form. Set aside. Whip chilled Jell-O until thick and foamy and double in volume. Gently fold gelatin until thick and foamy and double in volume. Gently fold gelatin and apricot pieces into whipped cream. Spoon filling into pie crust. Chill one hour or until set. Arrange reserved apricots, on pie just before serving. If desired, garnish with additional whipped cream. NOTE: to cut pie easily, place hot, wet towel under bottom and around sides of pan. Allow to stand a few minutes.

## Sour Cream Raisin Pie Filling

| | |
|---|---|
| 1 cup raisins | 2 eggs beaten |
| 1 cup brown sugar | 1 tsp. cinnamon |
| 1 cup sour cream | 1/2 tsp. cloves |

Pour into pie shell and bake.

## Sour Cream Rhubarb Pie Filling

| | |
|---|---|
| 4 cups rhubarb | Topping: |
| 1 cup sour cream | 1/2 cup brown sugar |
| 1 1/2 cups sugar | 1/4 cup butter |
| 1/3 cup flour | 1/2 cup flour |

## Surprise Rhubarb Pie

| | |
|---|---|
| 2 cups cooked rhubarb (sweetened with some sugar) | 1 pkg. whipped topping |
| 1/2 cup extra sugar | 1/2 tsp. lemon extract |
| 1 - 30 oz. pkg. strawberry Jell-O powder | 1 tsp. grenadine syrup (optional) |
| 1 cup miniature marshmallows | 1 prepared graham cracker crust |

Heat rhubarb and sugar to a boil. Add dry Jell-O and marshmallows, stir until dissolved. Cool. Add whipped topping and extracts and stir well then pour into prepared crust, allow to set 1/2 hour.

## Walnut Butter Tarts Filling

| | |
|---|---|
| 1 cup white sugar | 1/3 cup butter |
| 2 cups raisins | 4 Tbsp. cream |
| 2 eggs | 1/3 cup walnut crumbs |
| 1 tsp. vanilla | |

Beat eggs. Then combine with remaining ingredients, except the nuts, in a heavy saucepan. Boil at medium heat for 3 minutes. Add nuts. Fill unbaked tart shells and bake for 15 minutes at 375.

## Zucchini Pineapple Pie Filling

7 cups diced zucchini  
2 cups sugar  
1/4 cup lemon juice  

2 1/2 cups unsweetened pineapple juice  
4 tsp. pineapple flavoring  
Drop of yellow food coloring  

Boil for 10 minutes. Add 5 Tbsp. cornstarch diluted with water. Boil until thick. Add 1 Tbsp. butter. Pour into 3 baked pie shells; could prepare the zucchini and keep in fridge in jars, then thicken when needed for pie.

## Tips for Better Pie Making

1. Keep all your ingredients cold. Butter or shortening as well as the water you can add ice cubes.

2. The dough needs to be refrigerated after each step to absorb liquids, to relax the dough and prevent it from shrinking in the oven. Even the double crust, roll out the top crust, let it rest in the fridge on a plate while you prepare the filling.

3. Try not to overwork the dough too much.

4. Add only a sprinkle of flour when you are rolling out the dough.

5. Don't forget to vent a double crust. This is where you can be decorative and even use cutters instead of slits in the dough, cut a heart.

6. Aluminum foil or store bought pie shields will protect the crust edges from over browning.

7. Place a fruit pie on a bottom rack in the oven, on a preheated baking sheet, to prevent bubbling over into the oven. Fruit pies need to boil or bubble in order to thicken properly.

8. The hardest of all, let the pie totally cool before slicing so it will stay together.

# Dessert Squares

## Apple Crisp

6 sliced applies
1/2 cup flour (or 1/4 flour and 1/4 rolled oats)
3/4 cup brown sugar
1/4 cup butter
1/4 cup white sugar
Cinnamon

Butter dish, slice apples and sprinkle with the white sugar and cinnamon. Mix other ingredients together and spread on top. Bake at 350 for 30 minutes.

## Apple Crumble (Quick)

3/4 cup all bran cereal
1/2 cup all-purpose flour
1/4 cup firmly packed brown sugar
1 tsp. cinnamon

1/4 cup margarine or butter, softened
2 cans (20 oz. each or 4 cups) apple pie filling
1 Tbsp. lemon juice

In small mixing bowl, combine all bran, flour, brown sugar and cinnamon. Cut in margarine until crumbly. Set aside for topping. Combine pie filling and lemon juice. Place in a 9" x 9" baking pan sprinkle topping over apples. Bake at 375 about 30 minutes or until bubbly around edges. Cool slightly before serving.

## Banana Split Dessert

2 cups graham cracker crumbs (approx. 10 crackers crushed)
1 1/4 cups sugar, divided
1/3 cup butter, melted
2 pkgs. (8 oz.) cream cheese, room temperature
1 can (20 oz.) crushed pineapple, drained
1 cup strawberries, sliced thin

4 ripe bananas
2 cups cold milk
1 large box instant vanilla pudding
2 cups heavy whipping cream
2 tsp pure vanilla extract
1/4 cup powdered sugar
1 cup chopped pecans or walnuts

Mix graham cracker crumbs, 1/4 cup sugar, and melted butter. Press into the bottom of a 9" x 13" pan and set aside. Beat together remaining sugar and cream cheese. Spread over cookie crust and top with pineapple. Slice bananas and layer over the pineapple. Add sliced strawberries. Mix cold milk and vanilla pudding and set aside. Beat whipping cream, vanilla and powdered sugar until soft peaks form. Take 1 cup of whipped cream and fold into pudding. Layer pudding over bananas. Spread remaining whipped cream over pudding and sprinkle with nuts. Chill for 5 hours before serving. NOTE: You can also use 1 carton (8 ounces) Cool Whip, thawed instead of the whipped cream. *Contributed by Brent Matsalla.*

## Bavarian Apple Torte

Base:

| | |
|---|---|
| 3/4 cup margarine | 1/2 tsp. vanilla |
| 1/2 cup sugar | 1 1/2 cups flour |

Cream butter, sugar and vanilla. Mix in flour. Press into bottom of 9" x 13" pan.

Filling:

| | |
|---|---|
| 375 g or 8 oz. pkg. cream cheese softened | 2 eggs |
| 1/2 cup sugar | 3/4 tsp. vanilla |

Beat cream cheese and sugar together well. Add eggs and vanilla and continue to beat until combined. Pour over base in the pan.

Topping:

| | |
|---|---|
| 2 cups finely sliced peeled apples | 1 tsp. cinnamon |
| 1/2 cup sugar | 1/3 cup sliced almonds |

Mix together apples, sugar and cinnamon and spoon over cheese mixture in a pan. Sprinkle almonds over top and bake at 325 for 50 to 60 minutes. Cool in the pan.

## Blueberry Cobbler

| | |
|---|---|
| 1/2 cup sugar | 1 cup flour |
| 1 Tbsp. cornstarch | 1 Tbsp. sugar |
| 4 cups blueberries | 1 1/2 tsp. baking powder |
| 1 tsp. lemon juice | 1/2 tsp. salt |
| 3 Tbsp. shortening | 1/2 cup milk |

Heat the oven to 400, mix sugar and cornstarch in a 2 quart saucepan stir in blueberries and lemon juice, cook stirring until mixture boils and thickens. Pour into ungreased 2 quart casserole keep this mixture hot. Cut shortening into flour, add the 1 Tbsp. sugar, baking powder and salt. Stir in milk. Drop dough by spoonful on the hot blueberry mixture. Bake for 25-30 minutes or until topping is golden brown.

## Blueberry Dessert

| | |
|---|---|
| Graham wafers to cover bottom of pan plus | 1 can of blueberry pie filling |
| 1/2 cup graham crumbs | 1 pkg. cream cheese |
| 1 pkg. vanilla instant pudding | 1 large container of cool whip |
| 1/2 cup milk | |

Line bottom of 9" x 13" pan with whole graham wafers or crumbs. Mix together the pudding, milk and cream cheese. Add cool whip and top the graham wafers. Add blueberry pie filling on top, then add crushed graham wafers on top of the blueberry filling. *Contributed by Rosie Wolkowski.*

## Butter Chews

| | |
|---|---|
| 1 1/4 cups flour | 1 tsp. baking powder |
| 1/2 cup butter | 3 egg yolks (beaten) |
| Pinch of salt | 1 cup chopped nuts |
| 3 Tbsp. sugar | 3/4 cup shredded coconut |
| 1 1/2 cups brown sugar | 3 egg whites beaten stiff |
| 6 tsp. flour | |

Mix butter and flour as for pastry, add salt. Pat mixture in a pan and bake for 15 minutes. Mix remaining ingredients spread on top and bake for 30 minutes. Add cherries if desired.

## Butterscotch Brickle Bars

| | |
|---|---|
| 1 1/2 cups flour | 3/4 cup brown sugar |
| 1/2 cup soft butter | 1/4 tsp. salt |

Mix until crumbly, press into large pan. Bake in preheated oven to 375 for 10 minutes.

| | |
|---|---|
| Meanwhile, combine in double boiler. | 1 Tbsp. water |
| 1- 6 oz. pkg. butterscotch chips | 2 Tbsp. butter |
| 1/4 cup corn syrup | 1/4 tsp. salt |

Stir over hot, not boiling water until smooth, remove from water and stir in 2 cups coarsely chopped walnuts, spoon evenly over baked layer, return to oven for 8 minutes. Cut while warm. *Contributed by Rosie Wolkowski.*

## Carrot Spice Squares

| | |
|---|---|
| 4 eggs | 1/2 tsp. nutmeg |
| 1 1/3 cups honey | 1/4 tsp. allspice |
| 1 cup oil | 3 cups carrots |
| 2 cups flour | 1 grated apple |
| 1/2 tsp. salt | 1/4 cup chopped walnuts |
| 2 tsp. baking powder | 1/2 cup unsweetened coconut |
| 1/2 tsp. baking soda | 1/4 cup raisins |
| 2 tsp. cinnamon | |

Beat eggs well, and gradually add honey while beating. Mix in oil, and mix dry ingredients quickly into honey mixture. Stir in carrots, apple, walnuts, coconut and raisins. Bake at 325 for 45 minutes. *Contributed by Bev Zarazun.*

## Cherry Almond Nanaimo Bars

Bottom Layer:
1/2 cup butter
1/4 cup sugar
1/3 cup cocoa
1 tsp. vanilla

1 beaten egg
1 cup coconut
1 3/4 cups graham wafer crumbs
1/2 chopped almonds

For the Bottom layer; cook butter, sugar, cocoa, vanilla and beaten egg in a saucepan over low heat, stirring constantly, until mixture begins to thicken. Remove from heat and stir in coconut, crumbs and almonds. Press mixture firmly into a greased 9" x 13" pan. Chill for at least 1 hour.

Filling:
1/4 cup softened butter
2 Tbsp. cherry juice

1 tsp. almond extract
2 cups sifted icing sugar
1/3 cup chopped Maraschino cherries

For the filling cream butter, cherry juice and almond extract, gradually beat in icing sugar to make a smooth spreading consistency. Stir in cherries. Spread over first layer. Chill until firm.

Top layer:
2 squares semi-sweet chocolate

1 Tbsp. butter

Melt chocolate and butter together in a saucepan over low heat, stirring until it is a smooth consistency. Decorating drizzle chocolate over filling. Chill.

## Cherry Berries on a Cloud

3 egg whites
1/4 tsp. cream of tartar
3/4 cup sugar
1 pkg. 3 oz. cream cheese
1/2 cup sugar

1/2 tsp. vanilla
1 cup chilled whipped cream
1 cup mini marshmallows
1 can cherry pie filling, 1 tsp. lemon juice or 2 cups strawberries

Heat the oven to 275. Beat egg whites and cream of tartar until foamy. Beat in 3/4 cup sugar, 1 tsp. at a time, continue beating until stiff and glossy. Spoon meringue into building up sides of pan. Bake for 90 min. turn off oven, leave meringue in oven. (Door closed) until cool, finish cooling away from draft. Blend cream cheese, 1/2 cup sugar and vanilla. In chilled bowl, beat cream until stiff, gently fold in whipped cream and marshmallows with cream cheese. Pile into baked meringue shell, cover and chill at least 12 hours. Just before serving top with cherry berry topping. *Contributed by Linda Matsalla.*

## Cherry Cha-Cha

2 cups graham wafers

1/2 cup melted butter

*Continued on next page...*

Reserve 3/4 cup mixture for topping. Bake in a 9" x 13" pan for 10 minutes at 350.

|                              |                        |
|------------------------------|------------------------|
| Whip:                        | 2 Tbsp. icing sugar    |
| 1 1/2 cups whipping cream    | 1 tsp. vanilla         |

Pour over 4 cups miniature marshmallows and mix. Put 1/2 of mixture into a pan. Then add 1 can of cherry or blueberry pie filling. Then top with rest of cream and marshmallow mix. Add the reserved 3/4 cup of graham wafers on top. Chill overnight before cutting. *Contributed by Beatrice Ochitwa.*

## Cherry Slice Bars

|                              |                                          |
|------------------------------|------------------------------------------|
| 1/2 lb. margarine            | 6 eggs                                   |
| 2 cups white sugar           | 2 cups flour                             |
| 1 tsp. vanilla extract       | 1 tsp. baking powder                     |
| 1 1/2 tsp. almond extract    | 1 - 19 oz. can cherry or blueberry pie filling |

Cream butter, sugar, almond and vanilla. Beat eggs in one at a time. Add flour. Spread 2/3 batter in large cookie sheet. Top with pie filling. Drop remaining batter over pie filling. Bake at 350 for 40 minutes. Drizzle with thin icing while still warm. (1/2 cup icing sugar mixed with 1-2 Tbsp. water). *Contributed by Lil Popoff.*

## Cherry Triangles

|                              |                              |
|------------------------------|------------------------------|
| 1 cup milk                   | 1 cup butter                 |
| 1 pkg. dry yeast             | 4 egg yolks slightly beaten  |
| 4 cups flour                 |                              |

Cook milk to lukewarm, add yeast, let stand for a while, put butter into flour, and add milk liquid to dry ingredients, mix thoroughly. Turn out into floured surface and knead well. Divide dough in half. Roll first half large enough for a jelly roll pan, spread 1 can of cherry pie filling over the dough, roll out second portion of dough and cover the first dough and the pie filling. Pinch sides, allow to rise in warm place for 1/2 hour. Bake at 350 for 45 minutes. Cool. Spread icing on top.

|                              |                              |
|------------------------------|------------------------------|
| 1/4 cup butter               | 2 Tbsp. cream                |
| 1/2 tsp. vanilla             | 1 1/2 cups icing sugar       |

Sprinkle with 3/4 cup chopped nuts. Cut into 3" squares then cut each square diagonally to make 48 triangles.

## Chipit Cherry Bars

|                              |                                    |
|------------------------------|------------------------------------|
| 1 1/4 cups flour             | 1/2 tsp salt                       |
| 2/3 cup brown sugar          | 1 1/2 cups mixed nuts              |
| 3/4 cup margarine            | 1 1/2 cups halved candied cherries |
| 1 egg                        | 1 cup semi-sweet chocolate chips   |

*Continued on next page...*

Combine flour with 1/3 cup brown sugar, cut in margarine until mixture resembles coarse crumbs. Press mixture evenly and firmly onto a bottom of an ungreased 15' x 10' pan. Beat egg, stir in remaining 1/3 cup brown sugar and nuts, cherries and chips. Toss lightly to coat. Spoon mixture over bottom layer of pan. Bake for 20-25 minutes at 350. Cool and cut. *Contributed by Eleanor Hadubiak.*

## Chipits Crispy Chocolate Squares

| | |
|---|---|
| 3/4 cup honey | 3 cups rice cereal |
| 1 cup peanut butter | 1 cup or 6 oz. pkg. of Chipits semi-sweet chocolate chips |
| 1 tsp. vanilla | 1 cup salted peanuts |

Combine honey and peanut butter in a large sauce pan, cook over medium heat stirring constantly until smoothly combined and mixture just comes to a boil. Remove from heat, stir in vanilla, and add cereal, chips and nuts. Stir until well combined, press into a greased 9" x 9" pan, chill 1 hour.

## Chocolate Brownies

| | |
|---|---|
| 2 cups flour | 2 cups sugar |

Mix together.

| | |
|---|---|
| 1/2 cup margarine | 4 Tbsp. cocoa |
| 1/2 cup water | 1/2 cup oil |

Heat together in a saucepan until boiling point. Then pour over sugar and flour mixture, mix together and then add:

| | |
|---|---|
| 1/2 cup buttermilk | 1 tsp. baking soda |
| 2 eggs | 1 tsp. vanilla |

Mix well and put in a greased big cookie sheet. Bake for 20 minutes at 350, remove and ice while hot with:

| | |
|---|---|
| 1/4 cup margarine | Add: |
| 3 Tbsp. buttermilk | 1 1/2 cups icing sugar |
| 2 Tbsp. cocoa | 1/2 cup nuts |
| Boil together. | 1/2 tsp. vanilla |

Mix while hot and spread on hot cake. *Contributed by Lil Popoff.*

## Chocolate Lasagna (no-bake)

| | |
|---|---|
| 1 pkg. regular Oreo cookies (Not Double Stuff) – about 36 cookies | 2 Tbsp. cold milk |
| | 1- 12 oz. tub Cool Whip, divided |
| 6 Tbsp. butter, melted | 2 – 3.9 oz. packages Chocolate Instant Pudding. |
| 1- 8 oz. package cream cheese, softened | 3 1/4 cups cold milk |
| 1/4 cup granulated sugar | 1 and 1/2 cups mini chocolate chips |

*Continued on next page…*

Begin by crushing 36 Oreo cookies. I used my Manual food processor for this, but you could also place them in a large Ziploc bag and crush them with a rolling pin or meat mallet. When the Oreos have turned into fine crumbs, you are done. Transfer the Oreo crumbs to a large bowl. Stir in 6 Tbsp. melted butter and use a fork to incorporate the butter into the cookie crumbs. When the butter is distributed, transfer the mixture to a 9" x 13" baking dish. Press the crumbs into the bottom of the pan. Place the pan in the refrigerator while you work on the additional layers. Mix the cream cheese with a mixer until light and fluffy. Add in 2 Tbsp. of milk, and sugar, and mix well. Stir in 1 and 1/4 cups Cool Whip. Spread this mixture over the Oreo crust. In a bowl, combine chocolate instant pudding with 3 and 1/4 cups cold milk. Whisk for several minutes until the pudding starts to thicken. Use a spatula to spread the mixture over the previous cream cheese layer. Allow the dessert to rest for about 5 minutes so that the pudding can firm up further. Spread the remaining Cool Whip over the top. Sprinkle mini chocolate chips evenly over the top. Place in the freezer for 1 hour, or the refrigerator for 4 hours before serving. *Contributed by Brent Matsalla.*

## Chocolate Pecan Bars

| | |
|---|---|
| 2 cups flour | 2 tsp. vanilla (divided) |
| 1/4 and 2/3 cups of sugar (divided) | 1 cup corn syrup |
| 1/4 tsp. salt | 4 oz. semisweet chocolate (melted) |
| 2/3 cup margarine | 2 eggs |
| 5 - 6 Tbsp. ice water | 2 cups pecan halves |

Heat the oven to 375. Combine flour and 1/4 cup sugar and salt. Cut in butter until mixture is like coarse crumbs. Stir in water 1 Tbsp. at a time and 1 tsp. vanilla. Chill 15 minutes. Roll this dough into a 12" square. Put in bottom of pan. Fold edges of dough to fit. Melt syrup with remaining sugar, chocolate, and vanilla and then beat in 1 egg. Whisk together. Press pecan halves into the crust and pour filling over crust. Bake for 45 minutes or until center is set. *Contributed by Gladys Grodzinski.*

## Cinnamon Apple Squares

| | |
|---|---|
| 1 cup flour | 1/2 brown sugar |
| 1/4 tsp salt | 1 cup rolled oats |
| 1/2 tsp. baking soda | 1/2 cup vegetable shortening |
| 1/2 tsp cinnamon | Apples for filling. |

Mix like for pie or like a crumb mixture. Put 1/2 on bottom then apples then put the other half on top. Bake at 350. *Contributed by Eleanor Hadubiak.*

## Coconut Fudge Bars

Base:

| | |
|---|---|
| 1 1/4 cups all-purpose flour | 1/4 tsp. salt |
| 2/3 cup sugar | 1/2 cup butter softened |
| 1/4 cup cocoa | 1 egg beaten |

Base: combine flour, sugar, cocoa and salt. Stir well to blend. Cut in butter until mixture is crumbly, stir in egg. Press evenly into a greased 9" x 13" cake pan. Bake at 350 for 10 - 12 minutes or until surface appears dry.

*Continued on next page...*

Filling:

| | |
|---|---|
| 1 can sweetened condensed milk | 2/3 cup chopped walnuts |
| 1/4 cup flour | 1/2 cup flaked coconut |
| 1 tsp. vanilla | 1/2-1 cup chocolate chips |

Combine condensed milk, flour and vanilla stir in coconut and chips. Spread mixture over hot crust and bake again for 20 -25 minutes longer or until light golden. Cool and cut into squares.

## Coconut Squares Unbaked

| | |
|---|---|
| 1 cup brown sugar | 1/2 cup chopped walnuts |
| 1/2 cup butter | 1 cup fine coconut |
| 1 egg | 1 cup graham wafers (crushed) |
| 1/3 cup milk | And whole graham wafers |

Melt butter and sugar in saucepan. Beat egg then add with milk to first mixture. Heat stirring until thick remove from stove and cool to lukewarm. Stir in coconuts, nuts and wafer crumbs. Line a pan with whole wafers and spread the filling on top. Place a final layer of whole wafers on top and spread with icing if desired.

## Corn Flakes Squares

| | |
|---|---|
| 1/2 cup margarine | 1 pkg. marshmallows |

Melt together, add the following:

| | |
|---|---|
| 4 cups cornflakes | 1 cup coconut |
| 4 oz. pkg. sliced almonds | Press into an 8" x 8" pan. |

## Crab Apple Squares

| | |
|---|---|
| 1/4 cup plus 2 Tbsp. butter | 1/2 tsp. cinnamon |
| 2 eggs | 1 cup flour |
| 1 cup white sugar | 2 cups crabapples |
| 1 tsp. baking soda | 1/2 cup chopped walnuts (optional) |
| 1 tsp. vanilla | |

Combine butter, eggs, sugar, baking soda, vanilla and nuts. Add cinnamon and flour. Add apples and walnuts. Bake in a 9" x 13" pan for 40 to 50 minutes at 350. Cool sift icing sugar over top to serve. *Contributed by Eleanor Hadubiak.*

## Crunch Bars

Base:
| | |
|---|---|
| 1/2 cup butter | 3/4-1 cup flour |
| 3/4 cup sugar | 1/2 tsp. baking powder |
| 2 eggs | 1/4 tsp. salt |
| 1 tsp. vanilla | 1/2 cup walnuts |
| | 2 1/2 cups coconut |

Cream butter, sugar, beat in eggs and vanilla. Add sifted dry ingredients. Stir in walnuts and coconut. Spread in a greased 9" x 13" pan, bake at 350 for 10 - 15 minutes. Remove from oven. Spread 2 1/2 cups miniature marshmallows and return to oven bake for 2 minutes. Allow cake to cool for 30 minutes before adding topping.

Topping:
| | |
|---|---|
| 1 - 6 ox. Semi-sweet chocolate chips | 1 1/2 cups rice crisps cereal |
| 1/2 - 3/4 cup peanut butter | |

Melt chips over low heat in saucepan, add peanut butter and rice crisps. Add to baked crunch bars.

## Cuban Lunch Bars

| | |
|---|---|
| 350 g. Each of: Peanut butter, butterscotch and chocolate chips | 1 1/2 cups crushed ripple chips |
| | 1 1/2 cups chopped peanuts (unsalted) |

Melt all chips add ripple chips and peanuts. But into small paper cups to set.

## Diamond Delights

| | |
|---|---|
| 3/4 cup flour | 1 cup caramel or butterscotch sauce |
| 1/2 cup rolled oats | 1/4 cup flour, mix into the sauce |
| 1/2 cup brown sugar | 1 cup semi-sweet chocolate chips |
| 1/2 tsp. baking soda | 3/4 cup chopped pecans |
| 1/2 cup margarine | |

Combine 3/4 cup flour with brown sugar, and baking soda stir well to blend. Melt margarine and add to flour mixture. Press evenly into a greased 9" square cake pan baking for 10 minutes at 325. Sprinkle nuts and chocolate chips over the top and pour sauce over the nuts and chips. Bake an additional 20 - 25 minutes.

## Easy Delicious Chewy Gooey Rice Krispie Squares

| | |
|---|---|
| 7 cups Rice Krispies | 1 Tbsp. vanilla extract |
| 1 stick (1/2 cup) unsalted butter | 1/2 tsp. salt |
| 1 bag mini marshmallows | |

*Continued on next page...*

In a large pot, melt butter on med. stirring constantly. Butter will start to foam and bubble up. Keep stirring and color will change from bright yellow to golden, and finally to a brown toast color. Remove from heat. DO NOT let it burn. You will smell aroma of a nutty brown butter. Add marshmallows, salt, and vanilla. Place pot back on med. heat and stir until marshmallows are soft and melted. Using a spatula, pour mixture into Rice Krispies and mix until combined. Transfer mixture into a greased pan. With greased fingers, press into an even layer. Let cool at room temperature for 30 min. before eating. *Contributed by Braxten and Rylan Mudry.*

## Eatmore Bars

1/2 cup peanut butter
2 cups chocolate chips
1 cup corn syrup or honey
1 cup oatmeal
1 cup chopped peanuts

Melt the syrup with the chocolate chips over medium heat. Remove from heat when melted and add the peanut butter. Stir until combined. Add oatmeal and peanuts and mix until well blended. Pour into a parchment paper lined cookie sheet and refrigerate for 30 minutes before cutting into bars. *Contributed by Theresa Mudry and Brent Matsalla.*

## Eatmore Bars with Wheat Germ

3/4 cup chocolate chips
1/2 cup honey or corn syrup
1/2 cup peanut butter

Melt together:
Add 3/4 cup wheat germ
1/2 cup chopped walnuts
1 cup rice crisps cereal

Wax paper a cookie sheet and spread mixture onto pan cool and cut into bars.

## Fudge Brownies

1 1/2 cups all-purpose flour
1 tsp. salt
2 cups white sugar
1/2 cup cocoa
1 1/2 tsp. baking powder

2 tsp. vanilla
1 cup oil
4 eggs
1/4 cup cold water
1/2 cup chopped walnuts

*Continued on next page...*

Put all ingredients in a beater bowl in order given and beat on low speed, scraping down the sides of bowl as it mixes. Do not beat too long. Grease a 9" x 13" pan and turn batter into it and smooth the top. Bake at 350 for 30 minutes no longer. *Contributed by Shawna Sicotte.*

## Fudge Krispies

| | |
|---|---|
| 1 pkg. (2 cups) chocolate chips | 2 tsp. vanilla |
| 1/2 cup margarine | 1 cup icing sugar |
| 1/2 cup corn syrup | 4 cups Rice Krispies |

Combine chips, margarine and corn syrup in a saucepan. Stir over low heat until melted and smooth. Remove from heat, add vanilla and sugar then Rice Krispies. Spread in a 9" x 13" pan, chill until firm, store in fridge. *Contributed by Bernice Gulka.*

## Graham Wafer Squares (Unbaked)

| | |
|---|---|
| 4 eggs | 1 tsp. vanilla |
| 1 cup butter | 1 box graham wafers (crushed coarsely) |
| 1 cup brown sugar | 1/2 pkg. of small marshmallows |

Cook the butter and brown sugar and beaten eggs do not boil. Cool mixture. Pour over marshmallows and wafers. Add coconut mix inside or place on top. Do not mix too much after wafers are added. *Contributed by Mabel Popoff.*

## Graham Wafers #1

| | |
|---|---|
| 1 cup shortening or margarine | 1 tsp. vanilla |
| 1/4 cup brown sugar | 2 cups white flour |
| 1/4 cup liquid honey | 4 cups graham flour (whole wheat will work) |
| 2 tsp. baking powder | 1 tsp. baking soda |
| 3/4 cup sweet or sour milk | 1 tsp. salt |

Mix all ingredients together and roll out and cut into squares.

## Graham Wafers #2

| | |
|---|---|
| 1/2 cup white sugar | 1/2 tsp. salt |
| 1/2 cup sour cream | 1 cup graham flour or whole wheat flour |
| 1/2 tsp. baking soda | |

Mix all ingredients together and roll out and cut into squares. *Contributed by Evelyn Kowalchuk.*

## Harvest Pumpkin Squares

| | |
|---|---|
| 3/4 cup oil | 1 1/2 tsp. baking soda |
| 1 1/2 cups sugar | 1 tsp. salt |
| 3 eggs | 1 1/2 tsp. cinnamon |
| 1-14 oz. can pumpkin puree | 3/4 tsp. nutmeg |
| 2 cups flour | 1/2 tsp. ginger |
| 1/2 tsp. cloves | 1 cup raisins OR 1/2 cup dates |
| 1 cup chopped nuts | |

Combine all ingredients. Bake at 325 for 30 minutes in 2 pans 1 - 9" x 13" and 1 – 8" x 8". While still warm pour a glaze over. Make holes in cake with a wooden spoon before pouring.

Glaze:

| | |
|---|---|
| 1 cup icing sugar | 1/8 tsp. salt |
| 1/4 tsp. nutmeg | 1/4 cup milk |
| 1/4 tsp. cinnamon | |

## Honey Rocks

| | |
|---|---|
| 1/2 cup butter or margarine | 1 tsp. baking powder |
| 1/2 cup shortening | 1/2 tsp. salt |
| 1 cup honey (liquid) | 1 tsp. baking soda |
| 2 cups rolled oats | 1 tsp. cinnamon |
| 1 1/2 cups raisins or dry cranberries | 2 Tbsp. milk |
| 2 cups flour | |

Cream margarine, sugar and honey. Add rolled oats and raisins. Sift dry ingredients and stir in alternately with milk. Drop by teaspoon 2" apart on lightly greased cookie sheet. Bake for 10 to 12 minutes at 375. Makes 5 dozen.

## Lemon Dessert

2 cups graham Wafers for the crust on bottom of 9" x 13" pan.
(or layer with whole graham crackers)

| | |
|---|---|
| The graham wafer crust is: | 2 Tbsp. sugar |
| 2 cups wafer crumbs | 1/2 cup margarine melted. |

Bake at 300 for 5 minutes, cool.

| | |
|---|---|
| Partially set 2 pkg. of lemon Jell-O | 1 1/2 cups boiling water |
| 1/2 cup sugar | |

Beat 1 can of carnation evaporated milk until thick (not the light because it will not whip)
Add Jell-O that is partially set, pour over graham wafers, and sprinkle with wafer crumbs on top. Set in fridge before serving.

## Lemon Coconut Surprise Squares

1 lemon pie filling (substitute 2 yolks for 1 egg because no meringue is required)
1/2 cup butter or margarine
1 1/2 cups graham cracker crumbs
1/2 cup medium unsweetened coconut
1/2 cup flour
1/2 cup sugar
1 tsp. baking powder
1/8 tsp salt

Make pie filling as indicated above, cool to lukewarm. Melt margarine in an 8" x 8" pan. Combine crumbs, flour, baking powder, salt and sugar in mixing bowl. Mix well in the pan with melted margarine. Pat and press to make a bottom layer. Cover with lemon filling, sprinkle with coconut. Bake at 325 for 30 minutes or until lightly browned. Chill and cut into squares.

## Lemon Squares #1

4 eggs
2 cups sugar
1/3 cup lemon juice

1/4 cup flour
1/2 tsp. baking powder

Icing sugar for topping when cake is cooked

Base:
2 cups all-purpose flour

1 cup butter
1/2 cup sugar

Base: blend ingredients well and press into 9" x 13" pan. Bake for approximately 15 minutes at 350. Cool slightly. Beat eggs while gradually adding sugar. Add lemon juice. Combine flour and baking powder. Fold into the egg/lemon mixture. Pour over the base. Bake at 350 for 20 to 25 minutes or until lightly browned. Cool. Sprinkle with the icing sugar and cut into squares.

## Lemon Squares #2

1 box lemon cake mix
1 egg

1/3 cup oil

Reserve 3/4 cup of crumb mixture for topping. Mix and pour into a small cookie sheet, bake at 350 oven for 15 minutes. Then mix:

*Continued on next page...*

8 oz. pkg. cream cheese

1 tsp. lemon juice

1/2 cup sugar

Spread on top. With topping of reserved crumb mixture. Bake for 15 minutes. *Contributed by Josie Nelson.*

## Magic Cookie Bars

1/2 cup margarine

1 1/2 cups graham wafers

1 can 14 oz. eagle brand condensed milk

1- 16 oz. package semi-sweet chocolate morsels

1- 3.5 oz. can flaked coconut (1 1/3 cups coconut)

1 cup chopped nuts

Preheat the oven to 350. (325 for glass dish) use a 9" x 13" pan. Add margarine to melt in the pan in oven sprinkle crumbs over margarine. Mix together and press into the pan. Pour sweetened condensed milk evenly over crumbs. Top evenly with remaining ingredients. Press down firmly. Bake for 25 to 30 minutes or until lightly browned. Cook before cutting.

## Marshmallow Bars

1/2 cup butter

1/2 cup sugar

2 eggs (beaten)

In a saucepan combine, butter and sugar. Add eggs stir over heat and bring to a boil then add:

1/2 box graham wafers crushed coarsely

1/2 lb. miniature marshmallows

1/2 cup walnuts

Press into a greased 9" x 13" pan.

## Marshmallow Slice

6 oz. chocolate or butterscotch chips

1/2 cup margarine

1 egg

1 cup icing sugar

Whole graham wafers

2 cups mini marshmallows

Put 6 oz. chocolate or butterscotch chips. 1/2 cup margarine and 1 egg in double boiler. When melted add 1 cup icing sugar, then set aside and cool slightly. Line 9" x 13" Pyrex pan with whole graham wafers. Stir in 2 cups marshmallows into liquid mixture. Pour over wafers. If desire, you may sprinkle with coconut.

## Marshmallow Squares

3/4 cup butter
1/3 cup lightly packed brown sugar
1 1/2 cups flour
2 envelopes un-flavored gelatin
1/2 cup cold water
1/2 cup chopped red and green maraschino cherries

1/2 cup toasted chopped almonds
2 cups sugar
1/2 cup warm water
1 tsp. almond flavoring
Food coloring (if desired)

Preheat the oven to 325. Cream butter, blend in brown sugar. Add flour and combine well. Press evenly into 9" x 13" baking pan. Prick the dough. Bake about a 1/2 hour or until golden brown. Soften gelatin in cold water. Combine sugar and warm water in saucepan, bring to a boil and boil 2 minutes. Stir softened gelatin into hot syrup. Beat with beater or electric mixer until very stiff. Add cherries, almonds, flavoring and food coloring. Pour over baked shortbread layer, allow to cool for several hours until surface gloss disappears. Cut into 1" squares.

## No-Bake Bars

1 cup peanut butter
1/2 cup honey
1/2 cup un-refined coconut oil (be sure to use un-refined for the coconut flavor)
2 cups dry oats (not instant)

1 cup shredded coconut
1/2 cup chopped walnuts (optional)
1 1/4 cups dark chocolate chips
1 tsp. vanilla extract

Melt peanut butter, honey and coconut oil over medium-low heat. Once melted, remove from heat and add oats, shredded coconut, chocolate chips and vanilla. Stir until chocolate is entirely melted. Pour into a 9×13 pan and cool in the fridge. When it is set, cut into bars and enjoy. Store in the fridge. If they last that long! *Contributed by Brent Matsalla.*

## Oatmeal Chocolate Chip Bars

1 cup oatmeal
3/4 cup butter
1 cup brown sugar
2 eggs
1/2 tsp. salt

1/2 cup chocolate chips
1 1/2 cups boiling water
1 3/4 cups flour
1 tsp. baking soda
1 tsp. cinnamon

Pour boiling water over oatmeal, cool. Cream butter and sugar add eggs, mix well. Add dry ingredients adding oatmeal and chips last. Bake at 350 for 30 minutes. When baked spread on icing.

1 cup coconut
1 cup brown sugar

5 Tbsp. melted butter
Put back into oven for 10 minutes.

## Orange Bowknots

6 to 6 1/2 cups all-purpose flour
1 pkgs. active dry yeast
1 1/2 cups milk
1/2 cup butter, margarine or shortening
1/3 cup sugar

1/2 tsp. salt
2 eggs
2 Tbsp. finely shredded orange peel
1/4 cup orange juice
1 recipe of orange icing

In a large mixing bowl combine 2 cups of the flour and the yeast; set aside. In a medium saucepan heat and stir the milk, butter, sugar and salt just until warm and the butter is almost melted; add to flour mixture alone with eggs. Beat with an electric mixer on low speed for 30 seconds. Beat on high speed for 3 minutes.

Using a wooden spoon to stir in orange peel, orange juice and as much of the remaining flour as you can. Turn the dough out onto a lightly floured surface. Knead in enough remaining flour to make a moderately soft dough that is smooth and elastic. Shape dough into a ball. Place in a lightly greased bowl, turning once to grease the full surface of the dough. Cover; let rise in a warm place until double in size (approximately 1 hour).

Punch dough down. Turn out onto a lightly floured surface. Divide in half. Cover and let rest for 10 minutes. Lightly grease 2 large baking sheets; set aside. Roll each dough half into a 7" x 12" rectangle. Cut each rectangle into twelve 7" long strips. Tie each strip loosely in a knot. Place knots 2" apart on prepared baking sheets. Cover; let rise in a warm place until nearly double in size (about 30 minutes). Preheat the oven to 375 bake for 12 to 14 minutes or until golden. Immediately remove from baking sheets. Cool on wire racks. Drizzle with orange icing.

Orange icing:
1 1/2 cups powdered sugar

1 1/2 tsp. orange peel
2 -3 Tbsp. orange juice

In a medium bowl combine ingredients to make icing a drizzling consistency.

## Peanut Butter Squares

1/2 cup margarine
2 pkgs. butterscotch chips
Melt in a double boiler. Remove.

Add:
1 cup peanut butter or less
Pour over 1 pkg. miniature marshmallows.

Can add chopped nuts or coconut if desired. *Contributed by Eleanor Hadubiak.*

## Peanut Mallow Squares

1 - 12 oz. pkg. semi-sweet chocolate chips
3/4 cup peanut butter

3 cups mini marshmallows

Melt chips and peanut butter over low heat. Stir in marshmallows, cool. Press into a greased 8" x 8" pan. *Contributed by Bernice Gulka.*

## Pie Filling Bars

4 cups sifted flour
1/4 tsp. salt
1 cup sugar
1 cup shortening substitute 1/2 butter
2 eggs

1 cup sour cream
2 tsp. baking soda
1 egg for topping
1 can pie filling

Mix flour, salt, sugar and cut in shortening. Mix until fine crumbs. Beat 2 eggs and cream stir in soda and add to mixture, chill. Roll out 3/4 of dough into jelly roll pan adding some up the sides just a little. Spread a can of pie filling on top, roll remaining dough about ¼" thick cut in strips and crisscross the dough on top. Beat 1 egg and 1 Tbsp. cold water, and brush over strips. Bake for 30 minutes. *Contributed by Lucy Grodzinski.*


## Pineapple Cookie Sheet Squares

2 eggs
1 1/2 cups sugar
2 1/4 cups flour
1 tsp. vanilla

1/2 tsp. salt
1 1/2 tsp. baking soda
1 can crushed pineapple (partially drained)

Grease and flour 15" x 10" cookie sheet pan. Beat eggs and sugar until creamy and light and fluffy. Add flour, baking soda, salt, vanilla and pineapple. Beat on medium speed until blended. Spread in the pan and bake at 350 for 20 - 25 minutes.

1 1/3 cups flaked coconut

1/2 cup chopped walnuts

Spread on top after baking while still hot from the oven. Top with glaze below.
Glaze:

3/4 cup sugar
1/2 cup margarine

1/4 cup cream
1/2 tsp. vanilla

*Contributed by Albina Hrychenko.*


## Pineapple Zucchini Loaf

3 eggs
1 cup oil
1 tsp. vanilla
2 cups brown sugar or 1 cup white and 1 cup brown sugar
1 tsp. salt
2 cups shredded zucchini

2 tsp. baking soda
1/2 tsp. baking powder
1 tsp. cinnamon
1 cup walnuts
1 cup drained crushed pineapple

Mix well and bake at 350 for 1 1/4 hours this makes 2 loaf pans.

## Pistachio Dessert

| | |
|---|---|
| 1 cup flour | 1/4 cup chopped walnuts |
| 1/2 cup margarine | 1/2 tsp. each vanilla and almond extract |
| 2 Tbsp. sugar | |

Mix above ingredients. Press into 9" x 13" greased pan. Bake at 325 until golden brown about 20 minutes.

Filling:

| | |
|---|---|
| 1-8 oz. cream cheese (softened) | 2/3 cup icing sugar |

Beat well, fold in 1/2 of large cool whip. Spread over the top of cooked cooled crust. 2 pkgs. pistachio instant pudding mixed with 2 1/2 cups milk, spread over creamed mixture. Spread remaining cool whip on top. Top with roasted almonds. Refrigerate overnight to set. Also freezes well. Also could use 3 cups milk and 1 can of drained pineapple added to pistachios.

Alternate to Pistachio could substitute Chocolate filling:

| | |
|---|---|
| 1 6 oz. instant chocolate pudding | 3 cups milk |
| 1 4 3/4 oz. pkg. instant vanilla pudding | |

Grate chocolate bar over cool whip.


## Poppy Seed Dessert

| | |
|---|---|
| 1/2 cup flour | 1/2 cup melted butter or margarine |
| 1/2 cup wafer crumbs | 1/2 cup nuts |

Mix together and rub until crumbly. Press into a pan and bake for 10 minutes at 350.

Filling:

| | |
|---|---|
| 3 Tbsp. cornstarch | 2 cups milk |
| 1 envelope gelatin (Knox) | 4 beaten eggs separated for the recipe |
| 1/2 cup poppy seed, ground | 1 tsp. vanilla |
| 1 cup sugar | 1/4 cup sugar |

Cook filling until it thickens, stirring constantly. When filling thickens, beat 4 egg yolks, add to it, and then cook 1 minutes longer. Cover and let sit aside to cool, until partially set. Beat egg whites and 1/2 tsp. vanilla, then add your filling and egg whites to the cooled crust and put in the fridge overnight. Put whipped cream or cool whip on top. *Contributed by Minnie Rudachyk.*

## Prune Fruit Squares

| | |
|---|---|
| 2/3 cup soft margarine | 2/3 cup icing sugar |
| 3 cups flour | 2 tsp. baking powder |

Mix butter and flour like pie crust. Then add icing sugar and baking powder. Mix together. Put in fridge to chill for 1/2 hour. Roll out into 12" x 15" cookie sheet. Bake at 375 for 15 minutes.

Prune Filling:

| | |
|---|---|
| 1/2 cup water | Stir while cooking |
| 1/2 Tbsp. vinegar | 2 cups sugar |

Bring to a boil and boil for 5 minutes. Then add:

| | |
|---|---|
| 14 oz. 1 lb. prunes pitted and sliced | Rind of 1 lemon |
| 8 oz. slivered almonds | |

Cook all for 10 minutes. Stirring all the time. Cool for a few minutes before spreading on baked crust. Cool in the pan and cut into triangles.


## Puffed Wheat Squares (Peanut Butter) #1

| | |
|---|---|
| 1/2 cup butter | 1 1/2 Tbsp. peanut butter |
| 1/2 cup syrup | 8 cups puffed wheat |
| 1 tsp. vanilla | 1 tsp. honey (optional) |
| 1 cup brown sugar | |

Heat the butter, peanut butter, brown sugar and syrup until melted remove from heat and add vanilla. Mix with puffed wheat cereal press into a greased 9" x 13" pan.


## Puffed Wheat Squares (Cocoa) #2

| | |
|---|---|
| 1/2 cup butter | 1 tsp. vanilla |
| 2 Tbsp. cocoa | 1 cup brown sugar |
| 1/2 cup syrup | 8 cups puffed wheat |

Heat the butter, cocoa, brown sugar and syrup until melted remove from heat and add vanilla. Mix with puffed wheat cereal press into a greased 9" x 13" pan.

## Pumpkin Dessert

Crust:

| | |
|---|---|
| 1 cup flour | 1 cup coconut |
| 1/4 cup sugar | 1/2 cup margarine |

Mix together the above. Press into 9" x 13" pan. Build up the edge. Bake at 250 for 10 minutes until light brown.

| | |
|---|---|
| Filling: | 1/2 tsp. salt |
| 4 cups cooked or canned pumpkin | 1 cup evaporated milk |
| 4 eggs, slightly beaten | 1 1/2 cups sugar |
| 1 tsp. vanilla | 2 tsp. pumpkin spice or cinnamon |

Combine filling ingredients and spread evenly over the crust. Bake at 350 for 40 minutes. Top with whipped cream.


## Pumpkin Pie Squares

| | |
|---|---|
| 1 cup butter | 1 tsp. vanilla |
| 1 cup sugar | 2 cups flour |
| 2 eggs | |

Cream butter and sugar together. Beat in eggs one at a time. Add vanilla. Add flour mix until blended spread into a greased 9" x 13" pan. Set aside.

| | |
|---|---|
| 2/3 cup sugar | 1/2 tsp. ginger |
| 1 tsp. salt | 14 oz. canned pumpkin |
| 1 tsp. cinnamon | 1 cup milk |
| 2 eggs | 1 tsp. pumpkin pie spice |

Measure all ingredients into mixing bowl. Beat together until blended. Pour over first layer. Bake at 400 for 10 minutes reduce heat to 325 continue to bake an additional 40-50 minutes until set. Cut into squares when cool. Top with whipping cream. This freezes very well.

<u>Pumpkin Slice Dessert</u>

Base:

| | |
|---|---|
| 1 cup flour | 1/2 cup brown sugar |
| 1/2 cup quick oats | 1/2 cup margarine |

Mix together the above. Press into an ungreased 9" x 13" pan. Bake at 350 for 15 minutes until light brown.

| Filling: | 1 tsp. vanilla |
|---|---|
| 1 can (398 ml) pumpkin | 1/2 tsp. salt |
| 1 can evaporated milk | 3/4 cup sugar |
| 2 eggs, slightly beaten | 2 tsp. pumpkin spice or cinnamon |

Combine filling ingredients and spread evenly over the crust. Bake at 350 for 20 minutes or until a knife comes out clean.

| Topping: | 2 Tbsp. butter |
|---|---|
| 1/2 cup chopped pecans | 1/2 cup brown sugar |

Combine and sprinkle over filling; bake an additional 10 minutes. Cool to serve. Cut into squares. Garnish with a scoop of cool whip.

<u>Quick Coffee Cake</u>

| | |
|---|---|
| 1 cup sugar | 1 tsp. baking powder |
| 1 cup oil | 1/4 tsp. salt |
| 4 eggs | 2 cups flour |

Mix all ingredients, put half batter in small cookie sheet. Spread 1 can pie filling over and the drop by little pieces the remaining half of the batter like a patchwork style. Less sugar can be used. *Contributed by Olga Fullawka.*

## Rhubarb Honey Cobbler

8 cups chopped fresh or frozen rhubarb (if frozen run under cold water to thaw and drain)
1/3 cup honey

1/4 cup all-purpose flour
1/4 cup sugar
1 Tbsp. orange juice

Cobbler Topping:
1 1/2 cups all-purpose flour
2 Tbsp. sugar
1 tsp. baking powder

1/4 tsp. baking soda
Pinch of salt
1/4 cup cold unsalted butter, cubed
2/3 cup buttermilk

Orange sugar topping, mix together the following:
3 Tbsp. sugar

1 Tbsp. grated orange zest
1 Tbsp. butter, melted

In bowl, combine rhubarb, honey, flour, sugar and orange juice until well coated; scrape into greased 8" square baking dish. Set aside. Cobbler topping: mix together all ingredients and roll out the dough to an 8" x 8" square, cut into 2" squares and place on top of rhubarb mixture. Topping with orange sugar mixture. Cook at 350 for 1 hour and 10 minutes.

## Rhubarb Casserole Dessert

2 cups cut rhubarb
2 cups white bread cubes
2/3 cup sugar
1/4 tsp. cinnamon

2 eggs
1 1/2 cups milk
1 Tbsp. butter
1/4 cup brown sugar

Wash and cut up rhubarb in pieces to make 2 cups. Remove crust from 2-3 day old bread. Cube and add to rhubarb. Sprinkle fruit and bread with sugar and cinnamon. Mix lightly and turn into greased 6 cup casserole, beat eggs slightly, stir in milk and pour over fruit mixture, dot with butter and cover the casserole. Bake in oven 300 for 30 minutes then remove cover and continue baking until pudding is set about 30 minutes longer, test with toothpick when it comes out clean. Sprinkle brown sugar over top of pudding and broil until sugar is bubbly. Serve warm with cream or ice cream.

## Rhubarb Crisp #1

4 cups rhubarb
1/3 cup flour
2/3 cup rolled oats

3/4 cup brown sugar
1/3 cup butter

Sprinkle rhubarb with 1/4 tsp. cinnamon and 1/4 tsp. ginger and 2 Tbsp. water. Arrange rhubarb in greased baking dish, mix flour, oats and sugar, add butter until mixture resembles a crumble. Sprinkle mixture over rhubarb and bake at 375 until rhubarb is tender and topping browned about 30 minutes. *Contributed by Eleanor Hadubiak.*

## Rhubarb Crisp #2

Mix together:
| | |
|---|---|
| 6 cups rhubarb | 1 1/2 cups sugar |
| | 3 Tbsp. minute tapioca |

On top mix together:
| | |
|---|---|
| 1/3 cup flour | 1/2 cup margarine |
| 1/2 cup oatmeal | 1/2 tsp. baking soda |
| 3/4 cup brown sugar | 1 tsp. baking powder |
| | 1/4 tsp. salt |

Bake at 350 for 50 minutes.

## Rhubarb Crisp #3

| | |
|---|---|
| 4 cups cut up rhubarb | 3/4 cup flour |
| 1/2 cup sugar | 3/4 cup sugar |
| 1 Tbsp. ground orange rind | 1/8 tsp salt |
| 1 tsp. ground lemon rind | 1/3 cup margarine |

Place rhubarb in a greased baking dish. Mix in 1/2 cup sugar and orange and lemon. Mix other ingredients and place on top and bake at 350 for 45 to 50 minutes.

## Rhubarb Crumb Dessert

| | |
|---|---|
| 2 cups graham wafer crumbs | 1/4 tsp. salt |
| 1 1/2 cups sugar | 1/3 cup margarine |
| 1/4 tsp. cinnamon | 6 cups chopped rhubarb |
| 2 Tbsp. grated orange peel | |

Make crumb mixture from all ingredients except rhubarb and alternate layers of rhubarb and crumbs. Bake at 350 for 40 minutes.

## Rhubarb Dessert

Crust:
| | |
|---|---|
| 2 cups flour | 1 cup butter |
| Pinch of salt | 4 Tbsp. sugar |

Filling:
| | |
|---|---|
| 5 cups rhubarb | 4 Tbsp. flour |
| 6 eggs separated for the recipe | 1 1/4 cups sugar |
| 1 cup cream | 2 tsp vanilla |

Bake crust in a 9" x 12" pan at 350 for 10 - 15 minutes. Add ingredients of filling mixture (with only the yolks of the eggs) and pour over crust. Bake at 325 for 1 hour. Remove and cover with egg white meringue (6 whites, and 1/4 cup sugar beaten) bake for 10 minutes more or broil to brown.

## Rhubarb Torte

1 1/3 cups graham wafer crumbs          1/4 cup melted butter
1/4 cup brown sugar

Combine the above items, and press into 9" x 13" pan bake for 6 - 8 minutes.
4 cups diced rhubarb                    1 cup sugar
1 1/4 to 1 1/2 cups of water            4 Tbsp. cornstarch

Cook rhubarb and water until soft. Combine cornstarch and sugar, add to rhubarb, and continue to cook until thick. Spread over cooled crust.

Topping:                                1 pkg. 4 oz. vanilla instant pudding mixed with 1 1/2
1 pkg. dream whip or whipped            cups milk.
topping                                 1 1/2 cups miniature marshmallows

Prepare pudding and milk. Mix dream whip and marshmallows, fold in pudding. Spread over rhubarb and chill. *Contributed by Olga Fullawka.*

## Rocky Road Slice

1 pkg. 350 g. Semi-sweet chocolate chips    25 ml or 2 Tbsp. margarine
1 - 300 ml can eagle brand sweetened        500 ml or 2 cups dry roasted peanuts
condensed milk                              1 - 250 g. pkg. of miniature marshmallows

In heavy saucepan over low heat melt chips with condensed milk and margarine. Remove from heat, in large bowl combine nuts and marshmallows fold in chocolate mixture, spread in waxed paper lined 9" x 13" pan, chill 2 hours. Remove from pan, peel off wax paper. Cut in squares. *Contributed by Linda Matsalla.*

## Skor Squares

1 pkg. of Ritz crackers (not cheese) average    1 can of condensed milk
size box                                        1 pkg. of Skor bits

Crush crackers, add milk and Skor bits. Mix. Press hard into an ungreased pan or small cookie sheet. Hint: a wet spatula works well. Bake for 12-15 minutes at 350, cool and cut into squares. *Contributed by Theresa Mudry.*

## Smore Brownies

1 pkg. brownie mix
6 graham crackers or 1/2 cup graham crumbs
2 cups miniature marshmallows
2 Hershey chocolate bars broken into pieces or 1 cup chocolate chips

Bake brownies as per directions on the box. As soon as the brownies are removed from the oven, top with marshmallows, graham crackers/crumbs, and chocolate. Set oven to broil and place brownies 5" from heat. Broil until the marshmallows brown and chocolate melts. Remove from oven and let cool. Cut into squares. *Contributed by Brent Matsalla.*


## Strawberry Chiffon Squares

1 1/2 cups graham cracker crumbs
1/4 cup margarine
1 3 oz. pkg. strawberry Jell-O
3/4 cup boiling water
1 can condensed milk

1/3 cup lemon juice
1 carton (15 oz.) frozen sliced strawberries
3 cups miniature white marshmallows
1/2 pint whipping cream (whipped)

Melt butter and combine with graham wafer crumbs and pan into a 9" x 9" pan. In a bowl dissolve Jell-O in boiling water. Stir in condensed milk, lemon juice, strawberries and marshmallows. Fold in whipped cream. Pour over crust, chill 2 hours. Variations: lime chiffon squares use lime flavored Jell-O and substitute 1 -14 oz. can of crushed pineapple.


## Strawberry Delight Dessert

16 graham wafers (1 1/2 cups crushed)
1/2 cup sugar

1/3 cup melted margarine

Mix together for the crust and bake for 15 minutes. Cool
1 pkg. dream whip
1/2 cup milk

3 Tbsp. icing sugar

This can be frozen at this point. Add pie filling or glazed Strawberries to serve.

## Strawberry Dessert

1 3/4 cups graham wafer crumbs
1/4 cup icing sugar
1/4 cup margarine
1 tsp. cinnamon
1 pkg. Strawberry Jell-O (small size)

1 cup boiling water
1 pkg. frozen strawberries (about 1 1/2 cups)
24 large marshmallows
1 pkg. dream whip
1/2 cup milk

Mix and press in a 9" x 13" pan the first 4 ingredients. Stir frozen berries into Jell-O mixture (boiling water and Jell-O powder). Chill slightly and pour over crumbs. Combine in double boiler the marshmallows and milk. Heat and stir until smooth and marshmallows melted. Cool and pour over berries and Jell-O. Top with dream whip. *Contributed by Bev Zarazun.*

## Toffee Marshmallows

2 toffee bars
2 Tbsp. cream milk

2 Tbsp. margarine

Melt the 3 ingredients in a double boiler. Keep over hot water while dipping large marshmallows in it. Then dip the marshmallow in Rice Krispies, place on parchment to set, when cool cut with sharp knife or serve as is.

## Tracy's Poppy Bars

Step 1:

Soak 1 Tbsp. yeast in 1 cup warm water

2 tsp. sugar, let stand 10 minutes.

Step 2:

3 cups flour
1 tsp. baking powder
Pinch of Salt

4 Tbsp. sugar
1 cup shortening
2 egg yolks

Poppy seed filling:

2 cups poppy seed ground
1 1/2 cups sugar
1 cup hot water
1 tsp. lemon juice

1 tsp. vanilla
Flour to make a soft paste
2 egg whites beaten
1 pkg. instant vanilla pudding

Icing:

1 cup icing sugar
1 1/2 tsp. soft butter

Pinch of salt
1 tsp. vanilla

Rub together as for pastry, make a well in mixture and add heat and 2 beaten egg yolks. Mix all ingredients. Divide dough into 3 balls. Roll out one layer and place on small cookie sheet. Spread some poppy seed filling. Then a layer of dough and cover with another filling, then cover with another (3rd) layer of dough. Let rise 1 hour. Bake at 325 for 45 minutes. Add enough cream to spread the icing. Frost with butter icing also drizzle melted chocolate crosswise ½" apart then pull a fork across the opposite ways. *Contributed by Eleanor Hadubiak.*

## Trifle

1/4 cup wine added to cooled vanilla custard. Slice sponge or angel food cake in layers across and then cut the top layer into cubes. Put in a bowl and spread raspberry Jell-O over the cake. Sprinkle little bit of wine over the cubes with some jam and custard. Then repeat, cake, and so on. On very top of dessert put a straight piece of cake and place whipped cream on top. Refrigerate.

## Toffee Squares

| | |
|---|---|
| 1 cup margarine | 2 cups flour |
| 1 cup brown sugar | 1/4 tsp. salt |
| 1 egg yolk | 1/3 pkg. chocolate chips |
| 1 tsp. vanilla | |

Combine margarine, brown sugar, egg yolk and vanilla, sift flour and salt. Blend into margarine mixture. Press into 9" x 13" pan, bake at 350 for 30 minutes or until edges are golden brown and cents is soft. Remove from oven, immediately place chocolate chips on top let stand 5 minutes until chips softened, spread evenly over cake, let set before cutting. *Contributed by Bernice Gulka.*

## Unbaked Squares

| | |
|---|---|
| 1/4 cup butter | 2 Tbsp. cocoa |
| 1/2 cup sugar | 24 or 1/2 lb. graham wafers |
| 1 egg (beaten) | 1 tsp. vanilla |
| 3/4 cup walnuts | |

Melt butter in saucepan, add sugar, cocoa, egg and stir. Bring to a boil and simmer 1 minute, add nuts, vanilla and roughly broken wafers, press mixture into a 9" x 9" greased pan. Ice with frosting and sprinkle with nuts if desired. *Contributed by Bernice Gulka.*

## Walnut Slice

| | |
|---|---|
| Bottom Layer: | 1/2 cup butter |
| 1 cup flour | Pinch of salt |

| Top Layer: | |
|---|---|
| 2 cups brown sugar | 1 tsp. flour |
| 2 Tbsp. water | 1 tsp. baking powder |
| 5 eggs (unbeaten) | 1 cup walnuts |
| 1 tsp. vanilla | |

Pat the bottom layer into an 8" x 8" pan. Then mix top layer ingredients and pour on top. Bake at 375 for 45 minutes. The top layer will be soft in middle when it is finished baking.

## Almond Bark

1 sleeve soda crackers or enough to cover cookie sheet.
1 cup butter
3/4 cup brown sugar

1 1/2 cups milk chocolate chips
1/2 cup sliced almonds (can toast them a bit)

Preheat the oven to 350. Cover cookie sheet with foil. Layer crackers on foil. On top of stove combine butter and brown sugar and boil for 2 minutes. Stir constantly so it doesn't separate and until all melted together. Pour over crackers evenly. Put into oven for 5 minutes. Let crackers settle, straighten out into place with a fork. Sprinkle with chocolate chips and put back in oven for 1 minute. Remove and spread melted chips evenly with butter knife. Sprinkle with almonds and flatten into chocolate. Freeze then break up once frozen.

## Almond Cream Puff Ring

1 cup water
1/2 cup butter or margarine
1/4 tsp. salt

1 cup flour
4 eggs

In 2 quart saucepan over medium heat, heat water, butter and salt until butter is melted and mixture boils. Remove saucepan from heat. With wooden spoon, vigorously stir in flour all at once until mixture forms a ball and leaves the side of the saucepan. Add eggs to flour mixture, one at a time, beating after each addition, until mixture is smooth and satiny, cool mixture slightly. Preheat the oven to 400. Lightly grease and flour large cookie sheet, using 7" plate as a guide trace a circle in flour on the cookie sheet. Drop batter by tablespoons into ten mounds, inside the circle, to form a ring. Bake ring 40 minutes or until golden. Turn off oven; let ring remain in oven 15 minutes. Remove ring from oven; cool on wire rack. When cooled, slice horizontally in half with a long knife. Prepare the Almond Cream Filling for the center and prepare the chocolate glaze to drizzle hot on top of cream puff ring.

Almond Cream:
1 - 3 1/2 oz. package of vanilla flavor instant pudding and pie filling as label directs but use only 1 1/4 cups milk. Fold in 1 cup heavy whipping cream, whipped with 1 tsp. almond extract.

Chocolate glaze: in double boiler over hot, not boiling water, heat 1/2 cup semisweet chocolate pieces with 1 Tbsp. butter, 1 1/2 tsp. milk, and 1 1/2 tsp. light corn syrup until smooth, stirring occasionally. *Contributed by Bernice Gulka.*

## Baked Apples

4 large apples
4 Tbsp. (1/2 stick) butter, softened
1/2 cup brown sugar
3/4 tsp. cinnamon
1/4 cup chopped pecans or walnuts

Preheat the oven to 375 degrees. Wash and cut a top off the apple and core apples but not all the way through so it's able to hold the filling. Combine the butter, brown sugar, cinnamon and chopped nuts. Press into the apple cores. Fill a baking dish with 3/4 cup water. Place the apples upright in the dish. Bake until the apples are soft and the filling is browned, 1 hour. Top with salted caramel and ice cream or heavy cream to serve. Top with more chopped nuts. *Contributed by Brent Matsalla.*

## Basic Fruit Pizza

1/2 cup butter                                          1 cup flour
1/4 cup brown sugar

Mix ingredients well and press into a pie plate. Bake at 325 for 12 minutes.

Create a cream cheese spread:
1 pkg. cream cheese softened and mixed with 1/3 cup sugar. Put on cooled crust and arrange fruit on top. Glaze for fruit: Cook until thick. Pour on top of fruit while still hot.

2 Tbsp. cornstarch                                  1/2 cup sugar
1 cup pineapple juice                              1 tsp. lemon juice

Chill and serve.

## Bread Pudding

2 cups dry bread
1/2 cup sugar
1 pint cream or milk
4 Tbsp. butter

4 eggs
1/4 tsp. cinnamon
1/2 tsp. vanilla
Pinch of salt

Soak bread in cream. Add the rest of ingredients and bake.


## Cherry Blossom Snowballs

3 cups rolled oats
2 cups unsweetened coconut (divided)
3/4 cup cocoa (sifted)
1/2 cup walnuts (chopped)
Pinch of salt

1 1/4 cups evaporated milk
1 tsp vanilla
2 1/2 cups sugar
3/4 cup butter (cut in small cubes)
34 maraschino cherries

In a large bowl, combine roll oats, 1 cup of coconut, cocoa, walnuts and salt – mix well and set aside. In a large saucepan, med-low heat, combine milk, vanilla, sugar and butter. Stir until all ingredients are totally dissolved. Increase to med-high heat and bring to a gently boil (at this time do not stir mixture). Continue cooking for 10 minutes or until temperature reaches 230F on a candy thermometer or at the soft-ball stage. Remove from heat and let mixture settle (Approx. 1 minute). Add mixture to dry ingredients and mix thoroughly. Place mixture in refrigerator until cool enough to handle or overnight. Shape into round balls, insert a hole in center with finger, place a cherry in each and close. Coat by rolling in coconut. *Contributed by Brent Matsalla.*


## Chocolate Rice Krispies Balls

*Continued on next page…*

| 1/2 cup peanut butter | 1 cup Rice Krispies |
| 3 Tbsp. soft butter | 1/2 cup chopped pecans |
| 1 tsp. vanilla | 1 cup shredded coconut |

Mix together, refrigerate for a half hour or longer and then form into balls. Return to fridge and let chill at least an hour.

Melt the following together in a double –boiler:

| 1 package chocolate chips | 1 square sweet chocolate |

Keep on low so that chocolate remains soft. Drop balls into chocolate mixture one at a time using a fork to roll them so that the chocolate will cover. Let set on parchment paper in fridge. They freeze well. *Contributed by Brent Matsalla.*

## Cocoa Rice Pudding

| 2 cups milk | 1/2 tsp. salt |
| 1/2 cup sugar | 2 cups cooked rice |
| 3 to 4 Tbsp. cocoa | 1/2 tsp. vanilla |

Bake all together until done.

## Creamy Chocolate Pudding

| 1 1/4 cups sugar | 1/3 cup butter, cut into pieces |
| 1/2 cup cocoa | 2 tsp. vanilla |
| 1/4 cup cornstarch | Whipped cream + 1/2 cup icing sugar + 1 tsp. vanilla |
| 1/2 tsp. salt | |
| 2 1/2 cups milk | |

Mix sugar, cocoa, cornstarch and salt with whisk and add milk. Cook over medium heat 8 to 10 minutes, stirring constantly, until pudding boils and is thickened. Reduce heat to medium-low; cook 2 minutes longer. Remove from heat and stir in butter and vanilla until melted. Cover top directly with plastic wrap to avoid a skin from forming and set aside to cool. In another bowl mix whip cream, icing sugar and vanilla. Whip until stiff peaks form. Fold whip cream into cooled pudding. Cover and refrigerate and serve cool. *Contributed by Brent Matsalla.*

## Dad's Burnt Sugar Candy

| | |
|---|---|
| 2 cups sugar | 1/4 cup water |
| 1/2 cup light corn syrup | 1/4 tsp. cream of tartar |

Stir ingredients in a saucepan over medium heat until sugar dissolves. Increase heat to med.-high and bring to a simmer. Brush the sides of the pan occasionally using a wet brush to remove any sugar crystals that form, simmer 5 minutes. When mixture reaches boiling, do not touch or disturb mixture at all. Boiling mixture will become amber in 5 to 7 minutes of boiling. Remove from heat to stop the boiling. It will darken in color a bit as it cools. Pour in thin layer over snow or a parchment paper lined cookie sheet that has been in the freezer for an hour. Can also be used to color and sweeten moonshine/homebrew. *Contributed by Joe Matsalla.*

## Frozen Raspberries Dessert

Put partly frozen raspberries in a blender with sugar and almond flavoring, blend and serve with dream whip or ice cream.

## Fruit Pizza with Oatmeal Base

| | |
|---|---|
| 1 cup butter | 1 tsp. baking powder |
| 1 cup brown sugar | 1/2 tsp. baking soda |
| 1 egg | 8 oz. pkg. cream cheese |
| 1 cup fine coconut | 1/4 cup sugar |
| 1 1/2 cup rolled oats | 1 small cool whip |
| 1 cup flour | Fresh fruit |

Glaze:

| | |
|---|---|
| 1/2 cup sugar | 1 1/2 Tbsp. cornstarch |
| 1 cup juice (pineapple or orange) | |

Cream butter. Add brown sugar and egg. Beat. Add next 5 ingredients. Spread on 13" greased pizza pan. Bake at 350 for 10 -15 minutes. Cool. Mix cream cheese, 1/4 cup sugar and cool whip thoroughly. Spread on cooled crust. Arrange fruit. Cook glaze until bubbly. Drizzle over fruit.

## Ice Cream Sandwiches

| | |
|---|---|
| 1/2 cup corn syrup | 4 cups Rice Krispies |
| 1/2 cup peanut butter | 1 pint ice cream (cut into slices) |

Stir peanut butter, butter and syrup in saucepan until smooth. Remove from heat. Stir in Rice Krispies. Press into a buttered 8" x 8" pan. Place in freezer until firm, add ice cream slices, and cover with the other half of cake to make a sandwich. Place in individual foil and freeze. *Contributed by Margaret Charuk.*

## Jam Snacks

1 cup flour
1 tsp. baking powder
3 Tbsp. milk

1/2 cup butter
1 egg

Mix together like for pie crust and spread in a pan. Spread any jam over the bottom layer. Then mix the following ingredients and spread on top of the crust and jam.

1 egg beaten
3/4 cup sugar
1 1/4 cups coconut

1 tsp. vanilla
butter in a size of an egg

Bake in 325 oven for 40 min.


## Key Lime Dessert Bites

1 cup cashews
3/4 cup Medjool dates, pitted
1/2 cup coconut, shredded, unsweetened

2 Tbsp. lime zest
1 Tbsp. lime juice

Place cashews in a dry frying pan and toast until golden brown and fragrant. Put dates in a food processor and blend until they are chopped into small pieces. Add cashews, coconut, lime zest and lime juice to food processor. Process until mixture is smooth. Measure out 1 Tbsp. of batter and roll into balls. Let cool in fridge until set. Store dessert bites in fridge in an airtight container. Makes 24. *Contributed by Jim Matsalla.*


## Marshmallow Fruit Dessert

2 pkgs. dream whip
1/2 cup sour cream
1 can mandarin oranges drained

1 can crushed pineapple drained
1 cup coconut
1 cup miniature marshmallows

Make dream whip according to package. Mix all other ingredients together. Put in fridge to set.


## Peach Dessert

1 cup chopped peaches
2 cups whipping cream or 2 pkgs. dessert topping

4 Tbsp. coconut
4 Tbsp. chopped cherries

Mix all together and refrigerate. *Contributed by Eleanor Hadubiak.*

## Polish Chruschiki

1 cup flour
3 egg yolks
1 whole egg
1 Tbsp. sour cream

1 Tbsp. sugar
1/2 tsp. vanilla
Pinch of salt

Let dough sit in fridge 1/2 hour. Roll to 1/8" thick and cut 2 1/2" squares with a small cut in the middle, pull one corner thru the hole in the middle, fry 3 or 4 at a time in a medium heat oil, use 2 bamboo skewers to turn over, lightly brown remove from oil onto a paper towel lined tray. Arrange on a platter and dust lightly with vanilla powder sugar. *Contributed by Brent Matsalla.*

## Quick Dessert with Rhubarb and Jell-O

4 cups rhubarb
1 pkg. raspberry Jell-O
1 pkg. cake mix (white)

1/2 cup butter
1 cup water

Put rhubarb on bottom of 9" x 13" pan. Then dry Jell-O powder over top. Then dry cake mix over Jell-O. Then butter mixed with water. Bake at 350.

## Scuffles

Dissolve 1 pkg. yeast in 1/4 cup warm water and 1 tsp. sugar for 15-20 mins.

Mix as for pie crust:
3 cups flour
2 Tbsp. sugar

1/2 tsp salt
1 cup butter
Add 2 eggs and yeast mixture

Knead dough until soft. Place in bowl and let stand in fridge overnight. Divide dough into 6 parts. Roll dough as you would for pie crust. Sprinkle mixture of 2 Tbsp. cinnamon and 1 cup sugar on both sides of dough. Cut in wedges and roll from wide to narrow end. Pinch together at bottom. Bake for 15 min at 350. *Contributed by Jerraie Oberg.*

## Sponge Toffee

2 cups sugar  
1/2 cup corn syrup  
1/3 cup water  

1 tablespoon baking soda  
1 cup dark chocolate chips  
Sea salt, to taste  

Add sugar, water, and corn syrup to a large pot. Mixture will expand to three times the size so a very large heavy bottomed saucepan should be used. Stir on med. heat until sugar is dissolved, then leave to boil, unstirred. Mixture must reach 300F. Remove from heat and add baking soda and whisk vigorously into the mixture for 5 seconds, no more or you will deflate the mixture. Quickly pour onto a parchment lined cookie sheet or baking pan. Do not move mixture for 2 hours. Remove from pan and using a blunt object, smash into bite size pieces. Melt chocolate in double boiler. Dip toffee pieces into chocolate, sprinkle with sea salt and set to cool on lined tray in refrigerator for 15 min.
VARIANTS: Add a pkg. of Kool-Aid to flavor and color the toffee or add 3 Tbsp. tequila and 2 tsp. lime zest for a spiked adult version.

## Starburst-like Kool-Aid Candy

2 1/2 cups white sugar  
3 Tbsp. cornstarch  
1 1/3 cups water  
1 cup corn syrup  

2 Tbsp. butter  
2 pkg. unsweetened Kool-Aid drink mix  
1/2 tsp. vanilla  

Using a large pot, mix sugar and cornstarch. Add water, corn syrup, and butter and heat on med. Stir until boiling, then stop stirring. Cook until temp reaches 250F. When the temp hits 240, the mixture will rise. Remove from heat and stir in Kool-Aid. Pour mixture onto parchment lined cookie sheet or silicone mat. Cool 15 min. until cool enough to handle with greased hands. Break off small portions and stretch it until color gets pale and it hardens a bit. Form a rope and cut in smaller pieces. Wrap individual pieces in wax paper

## Stewed Rhubarb Berry Stew

2 cups rhubarb (diced)  
3/4 cup strawberries  
1/2 cup raspberries  
1 orange (with juice)  
1/2 cup sugar (more or less)  
1/2 cup water  
1/4 tsp. pumpkin spice or cinnamon  

*Continued on next page…*

Combine all ingredients into a saucepan. Stir as you cook for approximately 10 minutes, or until rhubarb is starting to soften and it thickens slightly. Variations: This recipe can be used hot or cold. Depending on sweetness of the fruit and rhubarb, sugar quantities may vary and sweetener can be substituted. Any combination of fruit may be used, fresh or frozen. Rhubarb alone with sugar, water, spice, orange and juice, is another variation. Serve as a topping on porridge or any breakfast coffee cake. Also serve, as a quick dessert on cheese cake, shortbread, ice cream, and yogurt or with whipped cream. Quantities can be doubled, this recipe makes about 2 cups.

*Josie loved to make this recipe with the first rhubarb in the season, or if she had some leftover cut up rhubarb, it was an added treat throughout the summer.*

## Strawberry Pavlova

| | |
|---|---|
| 5 egg whites | 1 tsp. vanilla |
| 1/4 tsp. cream of tartar | 2 cups whipping cream |
| 1 1/2 cups granulated sugar | 2 Tbsp. icing sugar |
| 1 tsp. cornstarch | 6 cups fresh strawberries (kiwi or bananas could be used) |

In large bowl beat egg whites and cream of tartar until soft peaks form. Beat in sugar 1 Tbsp. at a time until stiff and glossy peaks form. Beat in cornstarch and vanilla. On foil lined baking sheet spread mixture into 12" circle. Bake at 275 for 1 hour to 1 1/2 hours. Turn oven off and let meringue cool inside oven (do not open the door). Whip cream until stiff, beat in icing sugar (adding more or less to make stiff). Peel foil from meringue and place meringue on large platter, cover with whipped cream and arrange sliced strawberries on top and a few on sides. Cut into wedges to serve. Makes 8 servings. *Contributed by Irene Bahrey.*

## Striped Delight Jell-O Pudding Dessert

| | |
|---|---|
| 1 1/2 cups graham cracker crumbs | 2 Tbsp. milk |
| 1/4 cup sugar | 1 container cool whip or whipped topping |
| 1/3 cup melted butter or margarine | 2 pkgs. chocolate instant pudding |
| 1 8 oz. pkg. cream cheese, softened | 3 1/2 cups cold milk |
| 1/4 cup sugar | |

Combine first 3 ingredients and press firmly into 9" x 13" pan. Beat cream cheese with sugar and 2 Tbsp. milk until smooth. Fold in 1/2 of the whipped topping. Spread on crust. Prepare pudding and milk and pour over cream cheese mixture. Chill several hours. Spread remaining whipped topping over pudding, garnish with grated chocolate or nuts. Makes 12-15 servings. May substitute chocolate for lemon or pistachio flavors.

## Vanilla Ice Cream

1 cup full fat cream warm over heat, but do not boil. Stir in until dissolved 3/4 cup sugar, 1/8 tsp. salt. Chill then add: 3 cups cream whipped, 1 1/2 tsp. vanilla. You could add strawberries or pineapple. Freeze.

## Watermelon Rind Candy

| | |
|---|---|
| Watermelon rind | 2 + 1 cups of sugar, divided |
| 1 qt. water | 1 1/4 cups of water |
| 1/4 cup of salt | |

Cut watermelon rind cut into 2" by 2" cubes leaving a bit of red and remove outer skin with potato peeler. Cut into slices like French fries. Put in pot on stove and cover with water. Boil for 5 min and drain. Make brine with water and salt. Pour over rind until covered and soak overnight. Next day, drain and rinse brine off rind very well. Place back in pot and cover with water and simmer until rind is tender, about 15-20 min. Drain. Make syrup with 2 cups of sugar and 1 1/4 cups water. Heat until syrup is 240 degrees F. Temp will rise quickly. Add watermelon rind, careful not to splash. Temp will drop. Cook again until 240 degrees and rind is slightly translucent. Drop rind into 1 cup sugar to coat and place on parchment paper to cool.

## Ideas and Tips to Making Treats

1. Drop a marshmallow into the bottom of an ice cream cone before adding the ice cream to keep the ice cream from leaking out and what a treat in the end.
2. Use waxed, unflavored dental floss to slice a cake so you can add a filling.
3. Freeze whipped cream cookies or mounds to add to a special dessert or hot chocolate. Spoon the whipped cream into individual sizes, freeze on parchment paper on a baking sheet to use.
4. Cookie batter can be formed in a cup shape when baked on an upside down muffin tin to make a muffin size cup to serve ice cream and you eat the bowl.

## When Cooking with Younger Children

1. Premeasure the ingredients so the child can start the recipe and stay on task. You can monitor how many chocolate chips they are eating if you can have a tasting mini bowl on the side for them to try.
2. Pre-arranging the tools in advance with good handles, plastic or wood spoons and bowls for little bakers.
3. Children lose interest during the baking time, so remember to bring them back to observe the stages of their own baking when the treat is in the oven. They are little scientists after all.
4. The rewards of baking with children is being creative, building fine motor skills, using all sensory development, building their confidence and it is always quality time spent with you.

# Breads & Doughs

## Air Buns

| | |
|---|---|
| 1/2 cup warm water | 1/2 cup lard |
| 1 tsp. sugar | 1 tsp. salt |
| 1 pkg. yeast | 2 Tbsp. vinegar |
| 1/2 cup sugar | 8-10 cups flour |

Mix together; let rise 2 hours punch down let rise 1 hour. Make into buns. Let rise 3 hours. Bake. Brush with butter before and after baking for golden color. *Contributed by Mabel Gulka*

## Babka (overnight)

| | |
|---|---|
| 1 cup sugar (or less) | 1 tsp. salt |
| 1 cup butter | About 7 cups of Flour |
| 1 Tbsp. yeast | 1/4 tsp. turmeric |
| 1 1/2 to 2 cups warm water | Raisins |
| 5 eggs | |

Mix about 9 or 10:00 at night and leave overnight. In morning put in 2 loaf pans or 5-6 cans 1/3 full after it rises, bake. *Contributed by Violet Kyba.*

## Balloon Buns

1 cup scalded milk
1/4 cup sugar
1 tsp. salt
1/4 cup butter or margarine
1/2 tsp. vanilla
1 pkg. yeast dissolved in 1 cup warm water with 1 tsp. sugar
4-5 cups flour
2 eggs beaten
1 bag of large marshmallows
1/2 cup melted butter
1/2 cup white sugar
1 Tbsp. cinnamon

Beat eggs add sugar, then butter. Start yeast mixture to proof. Then add the rest of the ingredients together with egg mixture and add yeast. Knead well. Let rise, punch down, let rise again. When dough is ready take a large marshmallow and dip in 1/2 cup melted butter, then dip into a mixture of 1/2 cup white sugar, and 1 tsp cinnamon. Then pinch off a piece of dough, flatten and wrap the dough around the marshmallow. Dip the bun into sugar mixture and place into greased muffin tins. Or parchment lined baking dish. Let rise in warm place. Cover with wax paper while rising. Bake at 350 for 20 min. Makes about 35 buns. *Contributed by Adeline Dranchuk.*

## Basic Pizza Dough

1 Tbsp. active dry yeast
1/4 cup lukewarm water
1 Tbsp. sugar
1 tsp. salt

1 Tbsp. oil
1 cup boiling water
2 3/4 cups flour

Dissolve yeast and sugar in lukewarm water. Let rise 10 minutes. Mix all other ingredients kneading in the last of the flour. Let rise 5 minutes while you grease pizza pans or cookie sheets. This makes a very soft dough. Stretch and pull into place on the pan. Let rise slightly while you prepare your topping.

## Beetnik Bread or Buns

Bread dough (used for beatniks, frozen bread dough etc.)
Dried onion flakes (ground roughly to not have big pieces)
Garlic powder
Dried or fresh dill (if fresh dry the dill thoroughly)
Un-cooked Beet tops no stems (cut into bite size pieces dried thoroughly)
butter or margarine

Roll out the bread dough after the first rise, into a rectangle (like for cinnamon buns). Spread butter over the dough, then the dill, garlic powder, dried onion and beet tops as much as you prefer. Ensure you use dry ingredients as the only moisture in the roll should be the butter.

Carefully roll up the dough. For bread place in a bread loaf pan to rise then bake at 350 for about 45 minutes until golden brown. For buns cut the rolled up dough into slices (like for cinnamon buns) add extra butter on top. Let rise and bake in greased 13"x 9" pans. Bake at 350 for 20-25 minutes, until the buns brown. Serve with borscht. *Contributed by Harold Mudry.*

# Beetnik Dough

Dissolve and let rise 10-15 mins:
1 cup warm water
2 tsp. sugar
2 pkgs. or 2 Tbsp. yeast

1/2 cup butter or oil
2 eggs
1 tsp. salt
1 cup scalded milk
2 tsp. sugar
5-6 cups flour

Mix and knead. Let rise 3/4 hour. Punch down and let rise again. Make into small balls. Roll in beet leaves that have been washed the night before and left on a tea towel to dry overnight. Lay them on a greased cookie sheet. Let rise 1/2 hour or more. Bake at 375 degrees F. for 20-30 minutes. To serve, warm the beetniks in a casserole dish. Boil whipping cream with green onion and dill and pour over beetniks. You can use frozen bread dough to make these beetniks. *Contributed by Devon Dziaduck.*

## Blueberry-Lemon Scones

3 cups all-purpose flour
1/2 cup sugar
Zest of 1 lemon
1 tsp. baking powder
1 tsp. baking soda

1/4 cup cold butter, cut into small cubes
1 cup buttermilk
1/4 cup unsweetened applesauce
1 cup fresh or frozen blueberries

Glaze:
1 1/2 - 2 tsp. fresh lemon juice

3/4 cup confectioners' sugar

Preheat the oven to 400. Line 2 baking sheets with parchment. Put flour in a large bowl. Reserve 1 Tbsp. of the flour in a small bowl. Add granulated sugar, lemon zest, baking powder, baking soda and 1/2 tsp. salt to large bowl with flour. Cut in butter with pastry blender or hands until fine crumbs form. Combine buttermilk and applesauce. Gradually mix with dry ingredients. Stirring gently to form dough. Toss berries with reserved flour in the small bowl and gently fold into batter. Mix well, but do not overwork dough. Separate into 2 equal portions. Flour a clean surface. Press 1 portion of the dough at a time, into a 1" thick round cutting each round into 6 wedges. Transfer the wedges to prepared baking sheets. Bake until firm to the touch and golden brown on top. 15 to 18 minutes. Cool on wire rack. Prepare glaze: gradually mix lemon juice into the sugar, until just pourable in consistency. Drizzle over scones. Cover leftover scones with plastic wrap to store up to 3 days.

## Buttermilk Cinnamon Buns

Dissolve 2 Tbsp. yeast in 1/2 cup warm water with 1 Tbsp. sugar. Heat: 1 1/2 cups buttermilk, and 1/2 cup melted butter

2 eggs
1/2 cup sugar
1 tsp salt

2 tsp. baking powder
5 - 6 cups flour or more to knead well

Don't have to let rise, roll out with cinnamon and sugar mixture and then let rise before baking. This recipe makes 2 - 9" x 13" pans. *Contributed by Nellie Kitchen.*

## Chocolate Chip Banana Monkey Bread

3 bananas, (1 cut into slices, 2 cut into half-slices
1 cup dark chocolate chips

3 cans biscuit dough
1 cup sugar
3 tsp. cinnamon

Glaze:

2 sticks butter

1/2 cup brown sugar

Garnish:

Banana slices

Dark chocolate chips

Preheat the oven to 350°F/180°C. Cut 2 bananas into slices and again in half, set aside. In a bowl mix sugar and cinnamon, set aside. Cut each biscuit round in half and flatten into rounds. Stuff each round with one piece of the halved banana coins and chocolate chips. Close the round together by pinching at the seam and roll into a ball in your hands. Place the balls in the cinnamon sugar mix and gently toss to coat. In a saucepan over medium heat melt the butter and brown sugar until one, stirring occasionally. Set aside to cool. Grease a Bundt pan and line the bottom with full banana coins. Layer half of the balls in the pan and pour half of the glaze on top. Sprinkle a handful of chocolate chips over top. Repeat last 2 steps. Bake for 40-50 min. until the crust is a deep dark brown on top. (if browning too much you can cover it with aluminum foil) Remove from oven and allow it to cool or about 15-30 minutes before turning it over onto a plate. *Contributed by Brent Matsalla.*

## Cinnamon Buns

Soak: 1 Tbsp. yeast, 1 tsp sugar in 3/4 cup lukewarm water

1 cup sour cream
1/2 tsp. baking soda
1/4 cup white sugar
1/2 tsp. salt
1-1/2 Tbsp. butter
1 egg, beaten
3-1/2 to 4 cups flour

Bring cream to a boil and add soda. Remove from heat and add sugar, salt and butter. Then cooled to lukewarm, add yeast mixture, egg and flour. Allow to rise for 5 to 10 minutes. Roll dough, sprinkle with brown sugar and cinnamon mixture cut and put on a greased cookie sheet. Let rise and Bake at 350 for 10 to 15 min. *Contributed by Doris Slugoski.*

## Cinnamon Buns with Buttermilk

Dissolve 2 Tbsp. yeast in 1/2 cup warm water

| Heat: | 1/2 cup sugar |
| 1 1/2 cups buttermilk | 1 tsp. salt |
| 1/2 cup melted butter | 2 tsp. baking powder |
| In mixing bowl add | 1/2 cup water |
| 2 eggs | 4 1/2 - 5 1/2 cups flour add enough to be able to knead the dough |

Don't have to let this dough rise, you can roll it out right away and then let rise before baking.
This recipe makes 2 - 9" x 13" pans.

Cinnamon filling:
| 1/2 cup brown sugar | 2 Tbsp. corn syrup |
| 1/4 cup melted butter | Cinnamon |

NOTE: if you don't have buttermilk, substitute is 1 cup yogurt, 1 Tbsp. lemon juice and 1/2 cup milk.

## Easter Baba

1 cup milk
1/3 cup flour
2 tsp. sugar
1/2 cup lukewarm water
3 pkg. dry yeast
10 to 12 egg yolks
2 whole eggs
1 tsp. salt
1 cup sugar
2 tsp. vanilla
Grated rind of 1 lemon
1 cup melted butter
5 1/2 to 6 cups flour
1 cup raisins or other fruit

Bring milk to a boil, remove from heat and add to the 1/3 cup flour, beat smooth. To lukewarm water dissolve sugar, sprinkle yeast, let stand 10 minutes. Combine with milk flour paste. Beat well. Cover and let rise in warm place until light and bubbly, beat eggs together with salt and sugar until light. Beat in butter, vanilla and lemon. Combine with yeast mixture and mix well. Stir in enough flour to make a soft dough, work the dough with a spoon for 10 minutes. Raisins or fruit should be added after kneading. Cover and let rise in warm place until double in bulk, punch down and let rise again. Prepare tall round 48 oz. tins by buttering very well and sprinkling with cornmeal or fine bread crumbs (loaf pans can be used as well). Fill 1/3 full. Cover and let rise in warm place until it reaches the brim of the can, it should triple in bulk. Brush loaves with beaten egg diluted with 2 Tbsp. milk. Bake in moderate oven 350 for 10 minutes. Then lower the temperature to 300 for 30 minutes. Lower temperature again to 250 for 15 to 20 minutes. Tap each loaf gently from pan when baked. Do not cool loaves on hard surface this is very important. Make a pillow of tea towels. *Contributed by Rosie Wolkowski.*

## French Bread

1 1/2 Tbsp. instant yeast
1/2 cup warm water
1 1/2 Tbsp. sugar
2 cups water (room temp)
1 1/2 Tbsp. oil
2 1/8 tsp. sea salt
6 cups all-purpose flour
1 egg beaten, for egg wash

Combine the yeast, sugar and 1/2 cup warm water; let it proof for 10 minutes. In a stand mixer add 2 cups warm water, oil, salt and 3 cups of the flour. Mix until flour is incorporated, then add the remaining 3 cups of flour, mixing between. Knead for 4-5 minutes, this is a sticky dough so don't over add flour. Important to make the bread chewy: Turn onto a floured rolling surface, and every 10-15 minutes for the next hour, knead the dough with a little bit of flour. Cover the dough with plastic wrap between kneading to prevent drying. Divide the dough into 2 loaves (or more for smaller loaves). Spread each portion out into a rough rectangle and roll up like a jellyroll. Take the two ends and tuck under the long loaf. Place on a lightly greased cookie sheet. Spray a sharp knife with cooking spray and cut diagonal lines into the tops of each loaf. Brush the loaves with beaten egg wash covering it completely because this will provide the brown color. Let rise for 30 minutes. Bake at 425 for 10 minutes, then at 375 for 15-20 minutes, rotating pan halfway through. *Contributed by Theresa Mudry.*

## Grandma Francis Matsalla's Old Time Tea Biscuits

1 cup sour cream
2 eggs
2/3 cup sugar

3 tsp. baking powder
1/2 tsp. baking soda
Enough flour to make a soft dough.

Roll out - cut into circles, squares or rectangles any size you prefer. If desired, sprinkle with sugar before baking. Bake at 350 until brown. *Contributed by Ann Belitsky.*

## Hot Tea Biscuits

*Tea biscuits with cheese.*

7 to 8 cups flour
3/4 cup butter
3/4 cup Crisco
1 1/4 cups white sugar
5 heaping tsp. baking powder
2 tsp. cream of tartar
1 tsp. salt not too full
2 tsp. vanilla
4 eggs

Cold milk to make a dough not to soft. Could add currants or raisins. Rub the butter and Crisco into the flour mixture (dry ingredients). Roll out but not too thin. Just before baking brush the biscuits with cream or milk and sprinkle sugar on top (optional). Bake at 325 for 10 minutes then turn to 300 for 20 minutes, more or less see how your oven is. Look at the bottom of the biscuits, if they are light brown. This recipe makes 4 dozen small ones. They freeze very well. Option: add 1/2 cup grated cheddar cheese. *Contributed by Anna Romanow in 1982.*

## Jodi's Scones

500 ml all-purpose flour
50 ml sugar
15 ml baking powder
5 ml salt

75 ml cold butter or margarine
50 ml currants or raisins
125 ml milk
2 eggs

Measure the flour, sugar, baking powder, and salt into a medium bowl. Stir to combine. With a pastry blender or two knives, cut butter into flour mixture until the mixture resembles oatmeal. Stir in the currants. Using a liquid measure, measure mild and add 1 egg and 1 egg yolk; mix with a fork (reserve egg white for use as glaze later). Gradually add milk mixture to flour mixture, mixing lightly with a fork until the ingredients are a soft dough consistency. (More or less liquid may be required). Turn out onto lightly floured counter and knead 10 to 20 times. Roll dough into a circle so the dough is 2 cm thick. Brush with slightly beaten egg white. Sprinkle with sugar. Cut into 5 or 8 pie shaped wedges. Place on ungreased lightly floured cookie sheet. Bake at 220 deg. C. For 12 to 15 minutes. Serve hot or cold. Makes 6 – 8 scones. *Contributed by Jodi Ledding.*

## No-Knead Bread (Olive Bread)

3 cups sifted all-purpose or bread flour

1/4 tsp. yeast

1 tsp. salt

1 1/2 cups hot water, not boiling, use thermometer 125-130 degrees

2 Tbsp. extra flour for shaping

3/4 cup sliced black olives (optional)

Combine flour, yeast and salt in a large bowl. Stir in water until it's well combined. Stir in sliced olives if making olive bread. Cover with plastic wrap and let stand for 3 hours. Dough will become puffy and dotted with bubbles. Put on a well-floured surface and sprinkle dough with a little flour. Using your hands or a scraper fold dough over a few times & shape into a ball and flip over. Make a few score marks with a knife on the top. Place in a parchment paper-lined bowl (not wax paper) and cover with a towel. Let stand for about 35 minutes. Put a Dutch oven with lid in a cold oven and preheat to 450, about 20-30 min. minimum. Lift the parchment paper with dough from the bowl and put it into the hot pot with the parchment paper. Cover and bake for 30 min. Remove lid and parchment paper. Return, uncovered, to oven and bake for 10 – 15min. more. Let it cool at least 15 minutes before slicing. *Contributed by Brent Matsalla.*

## No Yeast Pizza Crust or Tea Biscuit Dough

*Continued on next page…*

2 cups flour (could be mixed with some whole wheat and some white)

4 tsp. baking powder

1 Tbsp. sugar for pizza crust and use 2 Tbsp. sugar for tea biscuits

1/2 tsp. cream of tartar

1/2 cup cold butter

1 tsp. salt

3/4 cup cold milk

Mix first 5 ingredients dry and then cut in the butter adding the milk. This makes a soft dough not sticky. For pizza crust spread on pan and top. To ensure the crust is crispier you could put into oven at 400 for 5 minutes without toppings, remove and add toppings return to oven. Cook with toppings 7 min. then remove from oven and add cheese. Broil until cheese browns and bubbles.

For tea biscuits you can add 1/2 cup raisins and roll out and cut into shapes. Bake at 350 for 12-15 minutes or until edges are light brown. Cooking time varies on the thickness of the biscuit. *Contributed by Theresa Mudry.*

## Noodle Dough

Put 12 cups flour in a big plastic bowl. In a blender break 12 eggs and add water to make 4 cups liquid. Pour egg mixture into flour and mix so all flour is mixed. Put in fridge in a plastic bag for about 2 hours or more. Then knead again but back in fridge in a plastic or bowl and its ready to cut next day.

Cheese:
5 1/2 cups cottage cheese
1 1/2 tsp. baking soda

1 1/2 tsp. paprika
1/2 cup butter
1/2 cup sour cream

First boil the cottage cheese, paprika, soda and butter until dissolved then add cream and boil until smooth.

## Pastry Dough

3 cups flour
1 Tbsp. sugar
1/2 tsp. salt

1 cup lard
2/3 cup milk
1 egg

*Contributed by Elsie Carsten.*

## Pastry for Pie

4 1/2 cups flour
4 Tbsp. brown sugar
1 Tbsp. baking powder

2 cups lard
1 tsp. salt

Mix lard and flour and then other ingredients above.

1 egg
Water

1 Tbsp. vinegar

In measuring cup, beat 1 egg slightly with a fork, add water to 1/4 cup mark, add vinegar.
Add to lard and flour mixture.

## Perishke (Baked) #1

1/2 cup oil
1/2 cup melted shortening
4 eggs
1/4 cup sugar
1 tsp. salt
2 cups warm water
2 Tbsp. yeast dissolved in 3/4 cup warm water
Enough flour to make a soft dough

Mix ingredients and knead as for buns. Let rise about 1 1/2 hours. Roll out and fill with potatoes (more or less a small Dutch oven full of boiled potatoes mashed with salt and pepper and butter) Bake in moderate oven until golden brown. *Contributed by Joe and Olga Fullawka.*

## Perishke (Baked) #2

1/2 cup Mazola oil
4 eggs
1 tsp. Salt
2 Tbsp. yeast dissolved in 3/4 cup warm water

8 cups flour (approximately)
1/2 cup shortening (melted)
1/2 cup sugar
2 cups warm water

Knead as buns (let rise) about 2 hrs. Roll out, fill and place on a cookie sheets. Bake for 20-25 minutes at 350 degrees. *Contributed by Olga Fullawka.*

## Perishke (overnight dough)

1 cup shortening
1/2 tsp. salt
3 Tbsp. sugar
4 cups flour

1 pkg. yeast
1/2 cup warm water
1 cup sour cream
3 eggs well beaten

Mix together salt and sugar and cut in shortening (as for pie) dissolve yeast in warm water and let stand 10 min. When yeast has risen add sour cream and well beaten eggs, then add liquid mixture to dry ingredients, mixing and kneading well. Refrigerate overnight and in morning make them out. *Contributed by Pearl Hadubiak.*

## Perishke (baked with buttermilk)

1 cup buttermilk
2 Tbsp. vinegar
1/2 lb. margarine
2 eggs
1/2 tsp. salt
3 cups flour
3 tsp. baking powder
1/2 tsp. baking soda

*Contributed by Caroline Boychuk.*

## Perishke Dough with Saskatoon Filling

| | |
|---|---|
| 1/2 cup soft butter | 3 eggs beaten |
| 1/2 cup sugar | 1 tsp. vanilla |
| 3 tsp. baking powder | 1 cup cream |
| 1/2 tsp. salt | 3 cups flour to make a soft dough that is stiff enough to roll |

Saskatoon filling:

| | |
|---|---|
| 2 cups fresh or frozen Saskatoons | 1 Tbsp. flour |
| 2/3 cup sugar | Mix together and use to fill each perishke circle. |

Mix first 8 ingredients to form the dough. Make into balls the size of walnuts. Roll each individually and fill with Saskatoon filling. Fold ends up and pinch ends leaving center open. Bake for 15-20 minutes at 350 degrees. *Contributed by Rosie Wolkowski.*

## Pie and Pastry Dough (No-Roll) (aka Koocha Dough)

4-5 cups of flour
1/2 tsp. baking soda
3/4 cup sugar (could use half white, brown or coconut sugar)
2 tsp. baking powder

4 cups margarine or 1 lb. lard
1 tsp. cinnamon (optional)
2 eggs
3/4 cup sour cream

Add first 6 ingredients and mix into a crumble. Add eggs and sour cream beat to combine the flour well. Press 1/2 the crumb mixture into 3 or 4 greased 12" pans making an edge on the sides to hold the filling. Depending on your filling, you can make the crust as thick or as thin as you prefer note that the crust is soft and flaky. Put any filling on top and cover with remaining crumb mixture dropped by 1/2 tablespoons on top. Bake in a 350 oven for 40-50 minutes until brown. Cool and serve sprinkled with vanilla sugar. This recipe freezes well.

## Pie Crusts

11 cups flour
2 1/2 cups butter or 1 1/4 lbs.
2 1/2 cups lard or 1 1/4 lbs.
1 tsp. baking soda

5 eggs
1 cup water
1 tsp. salt

Beat eggs well, add water. Mix remainder of ingredients.

## Pierogies (Fried with Cheese)

8 cups flour
4 cups fine dry cottage cheese
1 tsp. baking soda
4 eggs, beaten

2 tsp. salt
3/4 cup vegetable oil
2 1/2 cups water (approximately)

Mix and roll out like you would for pierogies. Fill with potato filling of choice. Fry each in oil. Serve with sour cream. *Contributed and a favorite of Grandpa Joe Zarazun.*

## Pierogi Dough with Instant Potatoes

5 cups flour
1 tsp. salt
1/2 cup instant potatoes

1/2 cup oil
2 cups hot water

Mix oil and water. (Tip: you may need to add more water to make a soft dough)

## Pierogi Dough with Mashed Potatoes

3 cups well mashed potatoes
3 eggs
1/2 cup oil

1 tsp. salt
4 cups flour

## Pierogi Dough with Baking Powder

**Bonus Video: How to Make Pierogies Fast**

Scan the QR Code to the left to see the video.

No scanner? Free code scanning apps are available at your app store.

Access the video directly here:
https://youtu.be/dVdED-UF2u8

2-1/2 cups flour in bowl
4 Tbsp. Mazola oil
1 egg

Pinch of salt
Pinch of baking powder
Add 3/4 cup or more boiling water to form dough.

See filling next page. *Contributed by Marlene Mudry.*

## Pierogi Sauerkraut and Potato Filling

3 medium potatoes cooked with 2 cloves of garlic and salt. Mash with pepper, butter/marg. and 1/2 an onion chopped fine. 2 cups of sauerkraut chopped fine, drained and fried on oil or margarine until color changes. This will make only about a cup when fried down. Mix together and cool. Using a tsp. size cookie scoop, shape the potato and sauerkraut into balls. Trying to make sure there is no long ends sticking out because this will catch in the edge of the pierogi and not seal. Roll out the dough making sure more flour is at the bottom of the dough. Place the balls on the dough ½" from the edge dough just enough apart to ensure your cutter is not to close. Fold and just cover up the ball with the edge of the dough. Gently form the dough around the ball to prevent any air bubbles from forming. Using the cutter press to cut the dough around the formed pierogi. My cutter is a can from tuna and crackers (or antipasto salad that comes with crackers.) This can seems to seal the edge. Place on floured sheet. This recipe will make 39-40 pierogies depending on the size you choose to cut. No waste of re-rolling dough or edges using this method.

Note: after rolling out the dough and cutting pierogies out leave the remained edges to rest on the side between rolling, this will soften for re-rolling at the end. *Contributed by Theresa Mudry.*

## Pierogi Sour Cream Dough

4 Tbsp. sour cream
4 Tbsp. margarine
2 eggs

6 to 7 cups flour
Enough warm water to make soft dough.

*Contributed by Gladys Grodzinski.*

## Pizza Dough

Dissolve 1 pkg. yeast in 1 tsp. sugar with 1/2 cup of warm water.
Set to proof 10 minutes and then Mix with
2 cups water

3 tsp. sugar
1/2 tsp. salt
3-4 Tbsp. oil
About 5 1/2 cups flour

Let dough rise about 3 hours until double in bulk. Make into shape of pizza pan. Set oven at 400 and add favourite toppings pepperoni, cheese, use spaghetti sauce or pizza sauce. Bake until cheese is melted and browning of crust occurs. *Contributed by Linda Dyck.*

## Poppy Seed Roll

Dough:

| | |
|---|---|
| 3 cups boiled milk | 1 cup butter |
| 1 tsp. salt | 3 Tbsp. yeast |
| 7 egg yolks | 1 Tbsp. sugar |
| 2 cups sugar | 1/3 cup warm water |

Mix butter, sugar, beaten egg yolks, and 4 cups flour. Add milk and salt. Don't let rise, sweet dough doesn't like rising in a warm area.

Filling:

| | |
|---|---|
| 7 egg whites | 2 cups sugar |
| 2 cups poppy seeds | A little cream |

Roll dough to ½" thickness and spread with filling. Roll tightly and tuck ends under. Let rise 1 hour. Bake at 350 for 20-30 min.

## Pumpkin Bread

| | |
|---|---|
| 2 cups canned pumpkin | 2 tsp. baking soda |
| 3 cups sugar | 2 tsp. cinnamon |
| 1 cup water | 1 tsp. salt |
| 1 cup vegetable oil | 1 tsp. baking powder |
| 4 eggs | 1/2 tsp. nutmeg |
| 3 1/3 cups all-purpose flour | 3/4 tsp. ground cloves |

Heat the oven to 350. Combine pumpkin, sugar, water, vegetable oil and eggs. Beat until well mixed. Measure the flour, baking soda, cinnamon, salt, baking powder, nutmeg and cloves into another bowl and mix. Slowly add the dry ingredients to the pumpkin mixture, beating until smooth. Grease two 9" x 5" loaf pans and dust with flour. Divide batter between the two pans. Bake for 60-70 minutes or until a toothpick inserted in center comes out clean. Cool for 10-15 minutes, then remove from pans. *Contributed by Brent Matsalla.*

4 cups flour
2 heaping Tbsp. quick rise yeast
3 cups water
1 tsp. salt
2 eggs, beaten
1/3 cup oil
3/4 cup sugar (for buns) or 1/3 cup sugar (for bread)

Mix 4 cups flour and 2 tablespoons yeast. Add the rest of the ingredients. Add 4 to 5 cups flour to form the dough. Knead the dough until it is not sticky. Cover and let it rise for 15 minutes. Punch the dough down, cover and let it rise for 15 minutes. Punch down and cover once again for 15 minutes so a total of 45 minutes of rising time.

Shape into buns or loaves. Place into greased loaf pans or cookie sheets and let rise for about 1 hour. Option: substitute 2 cups whole wheat flour for white flour. For cheese buns, roll the dough flat spread with melted butter, sprinkle 1 cup grated cheddar cheese and roll like for cinnamon buns.

Cinnamon buns would be: 1/2 to 3/4 cup sugar and 1/4 cup cinnamon or as much as you prefer. Cut into one inch pieces; put it cut side up on cookie sheets and sprinkle with more cheese over the top. Option for the cinnamon bun version; add butter to the top of the cinnamon buns mixed with a little cinnamon and 1 tablespoon sugar. Bake at 350 for 15 to 20 minutes for buns and 35 to 40 minutes for loaves.

## Stollen Bread for Christmas or Easter

1/2 cup raisins

1/2 cup orange peel

1/4 cup citron or lemon peel

Dust with 2 Tbsp. flour before adding:

1/4 cup warm water

1/4 tsp. salt

1 pkg. yeast

4 Tbsp. butter

Dissolve together and proof.

2 eggs beaten

1 tsp. lemon rind

3/4 cup milk

Warm the milk and mix with other

1/4 cup sugar

ingredients.

2 2/3 to 3 cups flour

Shredded almonds (optional)

1/8 tsp. cardoon, nutmeg and cinnamon

Mix all together let rise 1 hour punch down. Let rise again 1 hour. Divide into 2 loaves and let rise on cookie sheet until double in size to form long rectangular loaves. Bake. Ice with thin icing drizzle if desired, using icing sugar and milk.

## Tart Dough

2 cups flour

1 tsp. vanilla

2 Tbsp. brown sugar

1 beaten egg

3 tsp. baking powder

1/2 cup sweet milk

1 cup shortening

*Contributed by Stefka Zarazun.*

## Tenderflake Pie Crust

5 1/2 cups flour

1 Tbsp. vinegar

2 tsp. salt

1 egg

1 tsp. baking powder

Cold water

1 lb. tender flake lard

## Torn Pants (Easy Polish Chrusciki) Deep Fried Dough

| | |
|---|---|
| 2 eggs | 1 cup flour |
| Pinch of salt | |

Icing sugar and 1 Tbsp. cinnamon for dusting after cooking.

Mix flour, salt and eggs. Roll out the dough (thin like for pie dough) and cut into rectangles about 4" long x 1" long. Cut a slot in the middle of the rectangle. Pull one end of the rectangle through the slot. Deep fry in hot oil. When cooled dust with icing sugar.

## Two Hour Buns

| | |
|---|---|
| 3 cups warm water | 2 Tbsp. yeast |
| 1/2 cup sugar | 2 eggs, well beaten |
| 6 Tbsp. oil | 8 cups flour |
| 1 tsp. salt | |

Combine first four ingredients. Add beaten eggs. Mix flour and yeast thoroughly. Add flour and yeast to the rest of the ingredients to make a soft dough. Pat with oil, let rise 15 minutes. Punch down, on the fourth rise. Make into buns, let rise 1 hour. Bake at 350 until golden brown.

## Yorkshire Pudding

| | |
|---|---|
| 1/4 cup roast pan juices | 1/4 tsp dried oregano |
| 1 1/4 cups flour | 2 eggs |
| 1/2 tsp salt | 1 cup milk |
| 1/4 tsp dried thyme | |

Preheat the oven to 450. Coat 8 muffin cups with non-stick spray. Divide pan juices among cups. Transfer muffin cups to baking sheet. Place in oven until cups are hot. (1-2 minutes) Meanwhile, in medium bowl combine flour, salt and spices, set aside. In another bowl lightly beat eggs with milk; stir into flour mixture until combined. Evenly divide batter among hot cups; bake for 15-20 minutes or until puffed and golden. Serve immediately.

## Zucchini Loaf

| | |
|---|---|
| 1 1/2 cups white sugar | 2 tsp. vanilla |
| 2 cups grated unpeeled raw zucchini | 1/4 tsp. baking powder |
| 2 cups flour | 3 eggs |
| 2 tsp. soda | 2 tsp. cinnamon |
| 1 tsp. salt | 1 tsp. nutmeg |
| 1 cup oil | |

Chopped nuts, raisins or fruit. Mix together, dry ingredients and wet ingredients combine. Makes 2 loaves. Bake at 350 for 45-50 minutes. *Contributed by Eleanor Hadubiak.*

# Pickles & Preserves

## 3 Day Pickles

**Day 1.**

| | |
|---|---|
| 2 cauliflower | 8 or 9 cucumbers (long English) |
| 2 lbs. onion (pickling type) | 1 cup pickling salt |
| 2 red peppers | 1/4 tsp. alum (optional) |

Combine together. Add hot water to cover.

**Day 2.**

Drain the brine into pot and boil. Rinse vegetables and pour brine over again.

**Day 3.**

| | |
|---|---|
| 8 cups white sugar | 1 tsp. celery salt |
| 4 cups vinegar | 1 tsp. turmeric |

Drain and rinse and put into jars. Boil vinegar, sugar, celery salt and turmeric for 2 minutes and pour over the vegetables in the jars. *Contributed by Lena Skrepneck.*


## Bacon Jam

| | |
|---|---|
| 2 pounds bacon cut into 1" pieces | 4 cloves crushed garlic |
| 1 onion diced | 1 Tbsp. red pepper flakes |
| 1/2 cup brown sugar | 1 red bell pepper |
| 1/2 cup bacon fat | 1 cup brewed coffee |
| 1/2 cup red wine vinegar | Salt and pepper |

Cook bacon on med heat but don't let it get too crispy. Reserve 1/2 cup bacon fat. Sweat onions in a pan to reduce moisture and cook until soft. In a dry pan blacken the red pepper and finely chop. Put everything in a large pot on medium heat. Cook until reduced by 1/3 and it thickens. Let cool. Put half in the blender and pulse until smooth. Mix with other 1/2 and store in refrigerated mason jars. Will keep for 2 to 3 weeks. *Contributed by Brent Matsalla.*


## Beet and Horseradish Relish

| | |
|---|---|
| 1 cup of finely chopped pickled beets | 1/2 to 1/3 cup of prepared horseradish (either cream style or vinegar) |

Mix together and serve. Use more horseradish for stronger taste. Will stay in the fridge for 2 weeks or freeze and thaw to use. *Contributed by Harold Mudry.*

## Beet Pickles

3 cups vinegar  
2 cups water (juice which you boiled the beets can also be used)

1 cup sugar  
1 1/2 tsp. salt

Pickling spice and cinnamon stick to add to the boiling brine (in a bag, or spice diffuser)  
Boil together pour over beets in a jar and seal.  
Alternative: this recipe can be baked in the oven instead of boiling the beets on the top of the store. Bake for about 1 hour or until a fork can be inserted easily in the beets. Remove from oven cool, peel and cut into cubes or slices.  
See *Easy Beet Preparation* under *Miscellaneous* to assist with this recipe.


## Beet Relish

Grind 6 cups of cooked beets. Boil the following for 2 minutes:

1 3/4 cups vinegar  
2 cups sugar

1 Tbsp. pickling salt

Add 1 pkg. of Certo. Boil for 6 minutes more. Put in jars and seal. *Contributed by Marian Skoretz.*  
See *Easy Beet Preparation* under *Miscellaneous* to assist with this recipe.


## Canned Fish

1 gallon filleted fish  
1 1/2 cups Mazola oil (separated for the recipe 1/2 and then 1 cup)

1 can 28 oz. canned tomatoes  
3/4 cup vinegar (separated 1/2 and 1/4)  
2 Tbsp. pickling spice

Cut fish into pieces, put into a roaster. Add 1 can of tomatoes, 1/2 cup of vinegar, 1/2 cup oil and the salt. Bake for 4 hours at 350. Stir once or twice. Take out of oven and add: 1 can tomato soup with remaining oil and vinegar. Pack in jars and boil the quarts 2 hours, if you are using pints boil for 1 1/2 hours. *Contributed by Mary Rieger.*


## Canned Horseradish

2-4 cups shredded horseradish  
2 cups cream  
2 cups sugar  
1 tsp. salt

1/3 cup flour  
2 eggs  
1/2 cup vinegar

Boil the ingredients together (except horseradish). Add horseradish when done, pack into jars and refrigerate or freeze.

## Company Best Pickles

15 medium cucumbers

8 cups white sugar

2 Tbsp. mixed pickling spices (tied in a bag)

5 tsp. salt

4 cups vinegar

Cover whole cucumbers with boiling water let stand until morning. Drain. Repeat this procedure for the next 3 mornings. Fifth morning. Drain, slice in ½" pieces. Combine sugar, spices, salt and vinegar and bring to a boil. Pour over cucumbers. Let stand 2 days. On the seventh morning: bring all to a boil and seal.

## Corn to Freeze

10 cups corn off cob raw

1/4 cup sugar

1 pint water

1 Tbsp. pickling salt

Mix well and put in shallow pan or roaster covered in 350 oven until it starts to bubble. Leave in shut off oven for 1/2 hour.

## Crisp Pickles

6 quarts sliced cucumbers

1 quart sliced onions

Pour boiling water over cucumbers, let stand 1/2 hour. Drain water. Pour cold water over cucumbers add ice cubes to it and let stand 1 hour. Drain.

1 each of red and green pepper finely sliced

Brine:

1 1/2 cups vinegar

5 cups white sugar

5 cups water

1/2 cup salt

1 Tbsp. pickling spices in a cheese cloth bag

Boil brine ingredients together for 5 minutes. Remove pickling spice bag. Put all vegetables in brine and bring to a boil. Put into jars and seal. *Contributed by Eleanor and Twila Hadubiak.*

## Cucumber Chunks

5 quarts cucumbers cut into 1" chunks

1/2 cup salt

Hot boiling water to cover cucumbers. Leave this overnight.

*Continued on next page…*

Syrup:

| | |
|---|---|
| 3 cups sugar | 1 tsp. dry mustard |
| 3 cups vinegar | 1 tsp. celery seed |
| 1 cup water | 1/2 tsp. turmeric |
| 1 tsp. whole spice | 1 tsp. mustard |

Drain Cucumbers, boil syrup, add cucumbers. Heat to boiling point and put in jars and seal. *Contributed by Eleanor Ludba.*


## Cucumber Pickles #1

| | |
|---|---|
| 1 cup white sugar | Cucumber to fill 3 big jars |
| 1 cup vinegar | Dill and garlic |
| 1 cup salt | Picking spice |
| Water to fill the 3 big jars | |

Pour hot over cucumbers in jars and seal.


## Cucumber Relish

| | |
|---|---|
| 6 cups peeled and chopped cucumbers with the center seeds taken out. | 3 cups chopped onions |
| | 3 red peppers (chopped) |

After all this is done, pour 6 cups of sugar and 1 Tbsp. salt over and let stand until the sugar goes through the vegetables. Put on stove and pour 1 pint of vinegar over. Cook this for about 35 minutes, until the vegetables are clear in appearance.

Then mix:

| | |
|---|---|
| 1/2 cup flour | 1 Tbsp. turmeric |
| 2 Tbsp. mustard | 1 pint of vinegar |

Pour into the vegetables that are cooked and cook 10 minutes more. Pour into jars. *Contributed by Francis Makowsky.*


## Dilled Cucumbers

| | |
|---|---|
| 1 cup vinegar | 2 1/2 Tbsp. pickling salt |
| 1 Tbsp. sugar | |

For each 2 quart jar add garlic and dill and cucumbers with the above. *Contributed by Bernice Gulka.*

## Dilled Cucumbers with Carrots

To a 2 quart sealer put a little dill on the bottom, 1 clove garlic, a carrot or two and a few pickling spices. Fill the jar with cucumbers and add 2 Tbsp. brown sugar and 2 Tbsp. salt. Now cook 4 cups of water and 3/4 cup vinegar together. Fill the jars over cucumbers with the brine and seal. (To seal you can put the jars into a canner with hot water and tighten lids and store)

## Dill Pickles #1

Place cucumbers, dill, and garlic cloves in sterilized jars.

Make a brine of:
1/2 cup vinegar
1/4 cup white sugar
1/2 cup pickling salt
11 cups water

Bring brine to a boil and fill into Jars. Seal immediately and store in fridge after they cool. Makes about 5 quarts. *Contributed by Bernice Gulka.*

## Dill Pickles #2

| | |
|---|---|
| 1/2 cup pickling salt | 1/2 cup vinegar |
| 2 1/2 cups brown sugar | 10-11 cups water |

Bring to a boil and pour hot on cucumbers to seal jars. *Contributed by Evelyn Kowalchuk.*

## Dill Pickles #3

20 cups water
1 cup vinegar
Add to 2 quart sealer
Dill, garlic, pickling spice,
2 Tbsp. salt
2 Tbsp. brown sugar

Put in jars to seal.

## Dill Pickles #4

2 Tbsp. salt
2 Tbsp. vinegar
1 Tbsp. brown sugar

Dill, garlic and pickling spices
Add boiling water or cold water to each jar
filled with cucumbers

*Contributed by Mary Obodiak.*

Prepare a salt brine:

Dissolve 2 tsp of sea salt into 2 cups warm water and let cool. Take a quart size/large mason jar. Add a handful of fresh or frozen pineapple chunks. About 3 stalks of raw rhubarb peeled and chopped into 2" pieces. 2-3 large shallots (or small onions) peeled and halved. 2 large green jalapeno/chili peppers halved and stem removed. You want to be able to fill the jar with fruit/veg until there is a couple inches room left at the top. You can experiment with adding garlic, or different fruit or peppers depending on what you have available or in-season.

Cram all the ingredients into the jar tightly so they will hold each other in place below the brine once it is added. Pour brine over the fruit/veg adding enough to cover and have everything submerged. You may not need to use all the brine depending on how your jar gets packed. I also like to weigh down the items with fermentation weights, keeping everything submerged prevents spoiling during fermentation. Place the lid on, hand tighten, and leave on the counter for 3 days out of the sun in a cool place.

On the 3rd day open your jar. You will likely find it bubbling as you release the pressure of the jar. Blend everything together, adding salt if needed or other spices if desired. I like to add a bit of lime juice or lime powder at this stage. Store in fridge and eat on everything from eggs to tacos! *Contributed by Mandelle Waddell.*

## Freezer Corn

Cut corn from cobs raw to equal 2 cups.     1/4 cup sugar
Add 2 tsp. salt     2 cups water

Mix well and simmer 10 min. Cool in flat pans, package and freeze. The corn may darken with freezing but will come clear with cooking. To cook use a small amount of water.


## Freezer Pickles

7 cups thinly sliced cucumbers     1/2 tsp. celery seed
3 onions sliced fine     1 Tbsp. pickling spice
1 green pepper chopped     1 cup vinegar
2 cups sugar

Mix ingredients together well and pack into freezer container and freeze. Thaw completely before using.


## Half Hour Jam

5 cups diced rhubarb     1 cup sugar
1 pkg. strawberry Jell-O     1 cup drained crushed pineapple

Boil rhubarb and sugar for 15 minutes. Add pineapple and Jell-O powder and bring to a boil again. Put into jars and keep in the refrigerator.


## Homemade Canned Fish

1 gallon of fish     3/4 cup vinegar
1 1/2 cups vegetable oil     2 Tbsp. pickling salt
1 - 28 oz. can of tomatoes     1 can tomato soup

Cut fish into bite size pieces, put in a roaster for the oven. Add tomatoes, 1/2 cup vinegar, 1/2 cup oil and salt. Bake at 350 for 4 hours. Stir once or twice while baking. Take out of oven and add tomato soup, 1 cup oil and 1/4 cup vinegar. Pack in jars. Boil the jars to seal 1 to 1 1/2 hours. This can make 8 to 9 pints. (2 cups size jar)

### Ice Cream Pail Pickles

Cucumbers                                    Red pepper
Onion                                        Slice and layer in an ice cream pail.

Syrup:
4 cups white sugar                           1 tsp. celery salt
2 cups vinegar                               1 tsp. mustard seed
2 Tbsp. pickling salt                        1 tsp. turmeric

Mix ingredients for syrup and bring to a boil. Pour over sliced vegetables. Put in the refrigerator.

### Million Dollar Pickles

6 quarts of sliced cucumbers (24 cups)       12 minced onions
3 minced green peppers                       1 cup salt

Put the salt over the above vegetables and let stand 3 hours with water to cover. Drain, wash and put in a pinch of alum.

Dressing:
1 small can pimentos                         3 tsp. turmeric
1 1/2 quarts vinegar                         1/2 cup mustard seed

Boil the dressing and pour it over the vegetables, simmer slowly for about 20 minutes. Pour into jars and seal.

### Pickles with Oil

Add: 1 Slice of onion and 1 Tbsp. oil to each pint jar of round sliced cucumbers.

Boil:
2 cups water                                 1 tsp. turmeric
1 pint vinegar                               1/4 cup pickling salt
1/2 tsp. celery seed                         2 1/2 cups sugar
1 tsp. mustard seed

Pour over vegetables and seal. (Note: makes 7 pints. If you have the tops of the jars hot and then cover the jar to seal). *Contributed by Antonia Hladun.*

### Pickled Carrots

4 quarts water                               1 cup pickling salt
2 cups vinegar                               1/4 cup sugar

Boil this pack carrots in jar with dill and garlic. Put the 12 quarts that are prepared in hot water to seal. Do not boil carrots before packing in jars, place in slices.

### Pickled Eggs

12 hard-cooked eggs, peeled
1 medium onion, sliced
1 Tbsp. sugar
2 tsp. pickling spices
1 cup white vinegar
1 cup water
1 bay leaf
1 tsp. salt
1 tsp. dried pepper flakes (optional)

Prepare 2- 1 liter jars fitted with lids. Place the bay leaf and some sliced onion on the bottom of each jar. Alternate with layers of boiled egg. In a small saucepan, mix together vinegar, water, spices (pepper flakes if desired) and salt. Cover and bring to a boil. Reduce heat to low and simmer for 10 minutes. Strain liquid and pour half of the mixture into each jar; cover with a lid. Refrigerate for at least 2 days before serving. Pickled eggs will keep for one month in the fridge. Hint: if your jar doesn't have enough liquid to cover the egg and onion, you can heat equal parts of vinegar and water to add to the jar. *Contributed by Theresa Mudry*

### Pickled Fish

1/2 cup vinegar
2 tsp. brown sugar

1 tsp. pickling salt
1 tsp. pickling spices

Bring to a boil and pour over layers of onions and fish in 1 pint jar.

### Pickled Jalapenos and Hot Spiced Vegetable Pickles

1 cup white vinegar
1 cup water
2 cloves garlic smashed
2 Tbsp. sugar
1 Tbsp. salt
7-8 jalapeno peppers thinly sliced

*Continued on next page...*

Wash and slice peppers and place in sterile jars. Use 7 or 8 jalapenos per jar or use 2 or 3 peppers and add your vegetable of choice. Asparagus, carrots, sweet peppers, string or green beans, etc. Great for Caesar garnish! Combine the vinegar, water, garlic, sugar, and coarse pickling salt in a medium pot and bring to a boil. Remove from heat and let sit for a few minutes. Pour into jars and seal. Lasts in the fridge for up to two months. *Contributed by Brent Matsalla.*

## Pickled Sugar Snap Peas

3 cups water
1 cup vinegar

1/4 cup pickling salt (or a little less)
1 lb. snap peas

Dill and Garlic and if you'd like them spicy you can add some dry red pepper flakes, jalapenos or chili flakes. Add to a prepared quart jar. *Contributed by Brent Matsalla.*

## Pickled Watermelon Rind

2 qt. jars watermelon rind in 1/2" cubes
1 1/2 cups of water
1 1/2 cups of apple cider vinegar
1 1/2 cups of sugar

1/2 tsp. red pepper flakes
1 tsp. of black pepper corns
3 Tbsp. of picking salt

Leave 1/4" of red on watermelon rind. Peel the tough outer skin off rind with a potato peeler. Put cubes in sterile jars. Heat ingredients to make the brine and boil for a few minutes. Let brine cool for a few before pouring into jars. Refrigerate. They're ready in a day but leave for 4 days for best results.

## Raw Tomato Relish

5 1/2 quarts cut up pieces of tomato
1 quart onion chopped
1 quart celery chopped

2 red peppers chopped
2 green peppers chopped
6 peaches cut up in cubes

Sprinkle the above ingredients with 1/3 cup pickling salt, and let stand overnight. Next day put into a colander and drain well.

Brine syrup:
4 cups sugar

2 1/2 cups vinegar
2 oz. mustard seed

Boil the syrup and pour over vegetables. Bring to a boil and put in jars and seal.

## Refrigerator Pickles #1

8 cups thinly sliced cucumbers (not peeled)
1/4 cup or less pickling salt
1 tsp. mustard seed
1 tsp. celery seed
2 cups white sugar
1 cup vinegar
1 cup onion (sliced)
1 tsp. turmeric

Combine all ingredients and refrigerate 8 hours before using. Keeps in fridge for 4 to 6 months. *Contributed by Eleanor Hadubiak.*

## Refrigerator Pickles #2

4 cups sugar
2 cups vinegar
2 tsps. pickling salt
1 tsp. turmeric
1 tsp. celery seed

1 tsp. mustard seed
1 onion
1/2 red pepper
1 garlic clove

Peel and slice cucumbers into thin rounds fill jars. Boil the brine and pour over vegetables. *Contributed by Rose Arent.*

## Refrigerator Beet Pickles

Save juice from beets being boiled. Need enough beets to fill an ice cream pail. 2 sliced onions to mix with beets.

Brine:
2 cups beet juice
3 cups sugar or less
4 Tbsp. pickling salt
1 tsp. celery salt
2 cups vinegar
1 tsp. turmeric
2 tsp. pickling spice (in a cheese cloth bag)

*Continued on next page...*

Boil the brine for 5 to 6 minutes Take the bag of spice out Pour the brine over the beets (either cooled or warm) Store in fridge.

Alternative: this recipe can be baked in the oven instead of boiling the beets on the top of the store. Bake for about 1 hour or until a fork can be inserted easily in the beets. Remove from oven cool, peel and cut into cubes or slices.

See *Easy Beet Preparation* under *Miscellaneous* to assist with this recipe.

## Relish

| | |
|---|---|
| 6 cups sugar | 2 Tbsp. mustard seed |
| 6 cups chopped cucumber | 1 Tbsp. salt |
| 3 bunches of celery (6 cups chopped) | 1 pint (2 cups) vinegar |
| 3 red peppers chopped | Small head of cabbage chopped |
| 4 cups onions chopped | |

Mix the above ingredients and boil slowly for 35 minutes. Remove from the stove and mix together the following:

| | |
|---|---|
| 1/2 cup vinegar | 1/2 Tbsp. mustard |
| 1/2 cup flour | 1 Tbsp. turmeric |

Then add to the vegetables. Bring to a boil, put into jars and seal. Makes 14 pints. Recommended to chop vegetables with a knife not food chopper which makes it mushy. *Contributed by Linda Matsalla.*

## Sliced Pickles

Wash and slice cucumbers. Put garlic and dill and pickling spice in jar.
Brine:

| | |
|---|---|
| Boil brine and pour over hot and seal jar. | 2 cups white sugar |
| 3 cups water | 3 Tbsp. pickling spice |
| 2 cups vinegar | |

*Contributed by Minnie Rudachyk.*

## Strawberry Rhubarb Jam

5 cups rhubarb (approx. 3 large stalks, cut into 1/2" cubes)
2 cups hulled and halved strawberries
2 1/4 cups sugar
1 tablespoon or juice from half a fresh lemon juice

*Continued on next page...*

Combine all ingredients in a medium to large saucepan over medium heat. Once mixture starts to bubble, reduce heat to medium low and cook until thickened. May need to cook for an hour to reach 205F degrees. Transfer to sterile jars, makes about 4 cups. *Contributed by Brent Matsalla.*


## Sweet Dills #1

| | |
|---|---|
| 10 cups water | 1 Tbsp. salt into each quart jar |
| 1 cup brown sugar | Dill, garlic and pickling spice |
| 1 cup vinegar | |

Fill jars to seal: Have water hot in canner put jars in and let stand until cucumbers are whiter than the raw green color. Makes 6 quarts. *Contributed by Francis Makowsky.*


## Sweet Dills #2

Slice cucumbers lengthwise and put garlic, a bay leaf and dill into each jar.
Brine:

| | |
|---|---|
| 2 1/2 cups water | 2 1/2 to 3 cups sugar |
| 1 1/2 cups vinegar | 1/3 cup pickling salt |

Pour hot over the cucumbers in the jars and seal. *Contributed by Helen Brodziak.*


## Uncooked Cabbage Relish

| | |
|---|---|
| 1 cabbage shredded fine | 3 red peppers chopped fine |
| 6 medium onions chopped | 3 green peppers chopped fine |

Brine:

| | |
|---|---|
| 1/4 cup mustard seed | 3 cups sugar |
| 1 Tbsp. celery seed | 3 cups vinegar |

Combine the cabbage and onions with a rinse brine of 1/2 cup salt and 6 cups water to cover let stand overnight. Next morning drain well and if vegetables taste to salty rinse in cold water and drain well. Add the peppers to the cabbage and onions. Add celery seed, sugar, and mustard seed to the vinegar and heat to boiling. Stirring until sugar is dissolved. Cool. Pack jars with prepared vegetables and fill to cover with brine. Seal. This recipe will be ready in 3 days. (note: the vegetables and brine can be combined and packed into the jars at the same time)

## Yum Yum Pickles

6 quarts thickly sliced cucumbers

Make a brine of 1/2 cup pickling salt to 4 quarts cold water.

Pour over sliced cucumbers let stand 3 hours or longer. Drain do not need to rinse. Boil the brine:

6 cups cider vinegar
6 cups white sugar

1 Tbsp. turmeric
1 tsp. Celery seed.

Put cucumbers in solution to heat through but do not boil. Pack in jars. *Contributed by Pauline Scopick.*

## Zucchini Marmalade

Put in blender 3 1/2 cups steamed zucchini to chop fine
2 cups sugar
1/4 cup lemon juice
1 box apricot Jell-O powder

Bring to a boil zucchini with sugar and lemon juice, add Jell-O and boil 1 minutes. Refrigerate or freeze.

## Zucchini Relish

10 cups grated zucchini
4 cups ground onions

4 Tbsp. coarse salt

Let stand overnight. Next morning drain and squeeze juice out.

Dressing:

1 Tbsp. turmeric
1 Tbsp. dry mustard
1 Tbsp. nutmeg

1 1/2 to 2 Tbsp. cornstarch
6 cups sugar
2 1/2 cups vinegar

Mix dressing together bring to a boil. For a thicker dressing increase cornstarch and add 2 red and 2 green peppers ground up to the zucchini mix to total 10 cups. Boil for 20 to 30 minutes.

## Durable Bubble Solution

2 cups hot water

1/4 cup dish soap

1 packet gelatin (1/4 oz.)

2 Tbsp. glycerin


## Easy Beet Preparation

Cut the beet leaves and stems off of the beetroot without cutting into the beet, leaving 1 inch of stem. Place the beetroot into a covered large roaster adding a cup of water on the bottom for moisture. Bake the beets at 350 for about 45 minutes (depending on sizes of beets). When beets are tender remove from oven, cool slightly and skins remove easy, as well as the ends. The beets will be tender and all the juices remain within the beet. Beets are now ready for preparing borscht, pickles, relish or for freezing.


## Fluffy Slime

2/3 cup of Elmer's white glue

1/2 tsp. baking soda

1/4 cup water

2-3 cups shaving cream (not shaving gel)

1 1/2 Tbsp. Equate contact lens saline solution (must contain sodium borate or boric acid)

Food coloring

Mix white glue, water and baking soda. Add shaving cream. Add food coloring and mix well. Slowly add saline solution and stir to desired stickiness and thickness. Knead for 5 min. Use on mat, use latex gloves when mixing. Store in a container with lid.


## High Flying Bubble Solution

2 cups warm water

1/3 cup dish soap

1/4 cup corn syrup


## Hummingbird Food

1 part white sugar

4 parts water

Dissolve sugar in water. Let cool before placing in feeder. Make sure feeder is sterile and should be cleaned every few days to avoid passing bacteria on to birds. DO NOT use red dye, it's not good for the birds. Store any extra food in refrigerator. Clean and sterilize feeder between refills.

## Marshmallow (Edible) Play Dough

6 large marshmallows
1/4 cup cornstarch (heaping)

2 tsp. coconut oil (heaping)

Heat in microwave, then add food coloring. Coat hands in coconut oil then stir and knead. Add more cornstarch if too sticky. *Contributed by Theresa Mudry.*

## Microwave Drying Fresh Herbs

Any Herb of choice (examples: mint, cilantro, oregano, sage, lemon basil, thyme)
2 sheets of paper towel

If you are selecting the herbs from your garden, do so after the dew or rain in the morning, they are the freshest.
If herbs need to be rinsed, make sure all the excess water is removed (I use the salad spinner)
Place one layer of the herbs on a paper towel, and place another paper towel on top.
Microwave on HIGH for 1 minute then remove and test to see if the herb is dry. Sometimes you may need to turn the paper towel over as the bottom layer will absorb the moisture.
Thicker herbs may need more time. Most herbs require an additional 30 seconds but only do 30 seconds or less in intervals to ensure not to over-cook the herb.
Store in an airtight container or herb jar. This method traps the rich pure summer green color and flavor of the herb.

## Mom's Drain Cleaner

1 cup baking soda
1 cup salt

1/4 cup cream of tartar

Combine ingredients pour 1/4 cup of mixture down the drain follow with a pot of boiling water. Then flush with cool water. Repeat until drain is clean.

## Play Dough

2 cups all-purpose flour
3/4 cup salt
4 tsp. cream of tartar
2 cups lukewarm water

2 Tbsp. of vegetable or coconut oil
Food coloring
Medium sized Ziploc bags

Mix flour, salt and cream of tartar in large cooking pot. Add water and oil and cook over medium heat stirring constantly until thickened and dough forms a ball. Remove from heat and cool on parchment or wax paper and knead until a smooth texture appears. Divide into portions and put into separate Ziploc bags. Then add food coloring to dough inside the bag, starting with 5 drops of color and you can add more the brighter you want the color to be. Knead the dough and color inside the bag so it doesn't color your hands. Store in the bags, will keep up to 3 months.

## Sugar Body Scrub

1 cup Coconut oil
2 cups large granulated sugar
(I use organic raw sugar)
1/2 cup Epsom salts
Essential oils (optional)

Combine the ingredients above with a mixer, and place into a jar to use in the bathtub. About 1 Tbsp. of the body sugar is rubbed onto your skin to moisturize, and exfoliate with a gentle scrub. The coarser the sugar and the granulated
Epsom salts will assist with the scrub and soothe achy muscles. It is oily so be careful with using on slippery surfaces. This is great wrapped with a bow as a gift. *Contributed by Theresa Mudry.*

## Unicorn Slime

8 oz. bottle Elmer's white or glitter glue
1 1/2 – 2 Tbsp. contact saline solution
1 Tbsp. baking soda

Food coloring
Glitter if using white glue

Mix glue and food coloring in a bowl. Stir until well combined, then slowly mix in baking soda. Add the saline solution and stir. If slime is too sticky, add more saline. The more saline you add the thicker it will be. Knead the slime until it all holds together. Store in Ziploc bag or a container with lid. Best to play with on a table or mat.

# Conversion Charts

## Quick Alternatives

| | |
|---|---|
| 1 tablespoon (Tbsp.) | 3 teaspoons (tsp.) |
| 1/16 cup | 1 Tbsp. |
| 1/8 cup | 2 Tbsp. |
| 1/6 cup | 2 Tbsp. + 2 tsp. |
| 1/4 cup | 4 Tbsp. |
| 1/3 cup | 5 Tbsp. + 1 tsp. |
| 3/8 cup | 6 Tbsp. |
| 1/2 cup | 8 Tbsp. |
| 2/3 cup | 10 Tbsp. + 2 tsp. |
| 3/4 cup | 12 Tbsp. |
| 1 cup | 48 tsp. |
| 1 cup | 16 Tbsp. |
| 8 fluid oz. | 1 cup |
| 1 pint (pt.) | 2 cups |
| 1 quart (qt.) | 2 pints |
| 4 cups | 1 qt. |
| 1 gallon (gal.) | 4 qt. |
| 16 oz. | 1 pound (lb.) |
| 1 milliliter (ml) | 1 cubic centimeter (cc) |
| 1 inch (in.) | 2.54 centimeters (cm) |

## Capacity (U.S. to Metric)

| | |
|---|---|
| 1/5 tsp. | 1 ml |
| 1 tsp. | 5 ml |
| 1 Tbsp. | 15 ml |
| 1 oz. | 30 ml |
| 1/5 cup | 47 ml |
| 1 cup | 237 ml |
| 2 cups (1 pt.) | 473 ml |
| 4 cups (1 qt.) | .95 liter |
| 4 qt. | 3.8 liters |

## Capacity (Metric to U.S.)

| | |
|---|---|
| 1 ml | 1/5 tsp. |
| 5 ml | 1 tsp. |
| 15 ml | 1 Tbsp. |
| 100 ml | 3.4 oz. |
| 240 ml | 1 cup |
| 1 liter | 34 oz. |
| | 4.2 cups |
| | 2.1 pt. |
| | 1.06 qt. |
| | .026 gal. |

## Weight (U.S. to Metric)

| | |
|---|---|
| 1 oz. | 28 grams (g) |
| 1 lb. | 454 g |

## Weight (Metric to U.S.)

| | |
|---|---|
| 1 g | 0.035 oz. |
| 100 g | 3.5 oz. |
| 500 g | 1.1 lbs. |
| 1 kilogram (kg) | 2.205 lbs. or 35 oz. |

## Milliliters

| tsp | ml | | oz | ml | | cup | ml |
|---|---|---|---|---|---|---|---|
| 1/2 | 2.5 | | 2 | 60 | | 1/4 | 60 |
| 1 | 5 | | 4 | 115 | | 1/2 | 120 |
| | | | 6 | 150 | | 2/3 | 120 |
| Tbsp. | ml | | 8 | 230 | | 3/4 | 180 |
| 1 | 15 | | 10 | 285 | | 1 | 240 |
| | | | 12 | 340 | | | |

## Grams

| oz | g | lb |
|---|---|---|
| 2 | 58 | - |
| 4 | 114 | - |
| 6 | 170 | - |
| 8 | 226 | 1/2 |
| 12 | 340 | - |
| 16 | 454 | 1 |

| Spoons and Cups | | | | | | |
|---|---|---|---|---|---|---|
| tsp. | Tbsp. | fl. oz. | cup | pt. | qt. | Gal. |
| 3 | 1 | 1/2 | 1/16 | 1/32 | - | - |
| 6 | 2 | 1 | 1/8 | 1/16 | 1/32 | - |
| 12 | 4 | 2 | 1/4 | 1/8 | 1/16 | - |
| 18 | 6 | 3 | 3/8 | - | - | - |
| 24 | 8 | 4 | 1/2 | 1/4 | 1/8 | 1/32 |
| 36 | 12 | 6 | 3/4 | - | - | - |
| 48 | 16 | 8 | 1 | 1/2 | 1/4 | 1/16 |
| 96 | 32 | 16 | 2 | 1 | 1/2 | 1/8 |
| - | 64 | 32 | 4 | 2 | 1 | 1/4 |
| - | 256 | 128 | 16 | 8 | 4 | 1 |

# Recipes for a Crowd

Have a large party planned? Here's a hint to quantities.

## Lunch for 300

- 
- 12 Large sandwich loaves, sliced lengthwise, 6 white and 6 brown

**Sandwich Fillings**

- 4 dozen eggs - hard boil, make filling with salad dressing and seasoning.
- 4 tins of Spam or 1 lb. ham or bologna - Mix with salad dressing and dills, chopped or sweet relish.
- This can be used for rolled sandwiches or ribbon type with egg using alternate layers of white and brown bread.
- 1 1/2 lbs. White cream cheese - Mix with salad dressing. Spread on bread. Sprinkle with chopped maraschino cherries. Make in rolls. Takes one 12 oz. jar of cherries and 6 oz. jar of green cherries.
- 1 1/2 lbs. Velveeta - Mix with salad dressing. Make in rolls with olives, 4 per slice, or dill slices.
- 3 tins of shrimp - Mix with salad dressing and roll.
  2 large tins of salmon - Mix with chopped celery, salad dressing and seasoning. Roll center with dill.
- These should be tightly rolled in wax paper and refrigerated until cut. These amounts will make 800 sandwiches allowing 2-3 per person.

## Tea & Dainties for 300

- 3 per person usually allowed. 25 people supplying 3 dozen each should be sufficient if a group project.

## Other Requirements

2 lbs. Tea
3 lbs. sugar cubes
3 quarts Creamilk

1/2 gallon sweet pickles
1/2 gallon dill pickles

## Baked Pork and Beans for 100

8 quarts Dry beans
20 quarts Salad
4 lbs. butter
4 quarts Cream

4 lbs. Salt pork
20 doz. rolls/buns
20 Pies
2 lbs. coffee

## Hash Supper for 100

40 lbs. Corned beef
32 quarts Potatoes
20 doz. Rolls
20 quarts Chopped cabbage

5 quarts Salad dressing
4 lbs. Better
2 lbs. Coffee
4 quarts Cream

## Cabbage Salad for 175

20 lbs. Cabbage
1 1/2 quarts Salad dressing

4 Cans crushed pineapple
2 Bunches carrots

## Ham Supper for 225

48 lbs. Canned ham
24 Potato salads
48 pkg. Peas (1 lb.)
5 lbs. Coffee

9 quarts Creamilk
48 quarts Strawberries
6 pkg. Bisquick (mixed for shortcake)
6 quarts Heavy cream

## Braised Beef for 200

65 lbs. Stewing beef
60 lbs. Potatoes
36 Pies

Harvard beets
40 lbs. Turnips
2 lbs. Cheese

## Turkey Dinner for 250

7 Turkeys (approx. 120 lbs.)
75 lbs. Butternut squash
20 Large cranberry rings

75 lbs. Potatoes
10 Bunches celery
44 Pies

## Chicken Shortcake for 135

60 lbs. Chicken
30 Packages frozen peas
20 Large cranberry rings

3 Large packages Bisquick
17 Packages corn
2 Bunches celery

## Meats for 100

36-40 lbs. Beef- rib roast
36-45 lbs. Pork

36-40 lbs. Ham

## Quantities for 100 people

25-30 lbs. Mashed potatoes, 25 lbs for scalloped.
16 lbs. coleslaw
15-20 heads lettuce (shredded for salads)
3 gallons ice cream

1-1/2 rolls per person
3 lbs. of butter
2 lumps/person of sugar, approx. (120 lumps in a lb.)
50 cups - 1 lb. coffee plus 2-1/2 gallons water

## Cocoa for 50

1-1/2 cups cocoa
2 cups sugar

5 quarts of milk
4 quarts of boiling water

## Fruit Punch for 50

2 lbs. sugar
8 lemons
6 oranges
6 quarts water
1 pt. Shredded pineapple

1 quart Water
1 pt. Grape juice or tea
1 pt. Canned pineapple juice or other fruit juice
1 pt. Strawberries or cherries

# Substitutions

Substitutions for when you run short on an important ingredient and your nearest farm-neighbor lives at least a mile away. Plus, it's probably snowing and -50C with the wind-chill.

| | |
|---|---|
| **All Spice** | If a recipe asks for 1 1/2 tsp. of Allspice, you can use 1 tsp. cinnamon and 1/2 tsp. cloves instead. |
| **Baking Powder** | To substitute 1 tsp. of baking powder, combine 1/4 tsp. baking soda with 1/2 tsp. cream of tartar. Use immediately. |
| **Baking Soda** | To make 1/4 tsp. baking soda, substitute 1 tsp. baking powder. |
| **Bread Crumbs** | Substitute ground rolled oats, crushed croutons, or cereal in the same 1:1 ratio as the recipe calls for. |
| **Bread Flour** | Substitute ground rolled oats, crushed croutons, or cereal in the same 1:1 ratio as the recipe calls for. |
| **Brown Sugar** | Substitute 1 scant cup granulated sugar plus 1 Tbsp. molasses. |
| **Butter** | For baking, coconut oil, margarine, or lard in the same 1:1 ratio. Mashed avocado in 1:1 ratio. |
| **Buttermilk** | Substitute 1 cup plain yogurt, or 1 cup milk mixed with 1 Tbsp. vinegar or lemon juice. |
| **Cake Flour** | Remove 2 Tbsp. of flour from a cup of all-purpose flour and replace with 2 Tbsp. of cornstarch to make 1 cup cake flour. |
| **Chocolate** | To substitute 1 ounce chocolate or 1 square of chocolate, use 3 Tbsp. cocoa powder and ¾ tablespoon coconut oil or pure butter. |
| **Cornstarch** | To substitute 1 Tbsp. cornstarch, use 1 1/2 Tbsp. all-purpose flour. |
| **Cream of Tartar** | To replace 1/4 tsp. cream of tartar, use 1/2 tsp. lemon juice. |
| **Egg** | For waffles, pancakes, cookies, and yeast breads, mix 2 Tbsp. ground flax meal and 3 Tbsp. cold water for every egg in the recipe. Mixture must rest for 10 min. before being used. <br><br> Use 1/4 cup of applesauce per egg in the recipe. For a softer dough, add another tsp. of applesauce. <br> Half-and-half or heavy cream. |
| **Evaporated Milk** | Use 1 cup powdered milk with 1 1/2 cups warm water. <br><br> Coconut milk at 1:1 ratio. |
| **Gluten Free Flour** | Blend raw rolled oats to equally make 1:1 ratio. |
| **Ground Beef** | 1 lb. of ground beef can be substituted for a leaner protein, 1 lb. ground turkey. |
| **Half-and-Half** | To substitute 1/2 cup half-and-half, use 1/4 cup milk and 1/4 cup cream. <br><br> Use 1:1 ratio of non-dairy coffee creamer. |
| **Heavy Cream** | To substitute 1 cup heavy cream, melt 1/4 cup unsalted butter. Whisk in 3/4 cup whole milk or half-and-half. |

| | |
|---|---|
| **Honey** | Corn syrup, molasses, maple syrup, or agave nectar at 1:1 ratio. |
| **Ketchup** | To substitute 1 cup ketchup, use 1 cup tomato sauce + 1 Tbsp. sugar + 1 tsp. vinegar. |
| **Lemon Juice** | To substitute 1 tsp. lemon juice, use 1 tsp. lime juice; or 1/2 tsp. vinegar; or 1 tsp. white wine. Or, use cider vinegar at 1:1 ratio. |
| **Lemon zest** | To substitute 1 tsp. lemon zest, use 2 Tbsp. lemon juice; or 1/2 tsp. lemon extract. |
| **Lime juice** | To substitute 1 tsp. lime juice, use 1 tsp. lemon juice; or 1 tsp. vinegar; or 1 tsp. white wine. |
| **Lime zest** | To substitute 1 tsp. lime zest, use 1 tsp. lemon zest |
| **Mascarpone Cheese** | To make 16 oz. of mascarpone, use 12 ounces of room temperature cream cheese with 1/4 cup heavy whipping cream and 1/4 cup sour cream. |
| **Mayonnaise** | To substitute 1 cup of mayo, use 1 cup plain yogurt; or 1 cup sour cream. |
| **Powdered Sugar** | Grind table sugar in a blender at 1:1 ratio. |
| **Pumpkin** | To replace 1 15 oz. can of pure pumpkin you can use 1 1/2 cups mashed sweet potato. |
| **Ricotta** | Use 1 cup dry cottage cheese (strained through a sieve or cheesecloth to reduce liquid). |
| **Rum Extract** | If you do not like the taste of rum but the recipe is interesting, sub the rum extract equally with vanilla instead. |
| **Self-rising Flour** | To substitute 1 cup self-rising flour, use 7/8 cup all-purpose flour + 1/2 tsp. salt + 1 1/2 tsp. baking powder. |
| **Semi-sweet Chocolate** | To make 1 oz. semi-sweet chocolate, use 1 ounce unsweetened chocolate and 1/2 tsp. granulated sugar. |
| **Sour Cream** | Use plain yogurt as a 1:1 replacement; or 3/4 cup buttermilk + 1/3 cup butter; or 1 Tbsp. lemon juice or vinegar + 3/4 cup cream + 3 Tbsp. cream. |
| **Sour Milk** | To make 1 cup sour milk, use 1 Tbsp. vinegar or lemon juice + 3/4 cup milk + 3 Tbsp. milk. Let mixture rest for 5 minutes to thicken. |
| **Soy Sauce** | To make 1/2 cup soy sauce, use 1/2 cup coco aminos/liquid aminos + salt to taste; or 1/4 cup Worcestershire sauce + 1 Tbsp. water. |
| **Sugar** | To substitute 1 cup granulated sugar, use 1 cup brown sugar, packed or 1 cup honey or corn syrup. By using the honey or syrup in a recipe requires a reduction of other liquids by 1/4 cup. |
| **Vinegar** | To substitute 1 tsp. of vinegar, use 1 tsp. lemon/lime juice; or 2 tsp. white wine. |
| **Whole Milk** | To substitute 1 cup of whole milk, use 1 cup almond/soy/rice milk; or 1 cup water/juice; or 1/4 cup dry powdered milk + 1 cup water; or 2/3 cup evaporated milk + 1/3 cup water. |
| **Wine** | For substituting 1 cup wine, use 1 cup broth (chicken, beef, or vegetable); or 1 cup water. <br><br> Who are we kidding, there's no substitute for wine. |

*The Matsalla Barn, painted by Josie's daughter Eleanor.*

# Translations

How to speak Saskatchewanian Farm Kid

| Saskatchewanian Farm Kid | Translation |
| --- | --- |
| How's the **grids**? I wonder if the **grader**'s been down them and cleared those **drifts** yet, so we can do some **bumper skiing**? | **Grids** - gravel roads that run through the province in a grid pattern.<br>**Grader** - heavy equipment road grooming machine.<br>**Drifts** - wind-blown snow banks that cross over a road.<br>**Bumper skiing** - grabbing on to a vehicle bumper and having the vehicle pull you while boot-sliding on ice. |
| The **U** is down by the **slough**, or maybe it's by the **dugout**. | **U** - Minneapolis Moline model U tractor.<br>**Slough** - a low spot on a field that is marshy or filled with water.<br>**Dugout** - a big pit dug out in your field during road construction that will fill with water turning into a man-made pond. |
| I could sure use a **Vico** at **supper** but I had one at **dinner**, so I'll just have a **beep** instead. | **Vico** - a chocolate milk drink.<br>**Supper** - 6pm dinner.<br>**Dinner** - noon lunch.<br>**Beep** - an orange juice drink.<br>**Note:** The school drink program offered plain milk, Vico, or Beep |
| We're having **shishlicks** in the **summer kitchen** tonight. | **Shishlicks** - mutton marinated in salt, lemon, and onion. Referring to the word Shishliki.<br>**Summer kitchen** - a kitchen used to cook and bake in summer time outside of the main kitchen, usually in an out-building or old house. This keeps the main house cooler in hot prairie summers.. |
| It's cool enough for a **bunny hug**. | **Bunny hug** - hooded sweater or hoodie. |
| I was **goosin' her** and I almost **hit the rhubarb.** | **Goosin' her** - going fast or accelerating.<br>**Hit the rhubarb** - driving into the ditch. |
| I just got a **two-four of Pil** and a **box of Boh** down at the **LB** to go with that **mickey** of yours. | **Two-four of Pil** - 24-pack of Pilsner beer.<br>**Box of Boh** - 6-pack of Bohemian beer.<br>**LB** - liquor board store only open 10-6 M-F<br>**Mickey** - 12 oz. bottle of liquor |
| She's pretty **ripe** coming from the **nuisance ground.** | **Ripe** - smelly or stinks<br>**Nuisance ground** - garbage dump |

| Saskatchewanian Farm Kid | Translation |
|---|---|
| My cousin gave me a **wedgy** and it ripped my **gitch** and she only had **gotch** to lend me, but they were **long Johns**. | **Wedgy** - tactfully pulling someone's underpants past their waist so the cheeks are separated by the material.<br>**Gitch** - girls or woman's underwear.<br>**Gotch** - boys or men's underwear.<br>Long Johns – winter underwear with full legs like pants. |
| Are you gonna wear your **thongs?**. | **Thongs** - flip-flop shoes |
| I love my wife's **dainties**. | **Dainties** - sweet desserts like cookies and squares. |
| You see the price of **purple gazz** yet? | **Purple gazz** - gasoline/petrol/fuel designated for use in farm vehicles only, which is less expensive as regular gasoline and dyed purple for identification. |
| I'm stopping at **Timmies** for a **double double**. | **Timmies** - Tim Hortons restaurant<br>**Double double** - coffee with 2 cream and 2 sugar. |
| I **sunk her to the axles** and had to get a **Saskatchewan yank**. | **Sunk her to the axles** - got a vehicle stuck in mud.<br>**Saskatchewan yank** - pulling out a stuck vehicle with a truck or tractor using a tow-strap or chain. |
| My neighbor's rape is looking pretty good. He's already laid her down and should be combining soon. | Rape - canola aka rapeseed<br>Laid her down - cut the crops down and put them into wind rows using a machine called a swather.<br>Combining - harvesting grain with a machine called a combine. |
| I was hoping to **snag a few** big **Jacks**. | **Snag a few** - catch some fish<br>**Jacks** - a native Saskatchewan species of fish called a Northern Pike, sometimes called a Jackfish. |
| I'm hoping to **tag** a **jumper** this year. Then I can make some **koob**. | **Tag** - referring to a hunting license tag.<br>**Jumper** - wild deer.<br>**Koob** - sausage, taken from Ukrainian Kielbasa but pronounced "koo-bah-saw." |
| Don't step in the **cow pie**. | **Cow pie** - a pile of a cow's feces. Sometimes called a "cow patty." |
| After I **haul a few loads** to the **elevator**, I'm going **skidooing**. | **Haul a few loads** - hauling harvested grains to market<br>**Elevator** - where you sold grain, a grain storage elevator<br>**Skidooing** - Snowmobiling |
| My mom knit me a **siwash sweater** to match my **toque**. | **SiWash Sweater** - a heavy knit jacket usually with a pattern on it.<br>**Toque** - a thick knitted hat to cover the top of your head and your ears, in -40 below weather. Or in the summer at 40 degrees, if you want to look cool. |

| Saskatchewanian Farm Kid | Translation |
|---|---|
| You were just a **stubble jumper** back then. | **Stubble jumper** - When grain is harvested it is cut and leaves a stubble like a crew cut haircut. Children have to step high and hop when walking through a stubble field. |
| Neighbors are having a **bush party** Friday night. | **Bush party** - An outdoor bonfire, usually in a treed cow pasture. |
| Dropped into the neighbor's place, **porch light was on**. | **Porch light was on** - If the light on your porch is on, it means you're accepting company and it's ok to drop in unannounced. |
| My brother gave me a **huruska** and it hurt. | **Huruska** - a noogie given to others, at the top of the head by getting them into a headlock and rubbing two knuckles on their head and catching hair. Leaving the scalp sore minus some hairs. |

*Josie at her 90th birthday party.*

# Special Thanks

The Matsalla family would like to thank Josie's friends and family that contributed recipes to Josie's collection throughout the many years, you are part of the love that was folded into these memories. Your contributions have allowed us to pass on tradition that will forever commemorate our beautiful mom Josie.

Mary Anaka (*friend*)
Rose Arent (*friend*)
Irene Bahrey (*friend*)
Ann Belitsky (*sister-in-law*)
Caroline Boychuk (*sister-in-law*)
Jenelle Breker (*granddaughter*)
Mark Breker (*granddaughter's husband*)
Sammy Breker (*great grandson*)
Tina Brezinski (*niece*)
Helen Brodziak (*friend*)
Mary Bugera (*friend*)
Elsie Carsten (*friend*)
Frances Charuk (*friend*)
Margaret Charuk (*friend*)
Lindsay Craig (*great niece*)
Phyllis Dercach (*friend*)
Adeline Dranchuk (*niece*)
Pat Dubasoff (*friend*)
Linda Dyck (*friend*)
Devon Dziaduck (*great grandson*)
Caley Eikelenboom (*great granddaughter*)
Kyler Eikelenboom (*great-great grandson*)
Mary Fedorchuk (*friend*)
Olga Fullawka (*friend*)
Cynthia Fullawka (*friend*)
Debbie Gabora (*friend*)
Pauline Gogol (*friend*)
Gladys Grodzinski (*friend*)
Lucy Grodzinski (*niece*)
Bernice Gulka (*daughter*)
Mabel Gulka (*daughter's mother-in-law*)
Eleanor Hadubiak (*daughter*)
Pearl Hadubiak (*daughter's mother-in-law*)
Tanis Hadubiak (*granddaughter*)
Twila Hadubiak (*granddaughter*)
Antonia Hladun (*niece*)
Albina Hrychenko (*niece*)

Francis Makowsky (*friend*)
Brent Matsalla (*son*)
Jaedyn Matsalla (*granddaughter*)
Jim Matsalla (*son*)
Joe Matsalla (*husband*)
Linda Matsalla (*daughter-in-law*)
Aryah Miller (*step-great granddaughter*)
Ivy Miller (*step-great granddaughter*)
Braxten Mudry (*great granddaughter*)
Harold Mudry (*daughter's husband*)
Jill Mudry (*grandson's wife*)
Marlene Mudry (*friend*)
Rylan Mudry (*great grandson*)
Theresa Mudry (*daughter*)
Josie Nelson (*friend*)
Jerraie Oberg (*granddaughter*)
Elsie Obodiak (*niece*)
Mary Obodiak (*sister-in-law*)
Beatrice Ochitwa (*friend*)
Mina Ozerney (*friend*)
Lil Popoff (*friend*)
Mabel Popoff (*friend*)
Sandra Pridge (*daughter-in-law*)
Jamie Lynn Rawson (*granddaughter*)
Rachel Rawson (*great granddaughter*)
Mary Rieger (*sister*)
Anna Romanow (*friend*)
Minnie Rudachyk (*friend*)
Pauline Scopick (*friend*)
Shawna Sicotte (*granddaughter*)
Marian Skoretz (*friend*)
Lena Skrepneck (*friend*)
Doris Slugoski (*friend*)
Leslie Stanier (*niece*)
Adam Waddell (*granddaughter's husband*)
Mandelle Waddell (*granddaughter*)
Darla Wolkowski (*great niece*)

*Continued on next page...*

Violet Kyba (*friend*)
Kathy K. (*friend*)
Nellie Kitchen (*daughter-in-law's mother*)
Evelyn Kowalchuk (*cousin*)
Gerald Kwasny *(granddaughter's husband)*
Camden Ledding (*great grandson)*
Jodie Ledding (*granddaughter)*
Chris Loshak (*granddaughter's husband)*
Tracy Loshak (*granddaughter)*
Eleanor Ludba (*friend*)

Rosie Wolkowski (*niece*)
Sophie Yaworski (*friend*)
Bev Zarazun (*sister-in-law*)
Ernie Zarazun (*brother*)
Joe Zarazun (*father*)
Mona Zarazun (*sister-in-law*)
Pauline Zarazun *(mother)*
Shirley Zarazun (*sister-in-law*)
Stefka Zarazun (*aunt*)

Manufactured by Amazon.ca
Bolton, ON